French Bronzes in The Wallace Collection

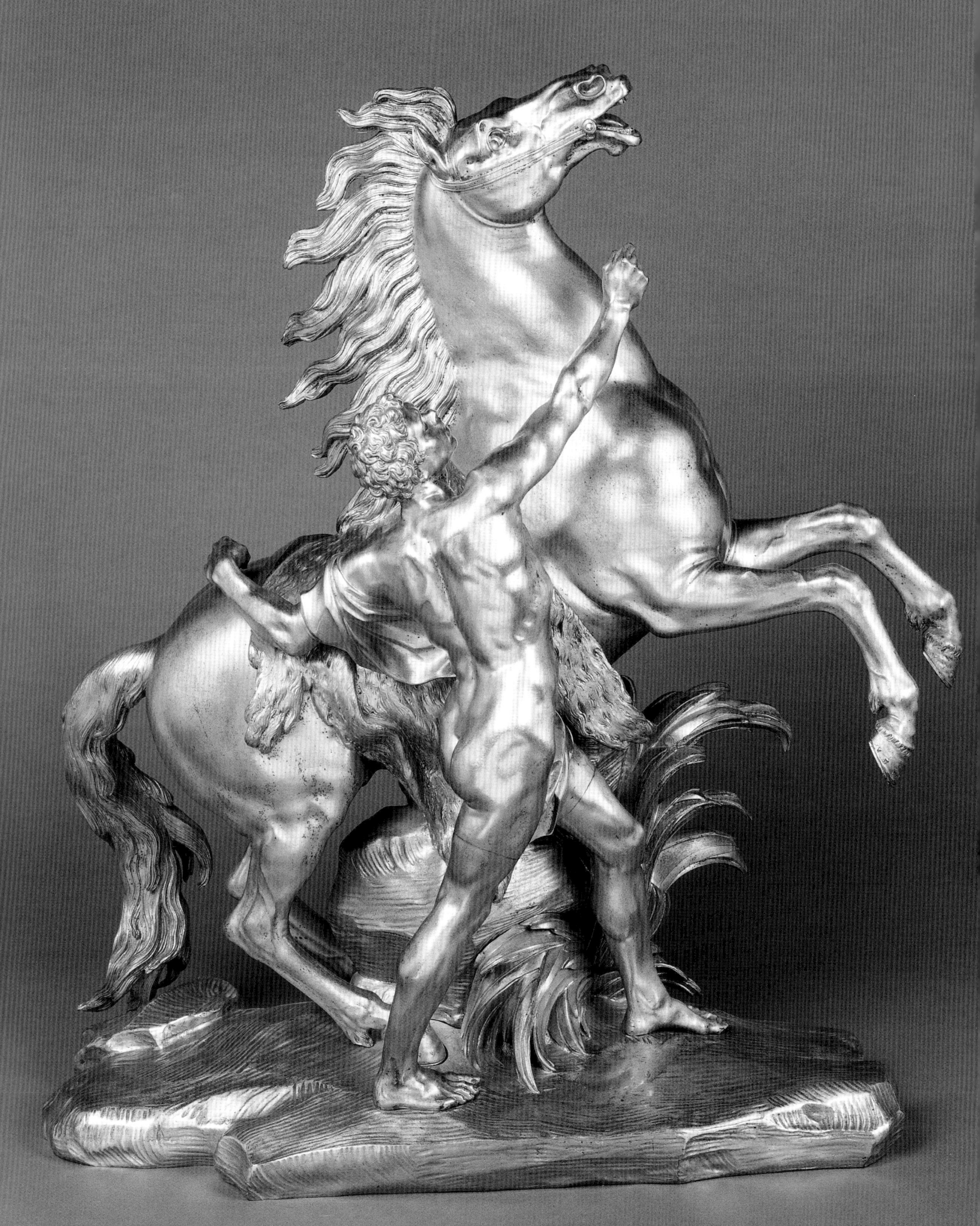

FRENCH BRONZES
IN THE
WALLACE COLLECTION

Robert Wenley

The Trustees of The Wallace Collection, London

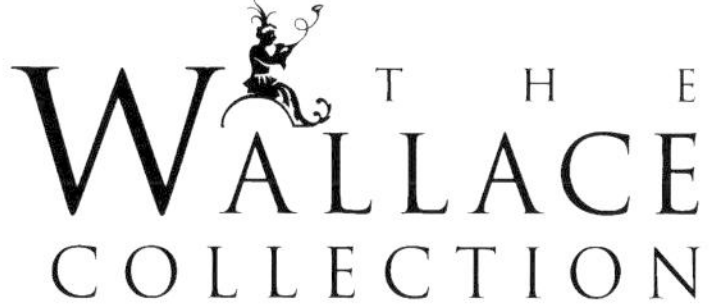

Published by The Trustees of the Wallace Collection,
Hertford House, Manchester Square, London W1U 3BN

Designed by Tim Harvey
Printed by BAS Printers Limited

Typeset in Albertina and printed on Hello Silk 170 gsm

ISBN 0 900785 78 0
British Library Cataloguing-in-Publication Data.
A catalogue record for this book is available from the British Library.

front cover
Venus and Adonis, attributed to Robert Le Lorrain, *c.*1704.
Wallace Collection (S185). See pp. 72–3.

back cover
A Mother and Child, attributed to Barthélemy Prieur, *c.*1600.
Wallace Collection (S129). See pp. 30–1.

frontispiece
One of *The Marly Horses*, after Guillaume I Coustou, *c.*1800–15.
Wallace Collection (S191). See pp. 94–5.

Contents

Foreword — 7

Preface — 9

The French Bronze Statuette to *c*.1815 — 11

The Taste of the Founders of the Wallace Collection for French Bronzes — 17

Techniques of Casting and Finishing French Bronze Statuettes *c*.1565–*c*.1815 — 20

The Bronzes — 24

Biographies of Principal Sculptors and Craftsmen (marked in bold in introductory essays and Index) — 106

Bibliography — 108

Index of Names and Places — 109

Photographic Acknowledgements and Author's Acknowledgements — 112

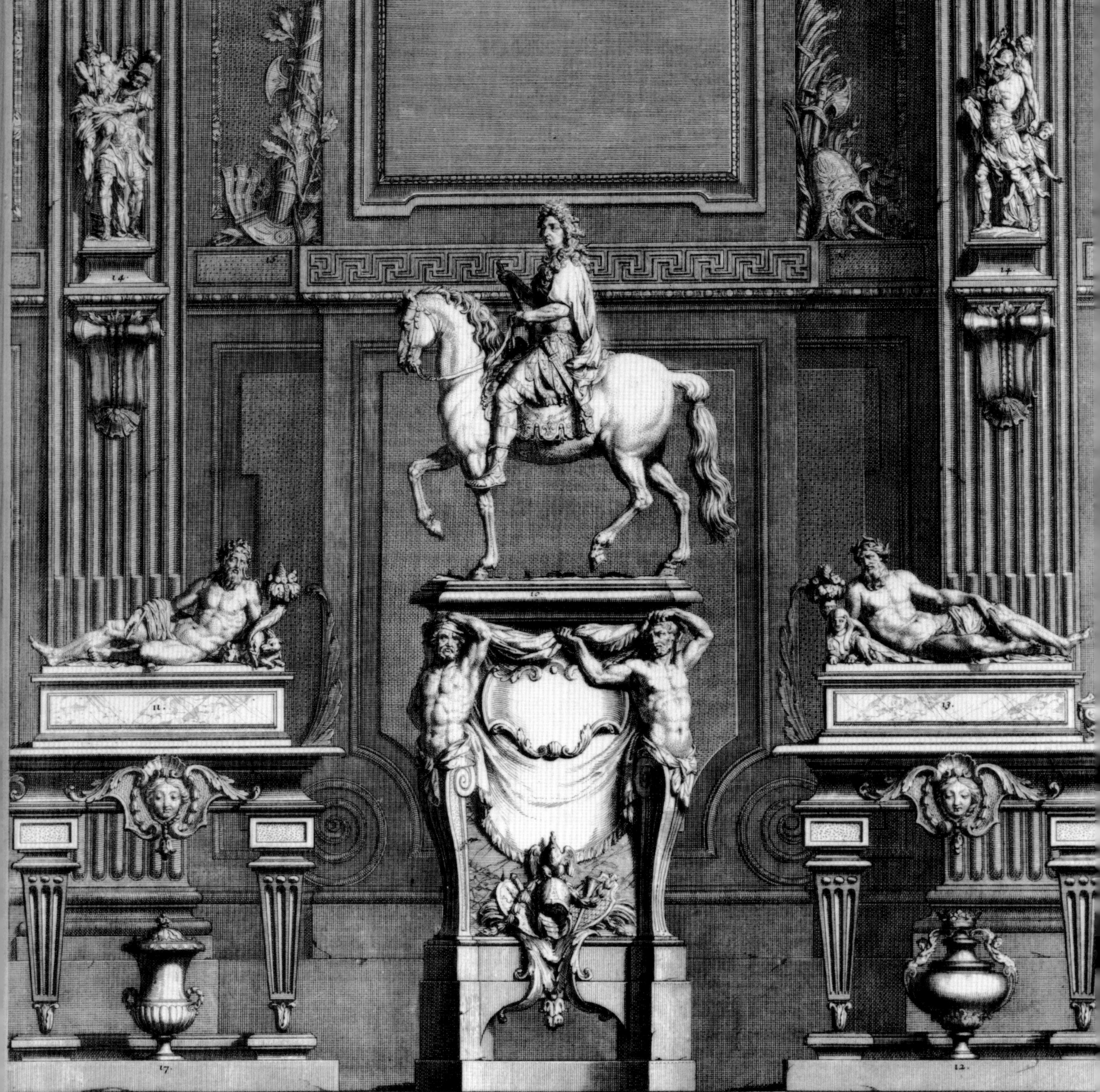

10...... Statüe Equestre en Bronze de Loüis le Grand poseé sur son pied
d'Estail de Marbre vert d'Egipthe, la Corniche est soutenue par quatre
Fermes de Bronze dorez, ainsi que les Draperies et les autres ornements, le
tout haut de 7. pieds ‡. Le modele de cette Statüe est placé dans la Biblioteque,
de Monseigneur de Pontchartrain Chancelier de France, et à servi à toutes celles
qui ont ête faites depuis. Le tout de F. Girardon .

11...... Le Tibre Figure de Bronze copiée a Rome d'apres l'Antique par
Cartier, poseé sur vn pied d'Estail d'Ebeine dont les panneaux sont de
Marbre vert d'Egipthe .

12...... Deux Vrnes de Bronze du Dessein de F. Girardon .

13...... Le Nil figure de Bronze copiée a Rome d'apres l'Antique par Carli[e]
poseé sur vn pied d'Estail d'Ebeine dont les panneaux sont de Mar[bre]
vert d'Egipthe .

14...... Enée et Anchise petit Groupe de Cire de F. Girardon qui a servi de M[odele]
à celui fait pour le Roy a Rome par le Pautre posé sur des Consol[es]
vû de deux côtez .

15...... Trophées Romaines et Syriennes du Dessein de F. Girardon .

16...... Autre Trophées des Couronnes Antiques du meme Modele de ceux de Vers[ailles]

17...... Deux vases d'Albatre du Dessein de F. Girardon

18...... Seize Méthopes de Trophées differentes .

F. Desbruslins Scrip.

Foreword

Generally speaking, during the last hundred years or so study of the bronze statuette has been focused on those by Italian artists. French bronzes have received comparatively little attention. Notable exceptions to this are the catalogue prepared for the 1968 M. Knoedler & Co. exhibition, *The French Bronze 1500 to 1800*, held in New York, and Professor Souchal's great dictionary, *French Sculptors*, on which work is still in course but which principally deals with monumental figures.

The reason for the apparent academic indifference to French bronzes of the *ancien régime* can be traced back to the twenty-five years either side of 1900 when the views of Wilhelm von Bode (of the Berlin Museums) held sway, as he advised many of the principal collectors and museums of the time in their choice of sculpture. His writings on and preference for Italian bronzes of the Renaissance were well known and influenced generations of scholars. This attitude did not always prevail as during the 18th and earlier part of the 19th century, French bronzes were highly regarded in their country of origin by *amateurs* and connoisseurs; in England, too, they were eagerly sought after by such collectors as the 3rd and 4th Marquesses of Hertford and George IV.

It is to be hoped that the attention currently being paid to French bronze statuettes by the French Bronze Study Group, comprised as it is of leading scholars in the field from all over the world, which is studying the principal international collections of these sculptures, will help to restore them to their rightful position. Similarly, this handsome and informative work by Robert Wenley is another step in the rehabilitation of this neglected area of art and will, in due course, be followed by a comprehensive catalogue of French Sculpture in the Wallace Collection.

I would like to thank Professor Andrew Ciechanowiecki who, for many years, was a lonely voice extolling the virtues of these bronzes. It is due to his generosity that this publication, the first substantial work on Wallace Collection sculpture since 1931, has been made possible.

John Lewis
Chairman of the Trustees of the Wallace Collection

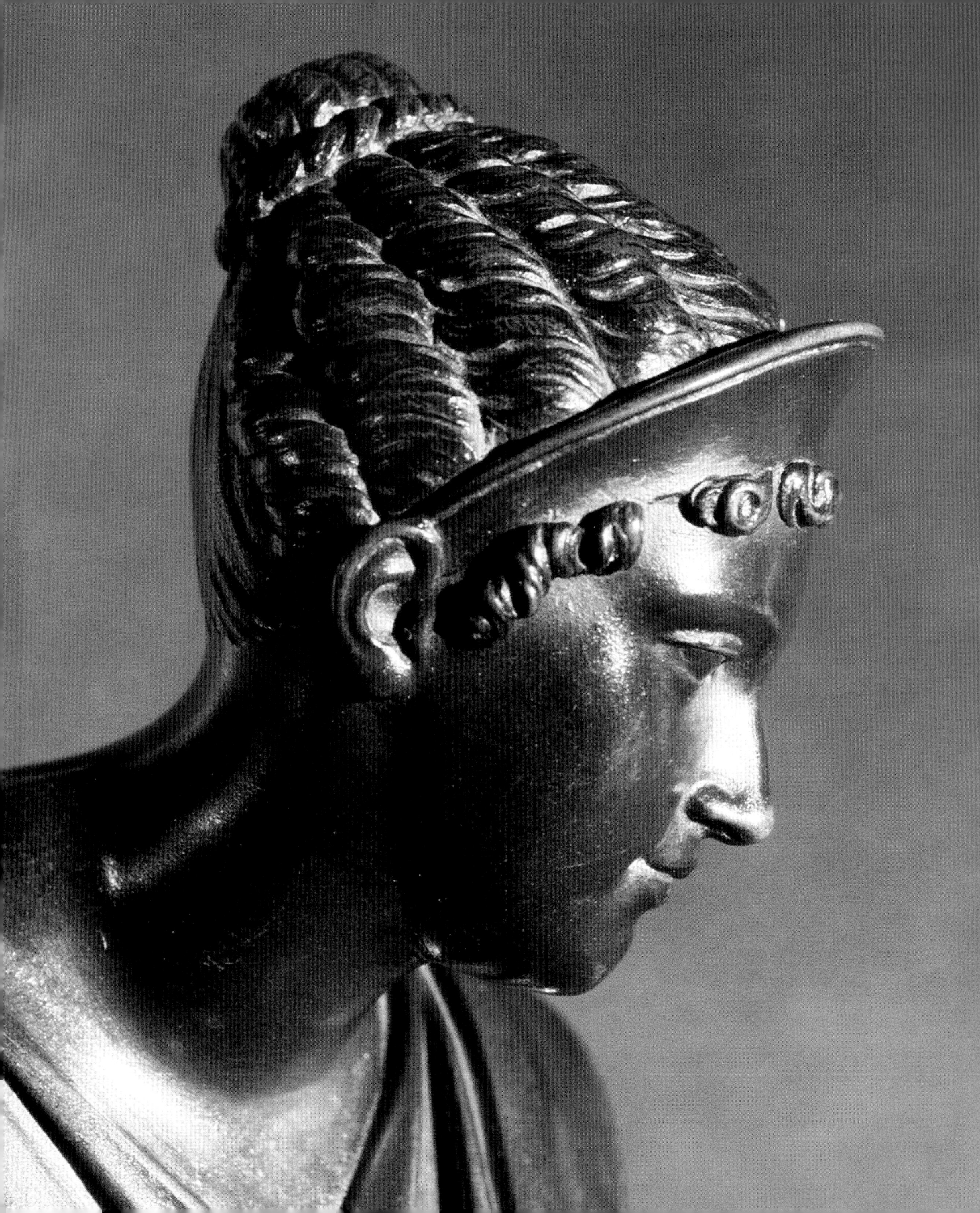

Preface

The Wallace Collection has long been celebrated for its outstanding array of French 17th and 18th century works of art. Bronzes – intimate small-scale statuettes, usually made for collectors – are a rich element of this cornucopia. The Collection contains almost one hundred examples, ranging in date from the late-16th century to the early-19th century. It is one of the largest such collections in the world – indeed probably more French bronzes of the period are on display here at Hertford House than anywhere else – and it includes several pieces of the finest quality.

In 1968, the late Sir Francis Watson, then Director of the Wallace Collection, lamented the neglect of French bronze statuettes as objects of study and forcefully argued the case for their reappraisal. Thirty-four years later, while there is more enthusiasm than in the 1960s for this class of object among art historians and collectors, research into the subject still trails far behind that enjoyed by Italian bronzes. The catalogue in which Sir Francis's essay appears (see Bibliography, p. 108, Fischer) remains one of the few texts of substance devoted to these beautiful works of art.

The intention of this publication is essentially threefold: to introduce French bronzes in general to a wider audience, to provide superb colour images of the finest examples in this Collection, and to publish new information on specific models and casts. It is hoped that this will stimulate wider interest and so act as a stepping-stone to the proposed complete and comprehensive new catalogue of all the sculpture in the Wallace Collection. The selection of statuettes, which form the greater part of the individual entries, is accompanied by examples of ecclesiastical statuary and portrait busts. Together they hint at some of the other categories of bronze sculpture that were created in the period covered by this book.

Kindled by the encouragement of John Lewis, Chairman of the Trustees of the Wallace Collection, the author Robert Wenley and Jonathan Marsden, Deputy Surveyor of the Queen's Works of Art, established the French Bronze Study Group in 2000. This aims to promote and foster research in the field, and I am both happy and proud for *French Bronzes in the Wallace Collection* to be published in recognition of the burgeoning international interest in these sensual and sophisticated works of art.

Rosalind Savill
Director, The Wallace Collection

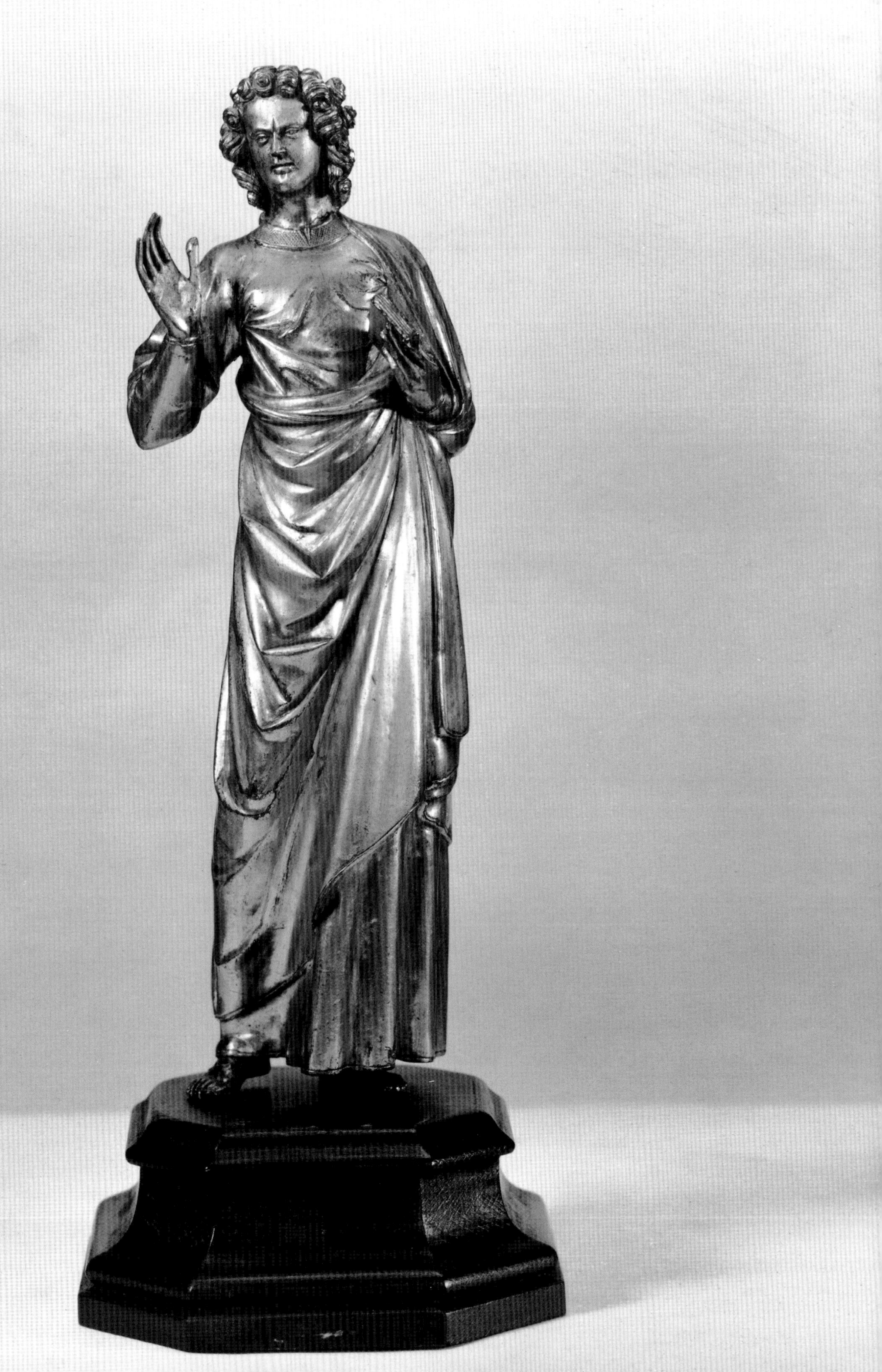

The French Bronze Statuette to c.1815

THE TRADITION of making small bronzes in France can be traced back to a famous 9th-century figure of Charlemagne now in the Louvre. However, bronze statuettes were not made specifically for collectors in France until the late 16th century. In the intervening years, small-scale pieces were made primarily for religious or dynastic purposes. Examples in the Wallace Collection include an exquisite gilt figure of *St John the Apostle* (fig. 1), from a late 13th-century reliquary casket, and a curious early 16th-century

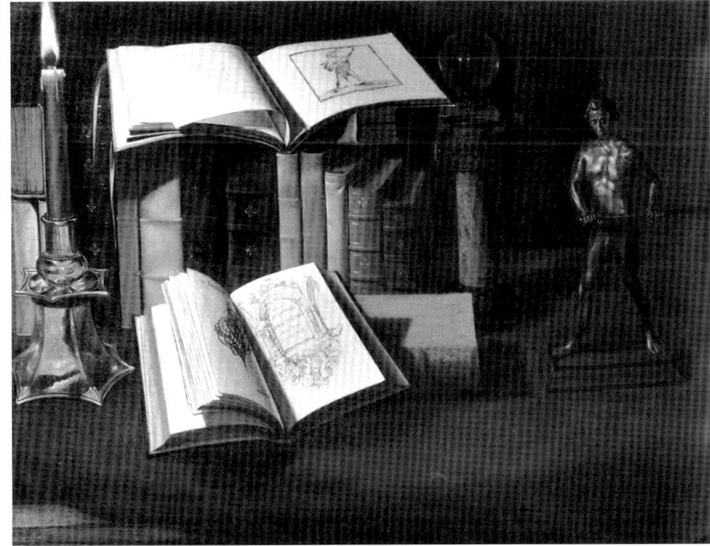

Fig. 3 *Still Life with Books, Candlestick and Bronze Statuette*, Sébastien Stoskopff (1597–1657), *c*.1635–45, oil on canvas, 51 × 69 cm. Musée du Louvre, Paris (RF 1980.22). The statuette is of a model attributed to Barthélemy Prieur

relief portrait-bust of *Louis XII* (reigned 1498–1515) (fig. 2). His successor, François Ier (1515–47) employed several prominent Italian artists in Paris and at his château at Fontainebleau, most notably Cellini and Primaticcio. Their work proved highly influential on such native sculptors as Germain **Pilon** and Ponce Jacquiot (see p. 30).

Italian influences undoubtedly also encouraged the taste for small bronzes, which had been made and collected since the mid-15th century in northern Italy in conscious emulation of classical practice. Barthélemy **Prieur**, who had worked in Turin in the 1560s, was perhaps the first French specialist manufacturer of statuettes and the most significant around 1600. Numerous casts survive of many of the models attributed to him. They were acquired in his own lifetime by the King, Henri IV, and continued to be collected in France long after his death: Louis XIV's garden-designer, André Le Nôtre (1613–1700), probably owned at least twenty-five. These were objects to be admired close to the eye, turned in the hand, or placed

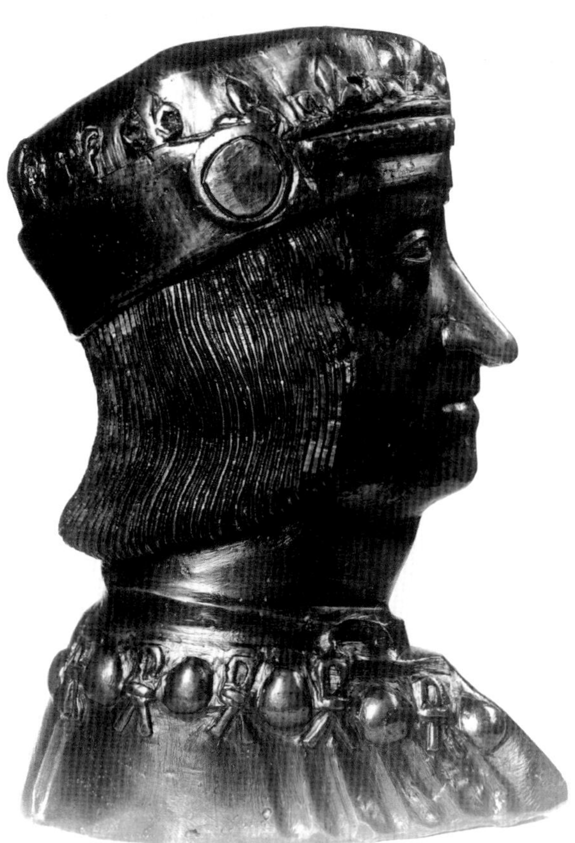

Fig. 2 Relief Bust of *Louis XII*, French early 16th century, bronze, h.: 23.5 cm. Wallace Collection (S153)

Fig. 1 *St John the Apostle* (originally from the *Châsse de tous les Saints*, Rouen Cathedral), French late 13th century, gilt copper, h.: 7.6 cm. Wallace Collection (S152)

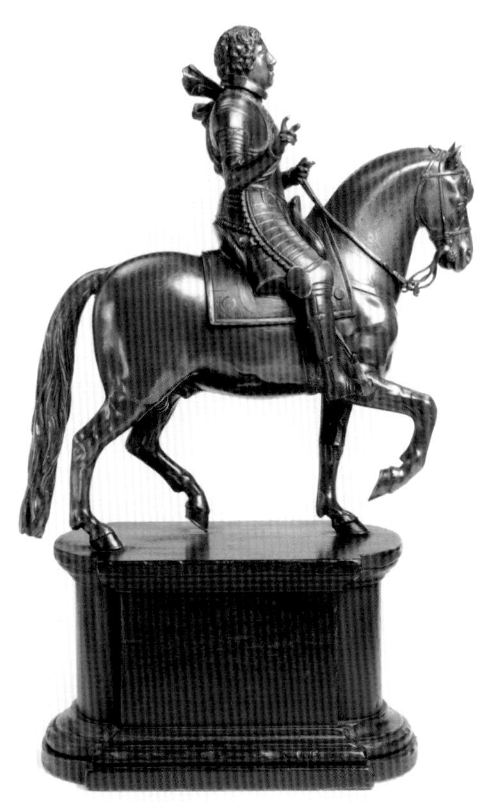

Fig. 4 *Louis XIII on Horseback*, H. Le Sueur, *c*.1620/5, bronze, h.: 20.5 cm. Victoria and Albert Museum, London (A.1-1994). Given by the Trustees of the Crescent Trust in memory of L. and R.J. Lewis

on a shelf, cupboard or desk in the collector's cabinet (fig. 3). Other contemporary sculptor-founders who made small bronzes included Prieur's own colleague and son-in-law Guillaume Dupré (*c*.1576–1643), today better known as a medallist.

Collectors of bronzes in France particularly favoured reductions of famous antique models, and casts after models by **Giambologna** or his followers in Florence – bronzes that had been prized since the late-16th century throughout Europe. Most were probably cast in Italy, but they were certainly also made in north European workshops, some perhaps in France (see fig. 11). Nevertheless, remarkably few *original* French bronze statuettes were created between the death of Prieur and the 1690s. French bronzes rarely amounted to more than five per cent of collections formed during the 17th century. Under Louis XIII (1610–43) the uncertain political climate may have contributed to a general dearth of sculptural commissions and thus of sculptors. One of the few who made small bronzes was Hubert Le Sueur (*c*.1585–*c*.1658), who served Charles I in England after a period working for Louis XIII (fig. 4). He was able to cast his own bronzes, but larger-scale works tended to be made by specialist founders, such as Henri **Perlan**.

Even in the early years of Louis XIV (1643–1715) very few bronze

statuettes cast from new models by French sculptors can be identified. The most significant were by Michel Anguier (1612–1686), who returned to Paris in 1651 after ten years in Rome, where he worked closely with Alessandro **Algardi**. In 1652, he modelled a series of figures of gods and goddesses, each about half a metre high, which were then cast as bronze statuettes. Many examples exist of the *Amphitrite* (fig. 5), by far the most popular model. Anguier's work, much influenced by antique sculpture and classical texts, provides an important link between the contemporary Italian baroque style, the earlier schools of Fontainebleau and the brand of French classicism that emerged in the years ahead.

In the 1690s, several factors coalesced to create an unprecedented – and unsurpassed – market for French bronze statuettes. One of the most important stimuli was the great flood of commissions for marble sculpture for the gardens and palace of Versailles, to where Louis XIV and his court moved in 1682. The fame of the resulting ensemble stimulated a desire among courtiers and *amateurs* for bronze reductions of the most famous works. In this way those who were unable to obtain their own marble sculptures could, perhaps, acquire something of the *kudos* of the originals – at about a tenth of the cost. The most frequently copied marbles were two *Abduction* groups intended for the *Parterre d'Eau* at Versailles (see pp. 54–7). Reductions after copies of famous antique marbles at Versailles were also made in some quantity, as were those after some of the marble sculptures for Louis XIV's château at Marly.

Many French bronze statuettes were made from the mid-1690s as a result of the 'statue campaign' in France of 1685–6. This saw the commissioning of nearly twenty monumental representations of Louis XIV, usually on horseback. The most successful were copied in bronze reductions and widely distributed as a mark of devotion to the monarch. Well-placed patrons could obtain large-scale casts, but table statuettes were the most popular, regularly appearing in 18th-century inventories and sale catalogues.

During the 1690s, François **Girardon**, Le Nôtre, the Grand Dauphin (see pp. 34–5), and the King himself, to name only some of the most prominent individuals, were all amassing sizeable collections. Girardon's *Galerie* became particularly well known from a series of prints representing it in a fictive setting (see p. 6 and figs 32, 36, 64). These collections were still dominated by casts after antique and Giambologna workshop models. But they must have stimulated a taste for small bronzes among courtiers, encouraging the production, as well as influencing the style, of independent French bronzes.

Contemporary Italian sculpture was also highly influential, not only the work of such sculptors as Bernini (1598–1680), **Algardi** and **Duquesnoy** in Rome, but also Florentine bronzes by

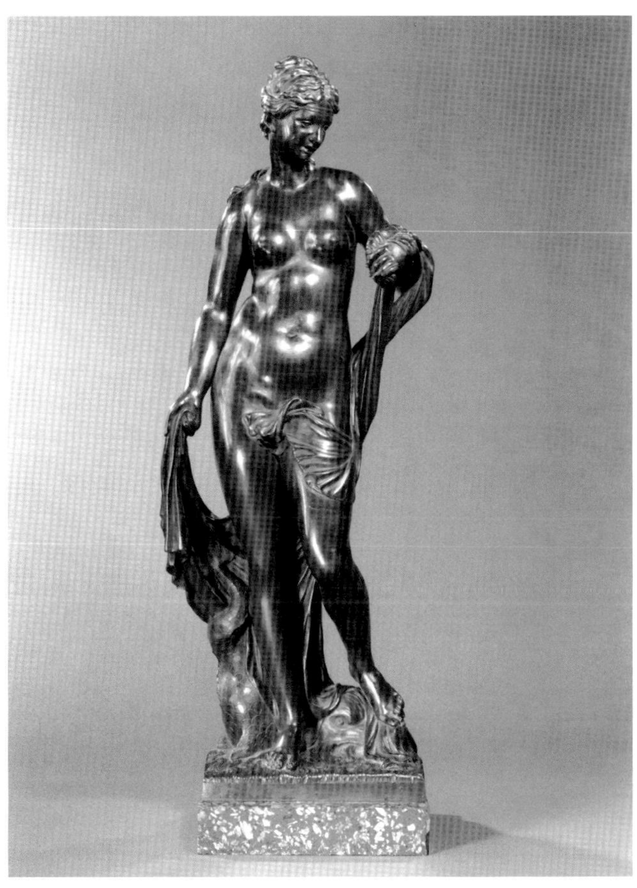

Fig. 5 *Amphitrite*, after M. Anguier, by 1693, bronze, h.: 53cm. Musée du Louvre, Paris (OA 11897)

Ferdinando Tacca (see p. 60), **Foggini** and Soldani (see p. 68). Tacca's two-figure groups engage in dialogue or dramatic contact and have an implied single, frontal viewpoint (fig. 6). Very often the subjects of such Florentine bronzes were taken from classical mythology and they were frequently conceived in pairs, so that they might be shown in a balanced, decorative display. The same traits can be seen repeatedly in French bronzes of the early 18th century.

One of Tacca's followers was the Frenchman François Spingola ('Lespingola'; 1644–1705), to whom are attributed a series of bronzes illustrating the story of Hercules. These may be dated to the late 1690s, the beginning of a long period of decline in official commissions for work at the royal palaces, to which the sudden outpouring of bronze statuettes from French sculptors was certainly in part a response. Their contemporary status can be gauged by the fact that only between 1690 and 1700 was a bronze statuette acceptable as a sculptor's admission piece (*morceau de réception*) to the Académie Royale (acceptance provided much greater opportunity for securing prestigious official commissions and positions). It is therefore perhaps unsurprising that the number of bronze statuettes exhibited at the Academy Salons peaked in 1704.

Several sculptors specialised in making bronzes specifically for private collectors, usually employing others to help cast or finish them. Philippe **Bertrand**, Robert **Le Lorrain**, and Corneille **Van Clève** favoured graceful mythological scenes, treated in a light manner, reflecting wider tastes during the early 18th century. Their bronzes often have compositions of a pictorial, even theatrical, nature, which bear a striking resemblance to those in contemporary French history paintings and in cabinet pictures by certain Dutch artists (fig. 7), a product of the shared influence of classical sculpture. In the 18th century these bronzes would have been displayed alongside the brass and turtleshell of fashionable boulle-marquetry furniture. This was often embellished with gilt-bronze mounts similarly depicting figures from Ovidian mythology, sometimes cast from models supplied by sculptors, and so created a harmonious ensemble (fig. 8).

Van Clève made his bronzes for speculative sale rather than on commission: he brought some of them to his apartment so as to 'the more easily show them to the public and sell them'. But this public can only ever have amounted to a few wealthy collectors, for these were luxury commodities, comparable in cost with the more valuable paintings and *objets d'art*. Casts of most models were as rare then as they are today. The largest collection was actually formed by a foreign monarch, Augustus the Strong of Saxony (1694–1733), one of several German princes who shared the taste for combining French bronzes, Dutch cabinet pictures and Boulle furniture. His agent bought about one hundred French bronzes in Paris in two purchases of 1699 and 1715, of which perhaps thirty were after

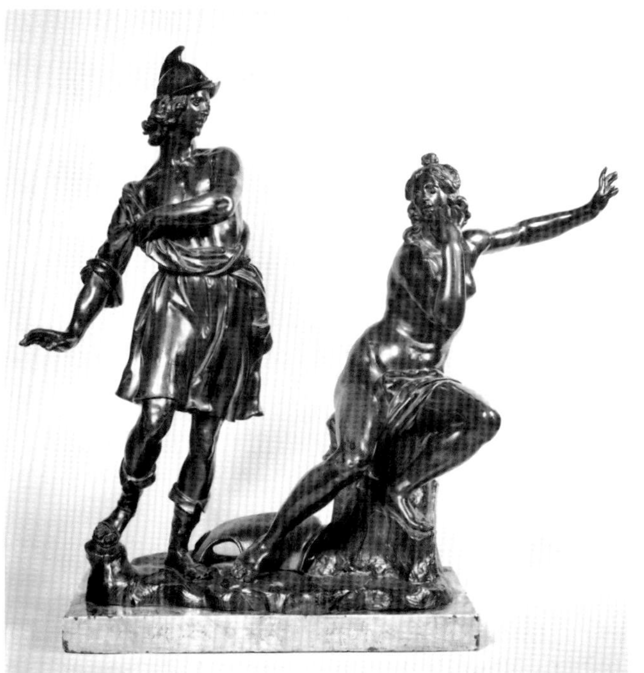

Fig. 6 *Roger and Angelica*, attributed to F. Tacca, mid-17th century, bronze, h.: 43 cm. Musée du Louvre, Paris (OA 7811)

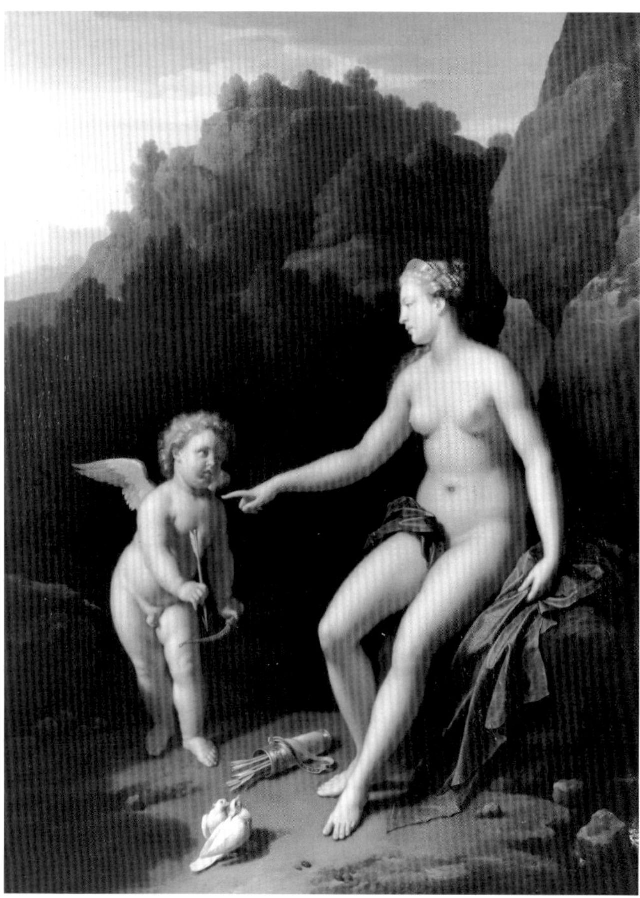

Fig. 7 *Venus and Cupid*, Adriaen van der Werff (1659–1722), 1716, oil on panel, 45.1 × 33.4 cm. Wallace Collection (P151)

dealers' stock books of the period. Probably their greatest connoisseur was Blondel de Gagny (1695–1776), in whose Paris townhouse about sixty were displayed in pairs on bookcases and cabinets. Sales usually contained at most twenty 'modern' pieces. The proportion of copies after the antique and Giambologna remained high, but those after the famous marbles at Versailles gradually lost favour to independent bronzes.

The widespread revival of interest in more strictly 'classical' forms in the late 1760s was marked in interior decoration and furniture. Boulle-marquetry cabinets and cupboards were again in favour, and with this came something of a regeneration in the production of French bronze statuettes. **Houdon** employed **Thomire**, a specialist *bronzier* (founder and chaser), to make small-scale casts after his models, while sculptors such as **Boizot** supplied Thomire, among others, with numerous models for the figural furnishing bronzes and clock cases that were so fashionable in the later 18th century (fig. 9). Generally it was the role of *marchands-merciers* (dealers) like Dominique Daguerre (d.1796) to co-ordinate such activity.

From the 1780s, bronze statuettes were cast in increasingly large numbers, indicating a broadening of the available clientele for small bronzes. The organisation and products of the Thomire and Feuchère foundries presaged the industrial casting in series practised by several French firms in the 19th century. Many popular 18th-century models were reproduced, in editions of various heights, for a market that socially and geographically had spread far beyond its traditional parameters.

specifically French models. However, their generally modest quality of finish confirms that they were intended for an essentially decorative display *en masse*.

In the mid-18th century there was a decline in the production of newly-conceived French bronzes. Not one was exhibited at over twenty Salons held between 1737 and 1769. Few can be attributed to sculptors active in those years. Bronzes that might be thought to relate to models of the 1750 or '60s, such as those sometimes attributed to **Falconet**, are usually much later casts. Under Louis XV (1723–74), furniture veneered with light woods replaced the dark and heavy Boulle marquetry, and brightly-coloured oriental, Meissen or Sèvres porcelain became immensely fashionable. Sculptors continued to supply figurative models for gilt-bronze furniture mounts and clock-cases, but patinated bronzes fitted less well into the new interiors. In 1748 the famous Parisian dealer Gersaint wrote of their 'dismal tone...for which they are ordinarily reproached'.

Nevertheless, copies of contemporary French sculpture, such as monuments to Louis XV, continued to be made during the mid-18th century. French bronzes were still widely collected, as demonstrated by their regular appearance in sale catalogues and

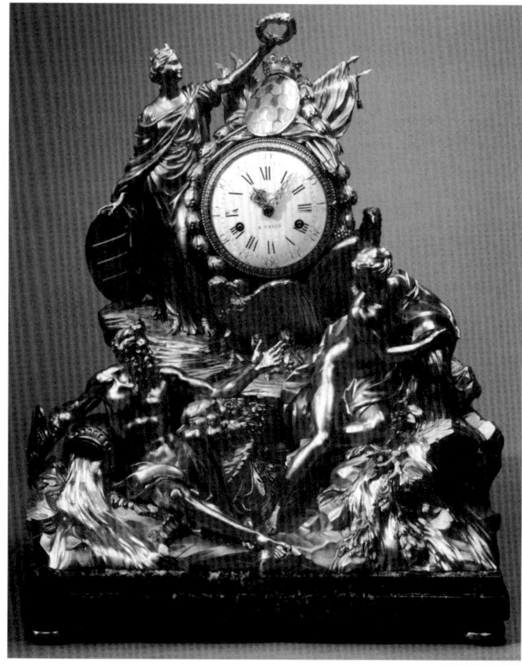

Fig. 9 *The 'Avignon' Clock*, (case) modelled by L.-S. Boizot, *c*.1771, gilt bronze, h.: 68.5 cm. Wallace Collection (F258)

fig. 8 *Apollo and Daphne*, gilt-bronze mount, h.: 25.2 cm; from an *armoire* (wardrobe) attributed to André-Charles Boulle (1642–1732), *c*.1700. Wallace Collection (F62)

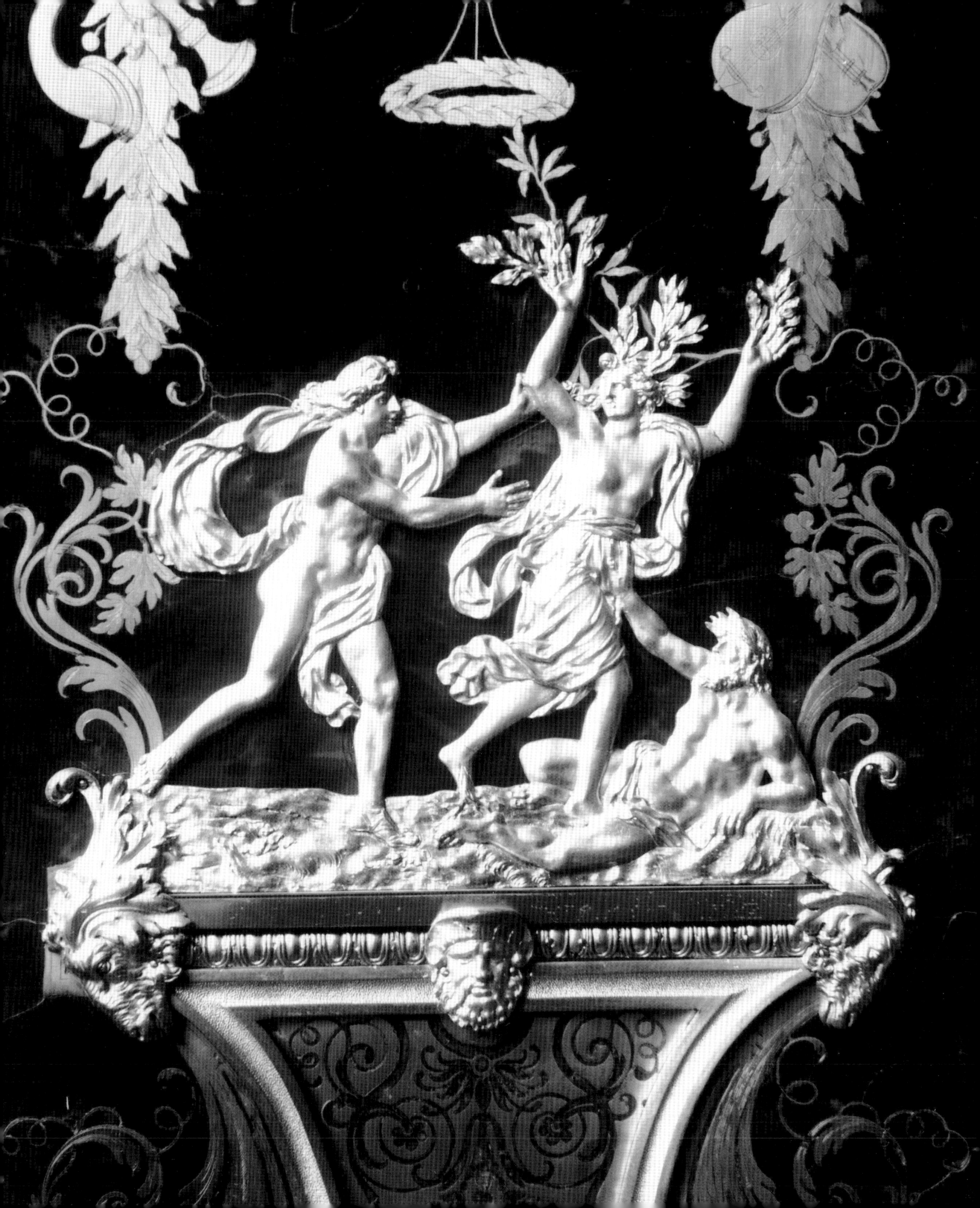

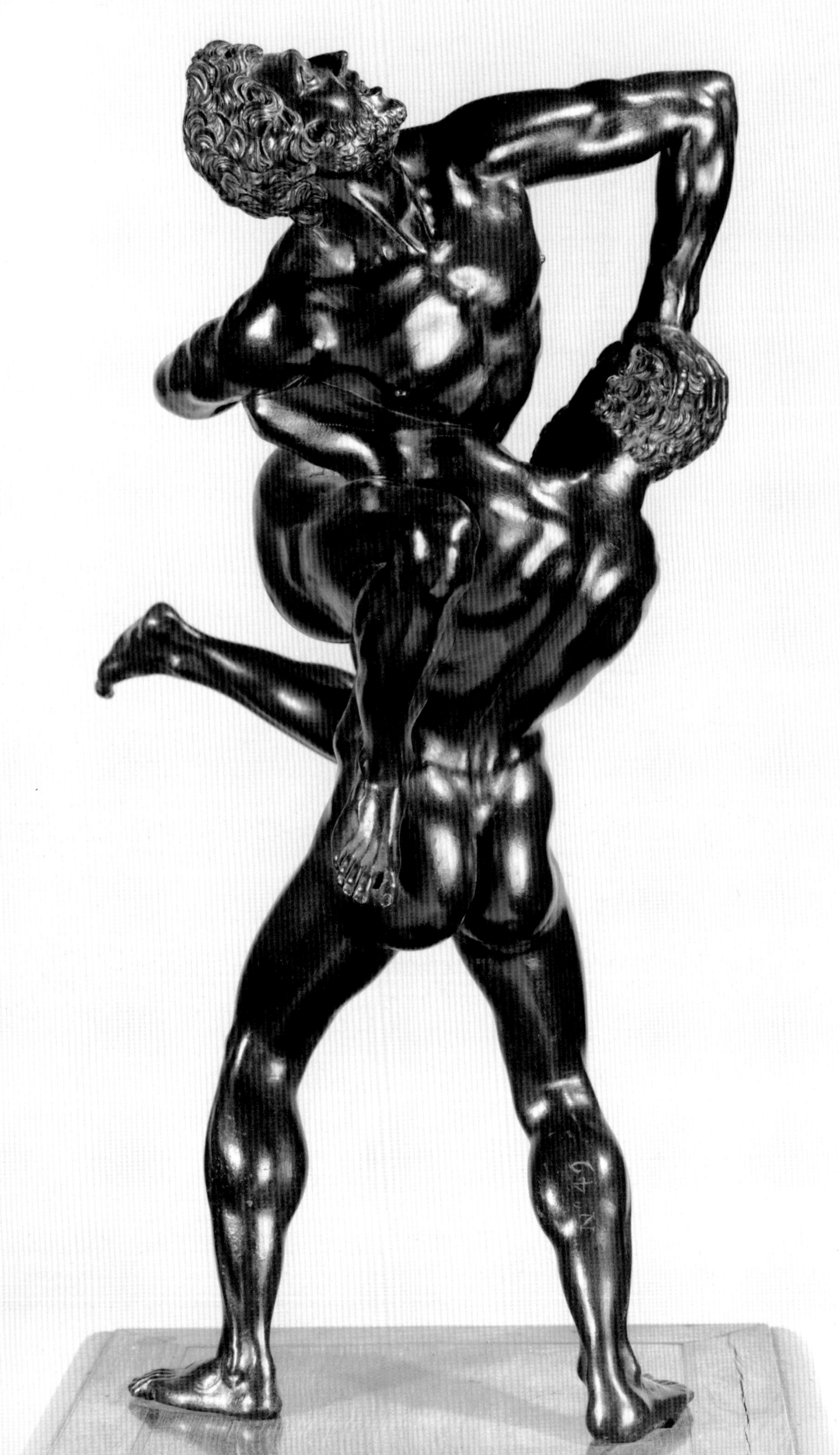

The Taste of the Founders of the Wallace Collection
for French Bronzes

THE FRENCH BRONZES in the Wallace Collection were obtained by the three principal Founders during the course of the 19th century. Their respective acquisitions were particular and distinct, and to some extent inevitably reflected broader patterns of taste among wealthy 19th-century European collectors.

Francis Seymour-Conway, 3rd Marquess of Hertford (1777–1842) (fig. 10) was most active as a collector in the 1800s and

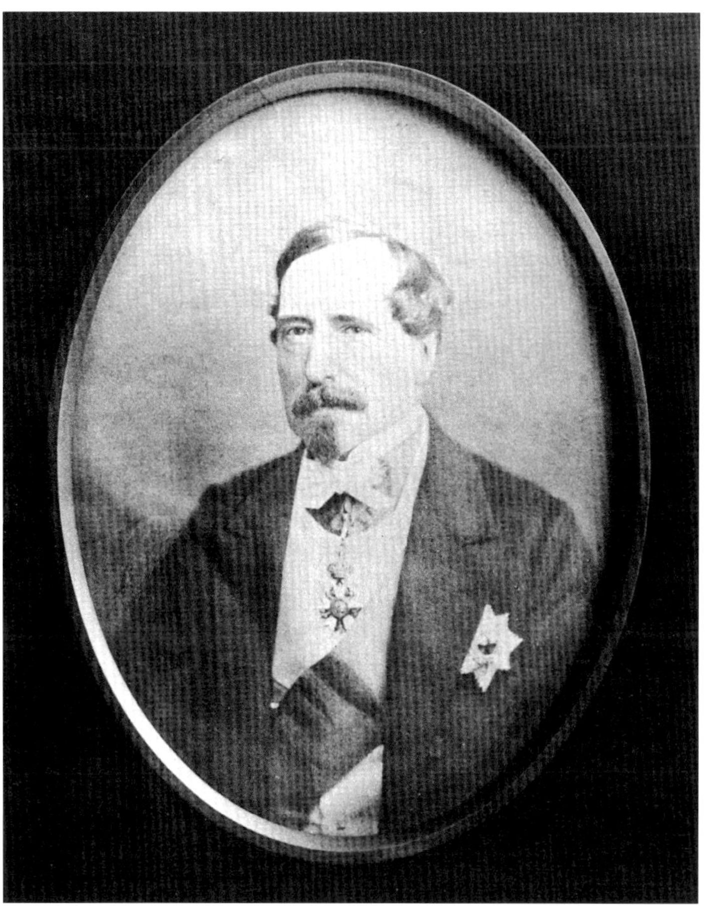

Fig. 12 *The 4th Marquess of Hertford*, Etienne Carjat (1828–?1906), *c.*1860, photograph. Library of Hertford House

1810s, when political and military upheavals across Europe broke up old collections and threw unprecedented quantities of high quality bronzes onto the market. He was a close friend at the time to the Prince Regent, later George IV (1762–1830) and, like him, built up a sculpture collection that was richest in French bronzes and casts after Giambolognesque models. His dozen or so bronzes in the latter category were mainly Florentine, but two that had been part of the French Royal Collection – partly dispersed during the Revolution – could be French casts (fig. 11). The French bronzes

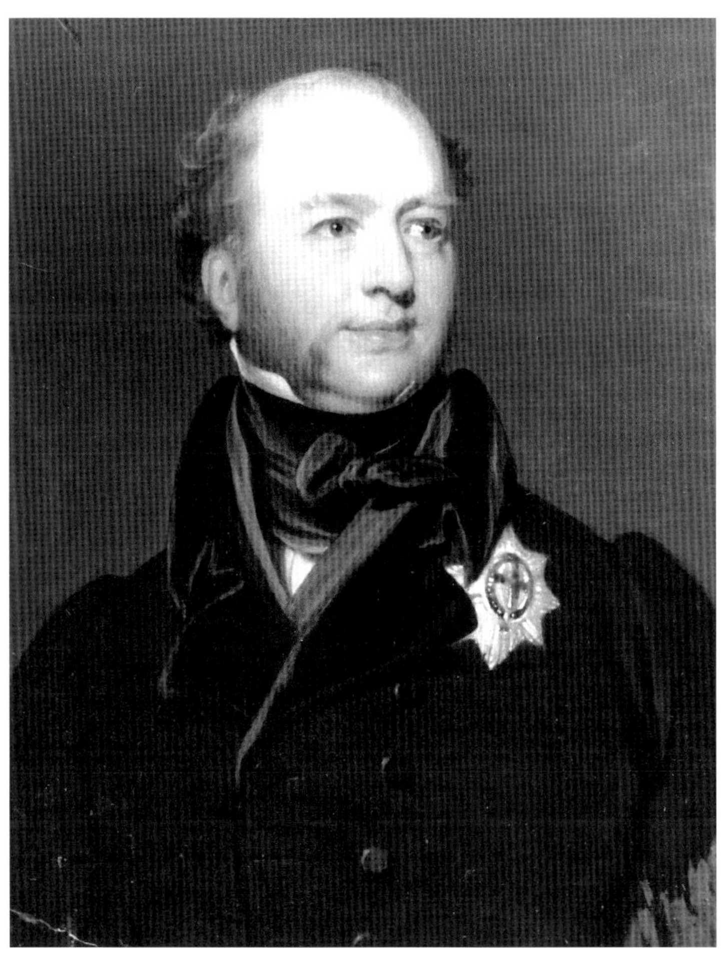

Fig. 10 *The 3rd Marquess of Hertford, after Lawrence*, Henry Bone (1755–1834), 1824, enamel, 9.7 × 7.5 cm. Library of Hertford House (MA3)

Fig. 11 *Hercules and Antaeus*, after Giambologna, possibly French, probably by 1662, bronze, h.: 39.4 cm. Wallace Collection (S120)

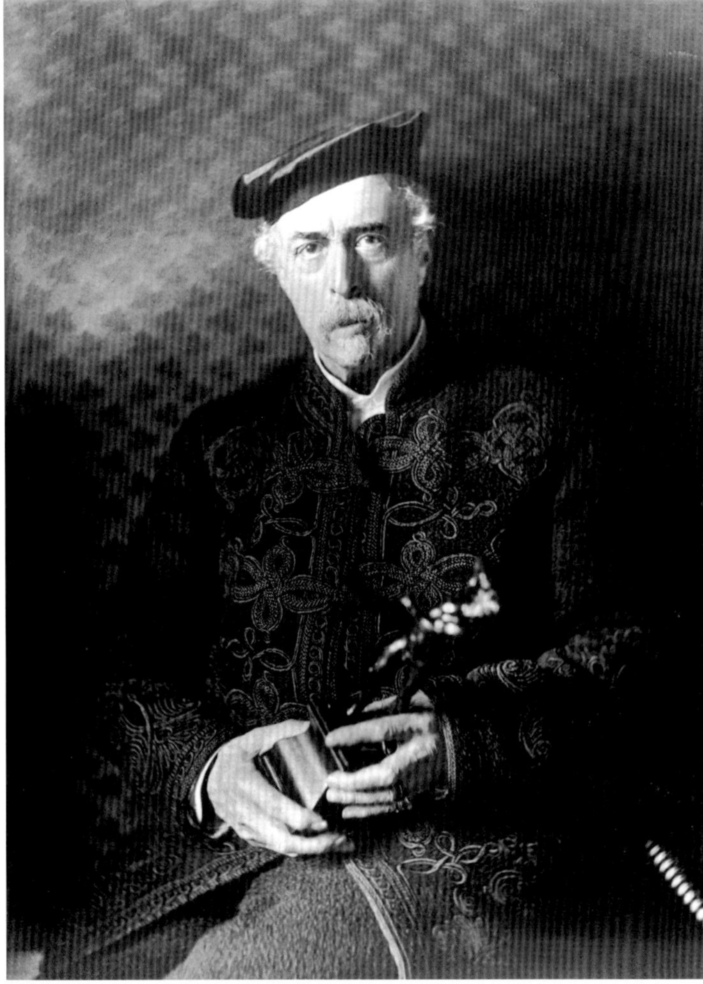

Fig. 14 *Sir Richard Wallace*, John Thomson (1837–1921), 1888, photograph. Library of Hertford House

included a gilt pair of *Marly Horses*, and reductions of famous marbles made for Versailles (pp. 54–7, 94–5). The superb version of the *Borghese Dancers* (pp. 32–3), a much greater rarity, may also have been acquired by the 3rd Marquess. The French bronzes were displayed together in his principal London property, Dorchester House. The majority passed to his son, the 4th Marquess.

Richard Seymour-Conway, 4th Marquess of Hertford (1800–1870) (fig. 12), was, with George IV, one of the great collectors of the 19th century, and similarly favoured French bronzes. Indeed, their respective collections in this sphere were probably the most important to have been formed anywhere since the early 18th century and have not since been surpassed. The 4th Marquess's bronzes were just one element of his lavishly-financed accumulation of works of art, especially of the 18th century, from France, his adopted homeland. They were mainly acquired in the 1850s and 1860s.

The 4th Marquess was unusual among his contemporaries in France and England not only for building a collection that contained relatively few Italian bronzes, but also in acquiring French bronzes ranging widely in date from the mid-16th to mid-19th centuries. Outstanding among the earlier works is the magnificent *Bust of Charles IX* by **Pilon** (pp. 24–5), his most expensive bronze, acquired at the celebrated Pourtalès-Gorgier sale of 1865, whence also came Hals's *Laughing Cavalier*. By then he had already bought three bronzes attributed to **Prieur** – although these were generally thought to be Italian at the time. One had been purchased at the Fould sale of 1860, where Lord Hertford obtained twelve of the 84 bronzes on offer, including the **Girardon** vases and the little group of *Drunken Silenus* (pp. 58–9, 78–9).

Like his father, the 4th Marquess acquired several bronzes after famous classical or Italian models. These included the superb *bronzes de galerie* representing the *Nile* and the *Tiber*, after the antique, and the magnificent casts after **Algardi**'s 'firedogs', which had belonged to the French Crown (pp. 34–41). More unusual were the several independent works, often unique casts, most notably the prize that the young Voltaire failed to win (pp. 70–1) and the extraordinary group commissioned by the notorious abbé Terray from Jean-Jacques **Caffiéri** (pp. 86–7). This was one of the first bronzes we know Lord Hertford to have bought, acquired in 1851 from the collection of another francophile Englishman, Lord Pembroke.

The later bronzes were no less remarkable. Fine life-size casts from the 1780s of two of **Houdon**'s most celebrated female compositions, 'La Frileuse' (now in the Metropolitan Museum of Art, New York) and *Diana the Huntress* (fig. 13), were kept in Paris, but did not form part of Lady Wallace's bequest. They complemented an extensive group of Houdon marbles – now also largely dispersed – just as the exquisite statuettes of Napoleon and his Empress (pp. 100–3) were part of a wider collection of works of art relating to the Emperor.

All these were inherited in 1870 by the 4th Marquess's only, illegitimate, son, Sir Richard Wallace (1818–1890) (fig. 14), the third great collector in the family, who had hitherto lived all his adult life in Paris. However, although he shared his father's interest in 18th-century French art, he appears to have acquired very few such bronzes. One of them may be identifiable with the gilt statuette of *Fidelity* (pp. 88–9), since a bronze of this description appeared in the (anonymous) sale of his youthful collection in 1857. More generally, Wallace's tastes, typical for his generation, were for medieval and renaissance art. It is therefore not surprising that his only certain contributions among the French bronzes are three Prieurs, including a cast of the delightful *Acrobat* (pp. 28–9), said to have been his last purchase: a suitably brilliant finale.

Fig. 13 *Diana the Huntress*, J.-A. Houdon, 1782, bronze, h.: 209 cm. Huntington Library and Art Gallery, San Marino, California

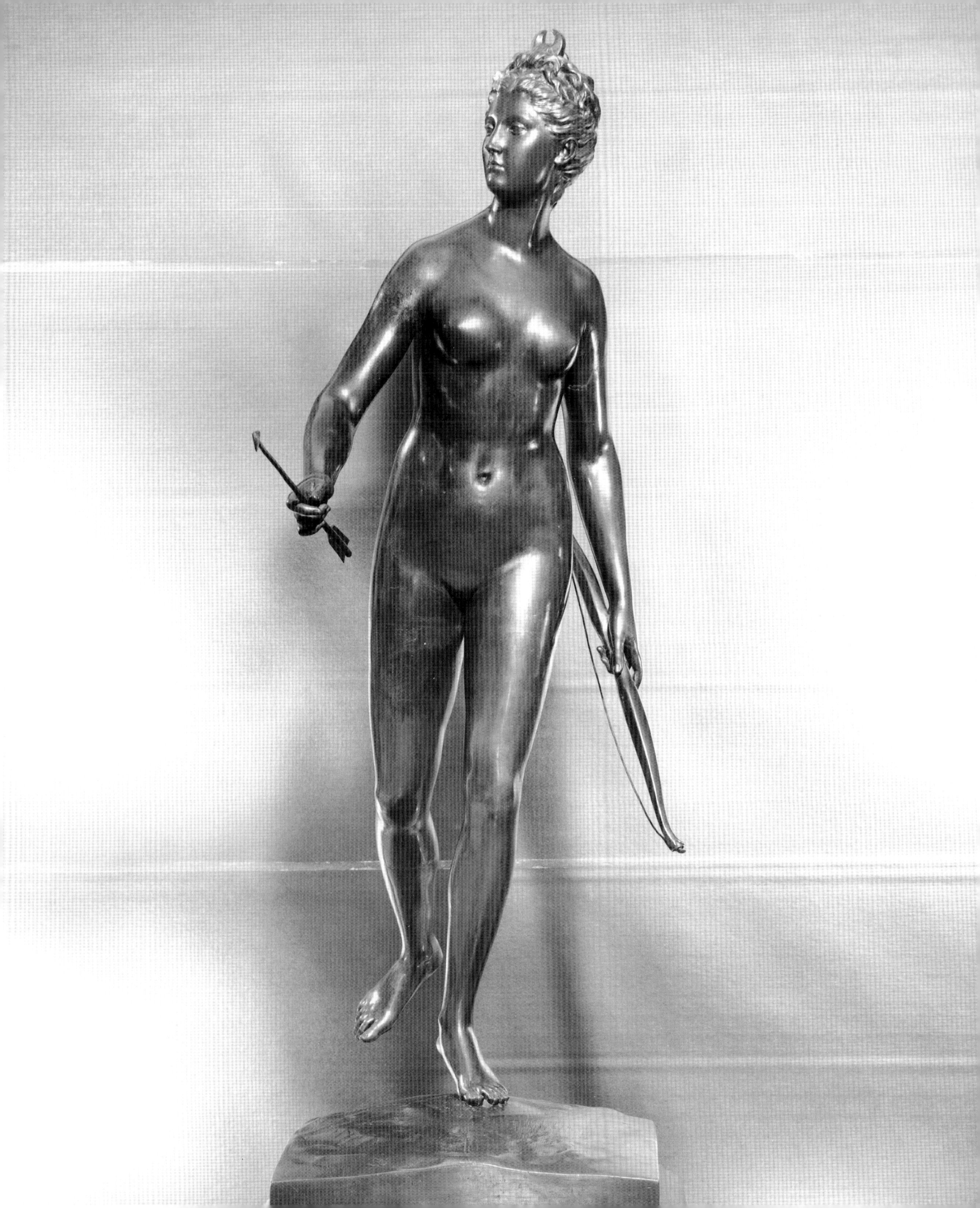

Techniques of Casting and Finishing
French Bronze Statuettes c.1565–c.1815

Until the late 18th century the majority of French bronze statuettes were made using the indirect lost-wax technique, which permitted the casting of numerous replicas of an original model (fig. 15). This began with the making of a plaster sectional piece-mould (B) from the model (A). Each section was lined internally with molten wax, typically by 'slush-moulding', to about 5mm thick for bronzes under a metre in height (C). The sections could be joined at the wax stage to reproduce the casting model, or some parts might be cast separately (Ci) and joined later in the metal. Refinements could easily be made to the wax model. Wire supports were employed to strengthen the core (inner mould) that was made of a refractory (fireproof) material, typically a mixture of plaster or unfired clay, sand or crushed fired clay and perhaps organic fibres (D). Core-pins (usually iron nails or wires) were inserted through the wax into the core and left projecting on the outside so as to engage with the investment (outer mould) and thus keep the model in place during the casting process. A casting-cup and a circulatory system of sprues (wax rods that would

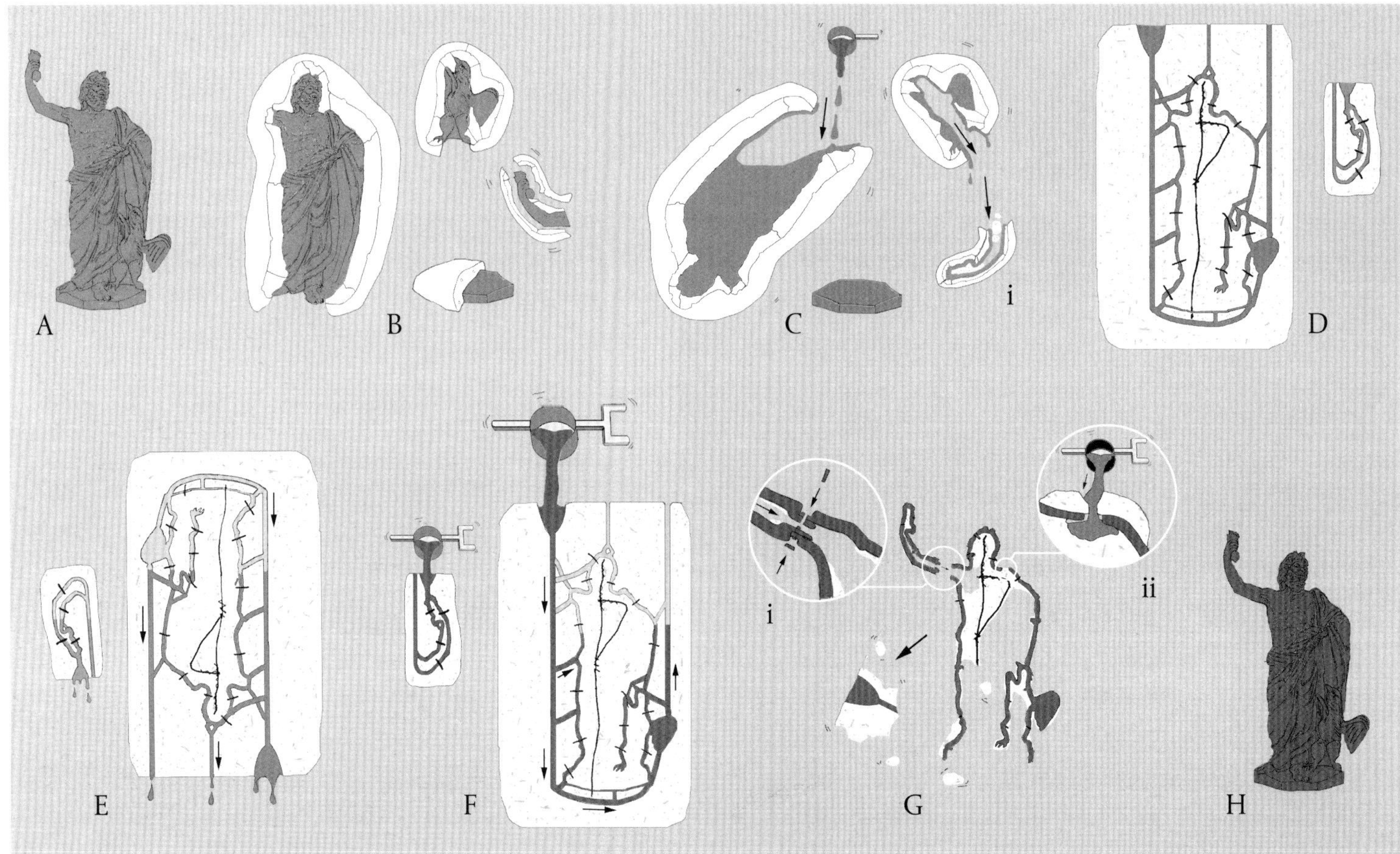

Fig. 15 Diagram of the lost-wax casting process used in France from the late 17th century to the late 18th century. © Francesca Bewer, Harvard University Art Museums

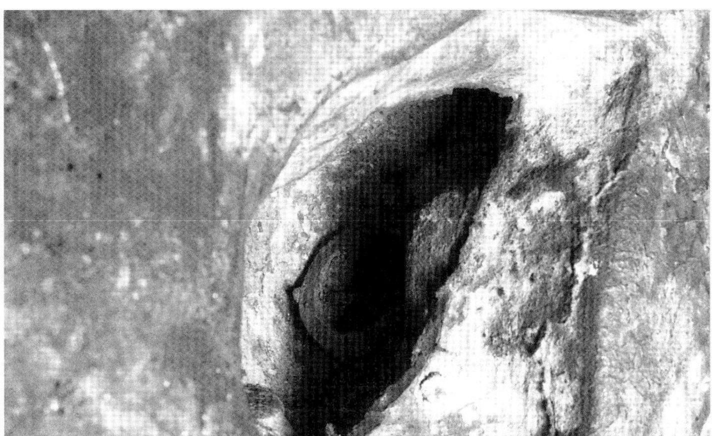

Fig. 16 Interior detail of *Crouching Venus*, after Coysevox (see pp. 42–4), showing sleeve-join. Wallace Collection (S188). photo: Alastair Johnson

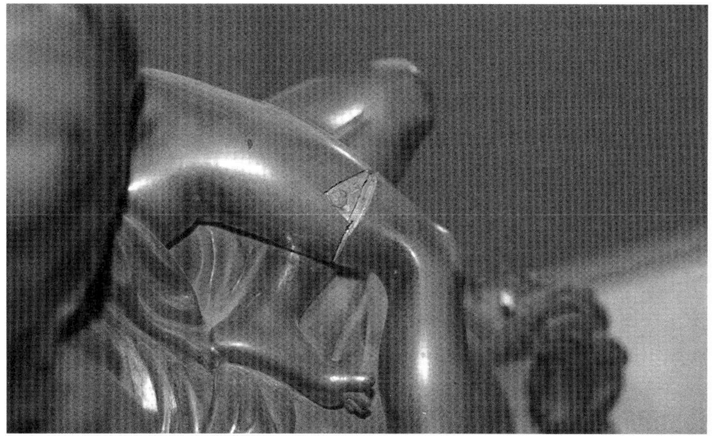

Fig. 17 Detail of *Roman Abducting a Sabine*, French c.1699. Grünes Gewölbe, Dresden (IX.26). photo: author

become channels in the mould) were joined by heat to the exterior of the wax model. The assemblage was coated with investment, (a refractory material similar to that of the core), which was built up into an outer mould and left to harden (D). The mould was heated to expel all moisture and wax, leaving a 'negative' of the model and the surrounding tubular network of 'sprues' (E).

The hollow mould could then be filled via the cup and sprues with the molten bronze (F). Bronze is an alloy made up primarily of copper with tin and, often, significant amounts of zinc and lead. The precise proportions of each element varied between workshops and from pour to pour. After the metal had cooled, the investment was broken away, revealing the cast bronze within its cage of sprues (see fig. 41), which were then cut off, together with other unwanted excrescences resulting from the casting process (G). Small faults were plugged with brass screws, larger gaps were repaired with cast-in fills of bronze or lead (Gii), and any separately-cast parts were joined to the figure (Gi) (see below).

Some of the smaller bronzes attributed to **Prieur** are of leaded brass (a copper-zinc alloy), and several were cast partly solid, although this increased the chance of casting flaws. However, French bronzes made in the late 17th and 18th centuries were often cast in (hollow) sections and joined together in the metal (as yet we know little about the alloys that were favoured). Typically each figure and its limbs, especially if extended, as well as any attributes or drapery that projected well beyond the main bulk of the composition, were cast separately. Individual figures, and smaller parts, could be simply screwed or slotted into the base or each other. Often this was done with 'sleeve' joins (Gi), in which a narrower tubular addition cast at the top of a limb is slotted into the torso of a figure and secured with iron pins, which sometimes are retained on the interior with a metal ring (fig. 16). Many of the bronzes in the documented collection in Dresden (see p. 13) have joins of this type but are, unusually, recessed. The pin 'heads' could

thus be concealed with a 'bracelet' of thin patches of bronze (fig. 17).

More prestigious bronzes, made on commission and thus existing in only a single example, could be cast in a single pour. This was the case with the superb *Borghese Dancers* cast by **Perlan** (pp. 32–3). **Pilon**'s *Bust of Charles IX* (pp. 24–5) was most likely made in two parts, as was **Caffiéri**'s *Cupid Vanquishing Pan* (pp. 86–7), probably principally to facilitate the meticulous tooling of the surfaces of these important works.

For once cast and shorn of its unwanted protruberances, a bronze was ready for more refined chasing and tooling, generally with delicate goldsmith's hammers, files and punches, and polishing, often using a wire-brush (fig. 18).

The final stage was the application of surface coatings, in the form of chemical patinas or varnishes, which helped to conceal joins and faults, and could be used to preserve the bright appearance of cast bronze (H). Bronzes attributed to Prieur usually show the remains of a reddish-gold varnish, imitating the finish of contemporary Florentine bronzes. This was probably achieved by

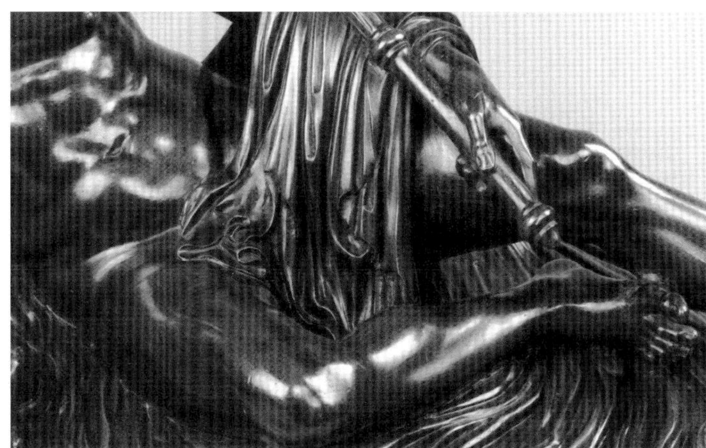

Fig. 18 Detail of *The River God Tiber*, after the antique (see pp. 38–41), showing wire-brush polished surfaces. Wallace Collection (S180)

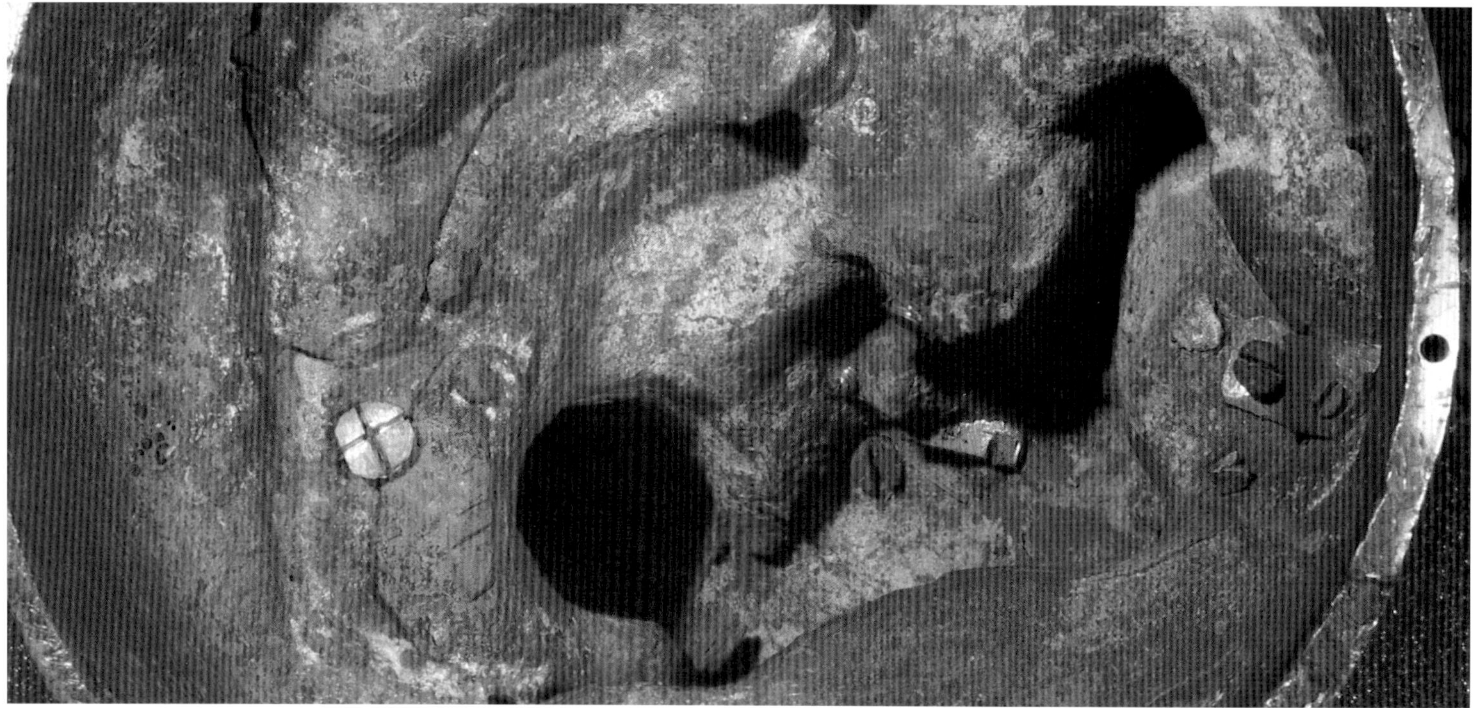

Fig. 19 Interior view of *Cupid Vanquishing Pan*, J.-J. Caffiéri (see pp. 86–7). Wallace Collection (S219). photo: Alastair Johnson

applying drying oils mixed with sanguine, the practice described as standard in France by André Félibien in his *Des Principes…de la sculpture* (1676). Traces of a translucent reddish coating, similar in appearance to that used in contemporary Florentine workshops, are often found on the finest French bronzes of the early 18th century. By the later 18th century a polished black-varnished surface was the prevailing aesthetic taste. A dark-green colour (achieved by applying vinegar), suggestive of archaeological origins and thus carrying antique associations, was sometimes given to later bronzes (see pp. 96–7). Many early patinas have since been concealed or destroyed by subsequent repatinations. Another option, though rarely found on independent French bronzes, was mercury (or 'fire') gilding (see pp. 88–9, 94–5).

Although much investigative work remains to be done using such scientific techniques as X-ray analysis, a great deal can be discovered with the naked eye about the facture of French bronzes from their interiors, where accessible. **Caffiéri**'s *Cupid Vanquishing Pan*, which we know to have been personally cast and finished by the sculptor, provides an excellent case study (fig. 19). The interior consists of a bewildering array of rough edges, pits and craters, threaded bronze bolts and soldered patches. All these are evidence of a defective cast that was nevertheless deemed too valuable to reject and that was instead literally patched up to make good.

Clues as to the dating of a bronze sometimes can also be found in the type of metal base and socle (support), if present, of a bronze. Around 1600, separately or integrally cast bronze bases, for instance those typically found on bronzes attributed to **Prieur**,

usually extended little beyond the footprint of the composition. They were essentially plain and functional, whether irregular or neatly finished. Later in the 17th century, low, naturalistically landscaped or terrain bases (*terrasses*), integral to the composition and sometimes to the cast, became commonplace, and remained so until the later 18th century. French bronzes are also often furnished with a socle, mount or pedestal, sometimes of a quite elaborate nature, and usually of an identifiable stylistic period. However, dating a bronze on this criterion alone is dangerous since this element may be a later copy or originally have been made for something else.

Bronze is by its nature a man-made medium and casting is a reproductive process, so there is no limit to the number of replicas that might be produced of a given model. It is certain that a few very popular examples were made over an extended period of not just decades but centuries. That this was sometimes done illicitly by sculptors and founders pirating the models of others is suggested by the need for the act of 'copyright' pertaining to the work of Academicians that was issued in 1676 and by subsequent regulations limiting the dissemination of specific designs. However, by the mid-19th century several celebrated models of the 17th and 18th centuries were reproduced commercially in large numbers by foundries in France and elsewhere, generally using cheaper, but cruder, sand-casting techniques that did not permit the sophisticated detailing of earlier bronzes. Although the 4th Marquess of Hertford seems rarely to have been fooled, they can deceive the unwary today.

French Bronzes

Charles IX (1550–1574), King of France

MODEL & CAST:

Germain Pilon (*c*.1525–1590), *c*.1570–9

H. (excluding socle): 62.2 cm (24½ in.), H. (including socle): 70.9 cm (28⅛ in.), W. (maximum): 60.5 cm (24 in.)

Heavy, lost-wax cast, open at back. The head (including collar) was probably cast separately from the bust, and inserted into it. Black varnish over mushroom-grey/chocolate brown oxidised metal surface.
On a black marble waisted socle of square section, apparently original to the bronze. Associated with a pedestal of white and coloured marbles of late 16th century design, but probably 19th-century French manufacture (not shown). H.: 111.5 cm (44¼ in.).

In 1560, Charles IX acceded to the French throne at the age of ten. Feeble in character and health, he was dominated by his mother, the scheming Catherine de'Medici (who acted as regent until 1563), and by the duc de Guise, leader of the Catholic faction during a prolonged period of religious civil war in France. The massacre by royal command of some five thousand Huguenots (Protestants) in Paris on St Barthlomew's Day in 1572 was perhaps its lowest point.

Charles IX died just two years later, aged only twenty-three.

The thin lips, shifty eyes and taut features of this portrait of the King brilliantly convey a sense of unease and youthful mistrust, which the grandiose presentation – crowned with laurel, swathed in a mantle embroidered with *fleurs de lis*, and armoured *à l'antique* – only serves to accentuate. As well as being psychologically penetrating, this bronze is also a work of great technical bravura, with the detailed surface treatment of the various parts boldly differentiated to striking effect. It is undoubtedly one of the great masterpieces in the œuvre of Germain Pilon, *Sculpteur du Roi* under both Charles IX and his successor, Henri III.

A marble version of the bust, in the Louvre (fig. 20), is closely related. It has a modern, variant head, but a near-identical body, which may derive from the Wallace Collection bronze, or a common model. Like the marble busts in the Louvre of Henri II and Henri III, similarly thought to be from the workshop of Pilon, it is dated *c*.1574–9. Also related is a bronze bust attributed to Pilon of Henri II (private collection). It has been proposed that all these busts, as well as a series of portrait medals of 1573–7 attributed to Pilon – appointed 'Controller-General of Effigies' at the Royal Mint by Charles IX – were commissioned as an act of self-promotion by Catherine de'Medici.

Believed to have belonged to the duc de Berry (d.1820), heir to the last of the Bourbon monarchs. Acquired in 1865 by the 4th Marquess of Hertford at the Pourtalès-Gorgier sale, Paris, for the enormous sum of 45,000 francs.

S154

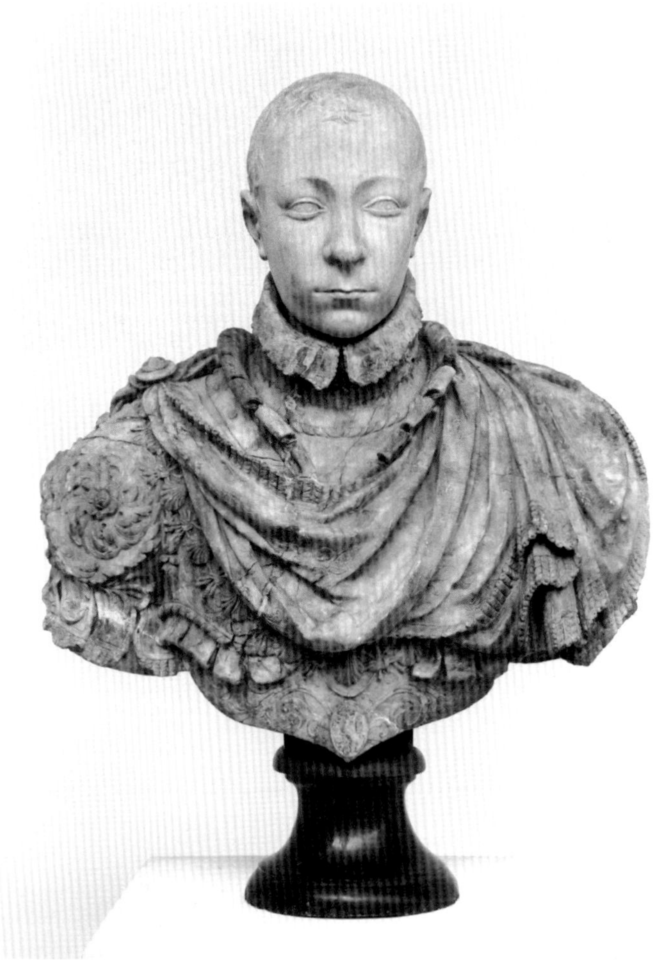

Fig. 20 *Bust of Charles IX*, attributed to the workshop of G. Pilon, *c*.1574–9, marble and alabaster, h.: 76 cm. Musée du Louvre, Paris (MR 1634)

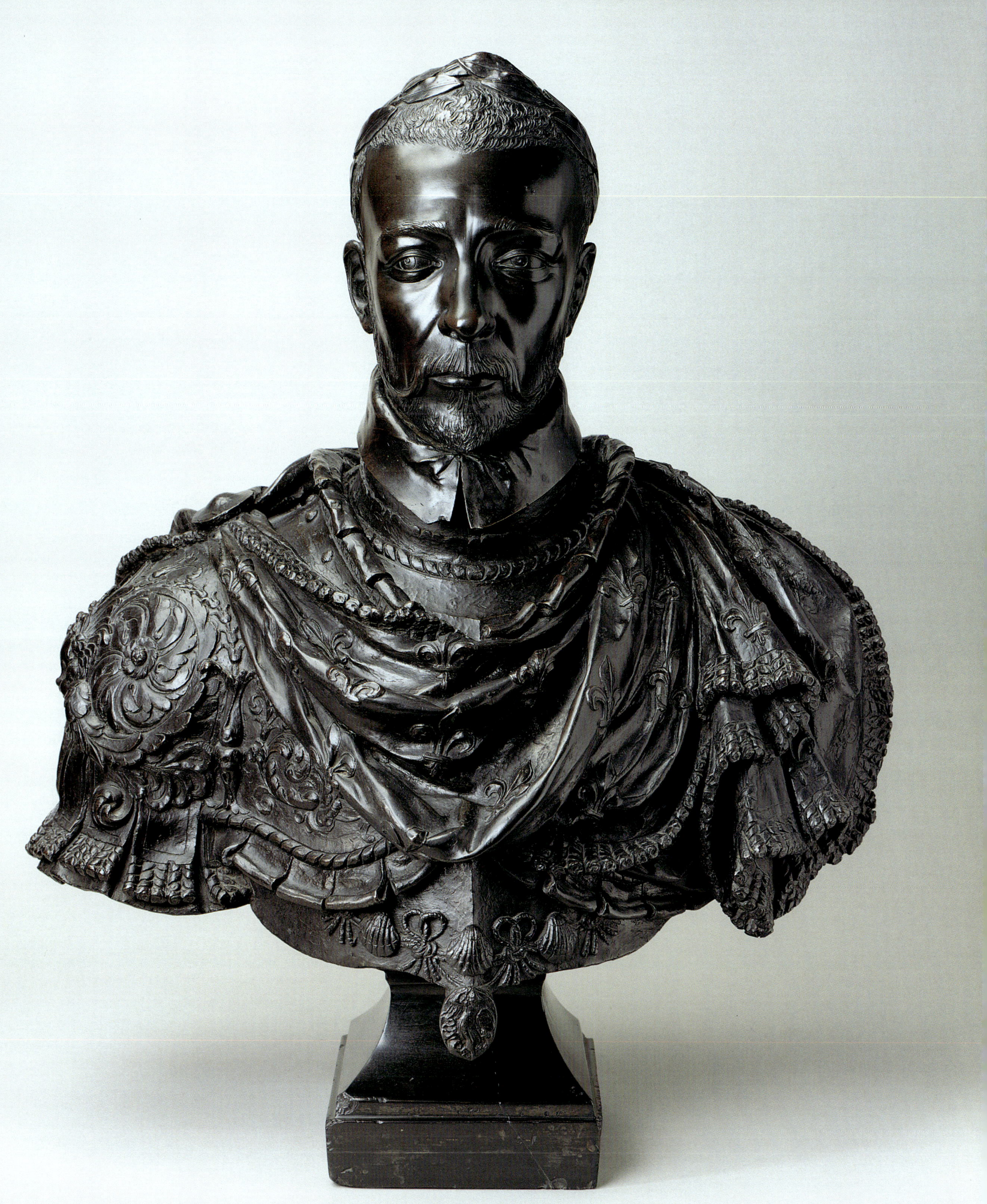

A Youth ('Narcissus' or 'Ephebe')

MODEL & CAST:
Attributed to the workshop of Barthélemy Prieur (1536–1611), c.1600

H. (excluding socle): 21.3 cm (8½ in.)

Heavy, lost-wax cast. Traces of ruddy translucent varnish, generally oxidised to black, over light-brown natural patina. Small ovoid integral base.
On a socle of verde antico *and yellow Siena marbles. H.: 14.0 cm (5½ in.).*

The appeal of this figure lies in its elegant simplicity of composition and subtle finish. The youth's body is lithe and supple, its sensuousness enhanced by the counterplay of smooth expanses of flesh with the sensitive detailing of hands and hair. The almost balletic stance, with arms crossed above the head is naturalistic but intriguing. His introspective expression of reverie, shared by certain classical and renaissance prototypes, has suggested an alternative title of 'Narcissus' (the mythological youth who fell in love with his own reflection). However, the essential *raison d'être* of this figure would seem to be as a study of a young male body (an *ephebe* was a young male soldier in ancient Greece).

Belying its simple pose and lack of pretension, the *Youth* may derive directly from the work of Michelangelo (1475–1564). It was possibly modelled after his celebrated marble *Slaves* (begun 1513) for Pope Julius II's tomb, either in their final or preparatory forms. Of the marbles, the closest in composition is the *Dying Slave* (Louvre) (fig. 21). Together with the *Rebellious Slave* (Louvre), this was brought to France in 1546, and presented by the King to his commander-in-chief, Anne de Montmorency (d.1567). Another possible source was a classical marble now in the Louvre, the *Spirit of Eternal Rest*, also a youthful figure with arms on head in a posture of languid repose.

The *Youth* is one of several distinctive and related male and female genre figures and groups that betray a combination of classical and 16th-century Italian influences. Their style and facture are regarded as typical of French bronzes of *c.*1600, in particular the products of the workshop of Barthélemy Prieur. Among Prieur's large-scale works were two bronze figures (1571; Louvre) for the monument for the heart of Anne de Montmorency, commissioned by his widow, and also their tomb (*c.*1576/86; effigies only in Louvre). Of more than twenty casts of the *Youth*, this is one of the finer examples.

First documented in 1865, when exhibited at the 'Musée Rétrospectif', Paris, by Alfred-Émilien, comte de Nieuwerkerke (1811–1894); sold by him, with much of the rest of his collection, to Sir Richard Wallace, in 1871.

S74

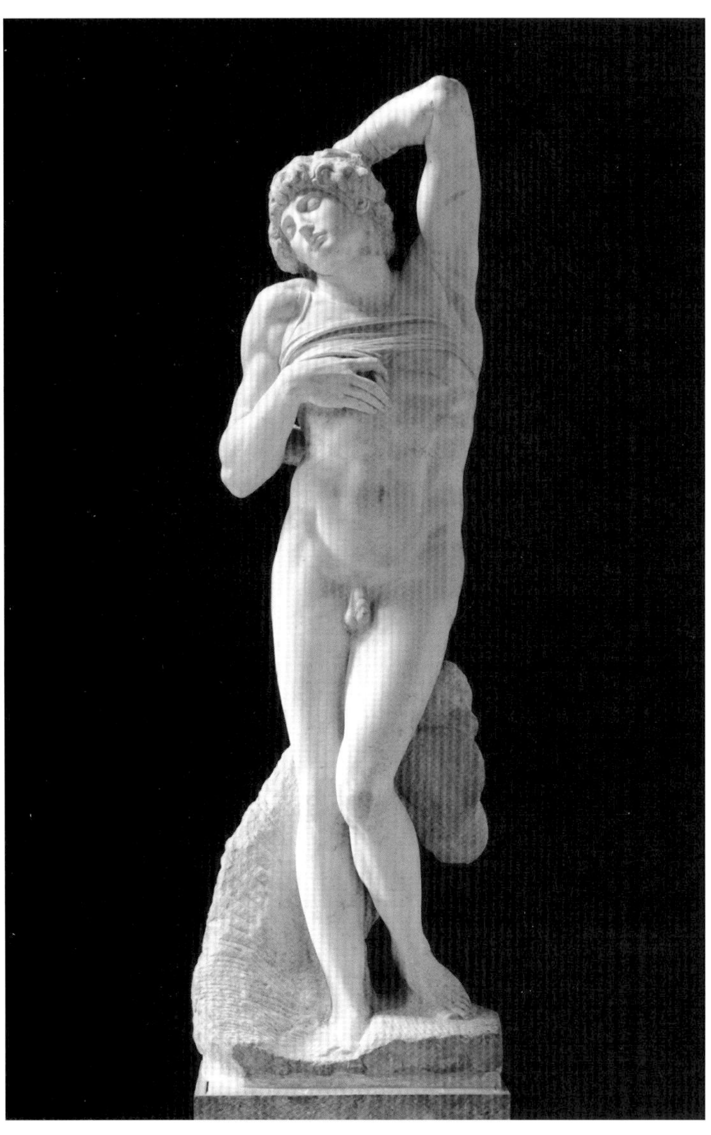

fig. 21 *Dying Slave*, Michelangelo, begun 1515, marble, h.: 209 cm.
Musée du Louvre, Paris (MR 1589)

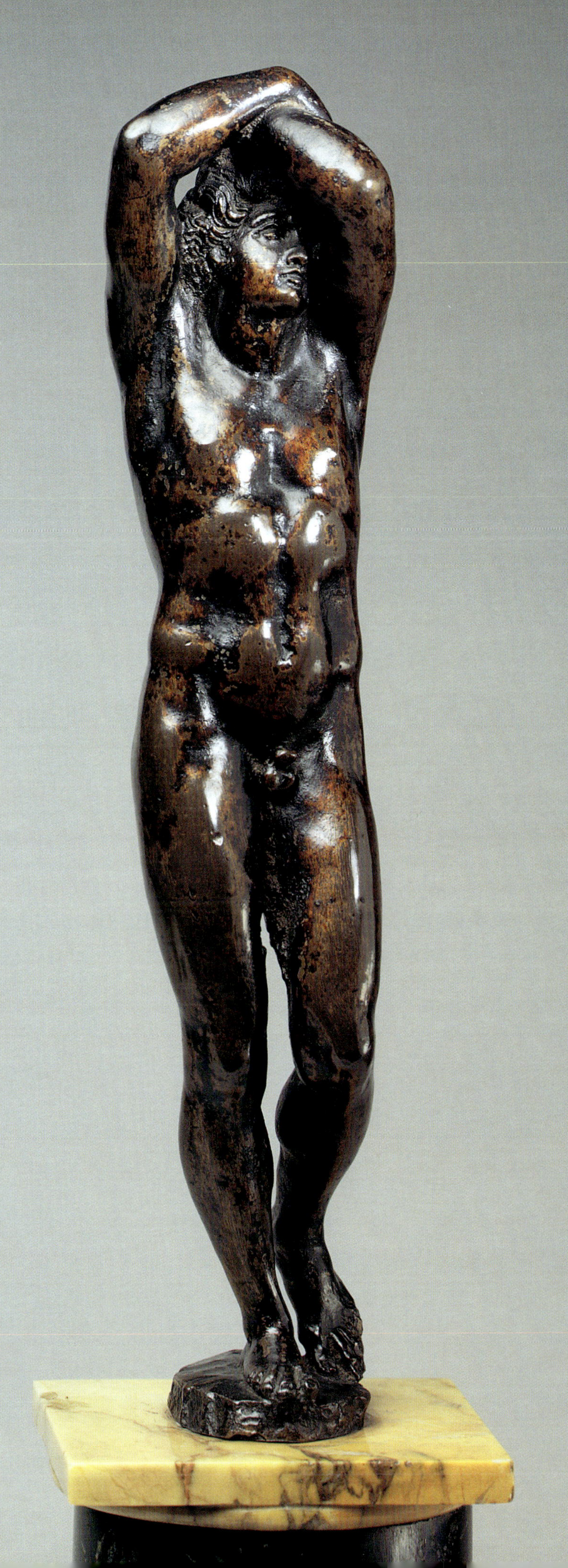

An Acrobat

MODEL & CAST:
Attributed to the workshop of Barthélemy Prieur (1536–1611), c.1600

H. (excluding socle): 29.2 cm (11⅝ in.)

Lost-wax cast. Yellow-brown metal, with substantial traces of ruddy-gold varnish, oxidised black in the recesses. No integral base.
On a cubic socle of verde antico marble. H.: 10.1 cm (4 in.).

The striking pose of this delightful statuette appears to have been unprecedented in sculpture. It may have been influenced, however, by a painting of 1541/4, known only by a preparatory drawing in the Louvre (fig. 22), representing the *Masquerade of Persepolis* by Primaticcio (1504–1570), a North Italian artist who worked in France. This includes a depiction of a youth performing a handstand, in reference to the *acrobatoi* (dancing priests) of the Temple of Artemis at Ephesus. Such a daring composition for a sculpture literally upends our preconceptions of a bronze statuette, and much of the impact of the figure lies in the novelty of encountering arms in the place of legs, and vice versa. The inherent instability of the posture is observantly expressed in the angle of the legs, and the backwards, off-centre turn of the head, from the crown of which a mass of curls cascades in an abstract detail of great beauty.

Once thought to be a 16th-century Italian work, the *Acrobat*, of which more than a dozen other casts are known, is now generally attributed to the French sculptor Barthélemy Prieur. It may be compared specifically with the two – much larger – reclining

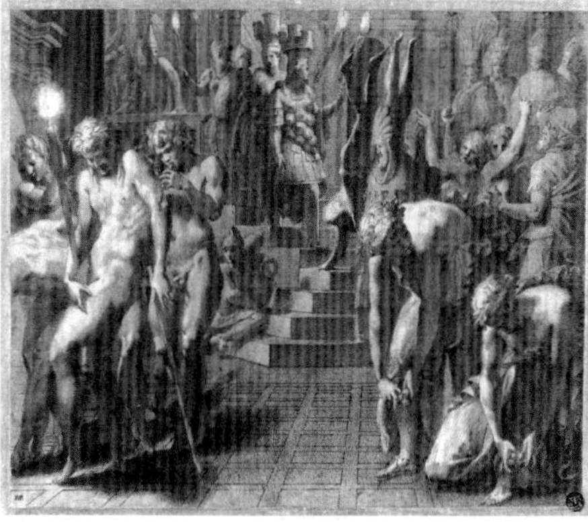

Fig. 22 *The Masquerade of Persepolis*, Primaticcio, 1541/5, pen and ink, grey wash, on paper, 25.5 × 30.5 cm. Musée du Louvre, Paris (inv. no. 8568)

statues of naked funerary *'génies'* from Prieur's documented tomb of *Christophe de Thou* for Saint-André-des-Arcs, Paris (principal sculptures now Louvre), executed c.1585 (figs 23ab). The facial types, treatment of hair and modelling of anatomy are all very close.

Acquired for £200 in 1888 by Sir Richard Wallace, and said to have been his last ever purchase.

S91

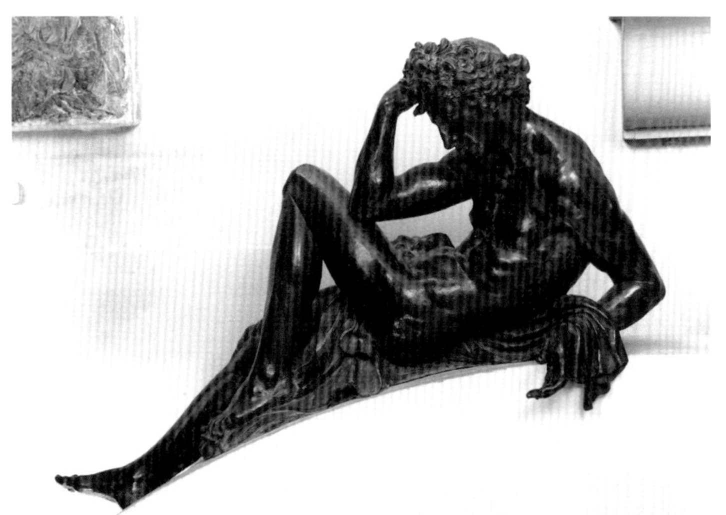
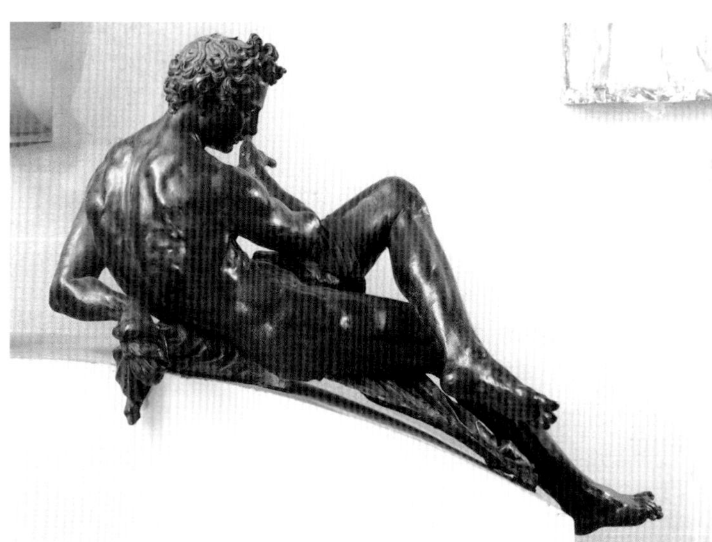

Figs 23ab Pair of *Funerary Spirits*, B. Prieur, c.1585, bronze, (left) l. 107 cm, (right) l. 99.5 cm. Musée du Louvre, Paris (MR 1684, 1685)

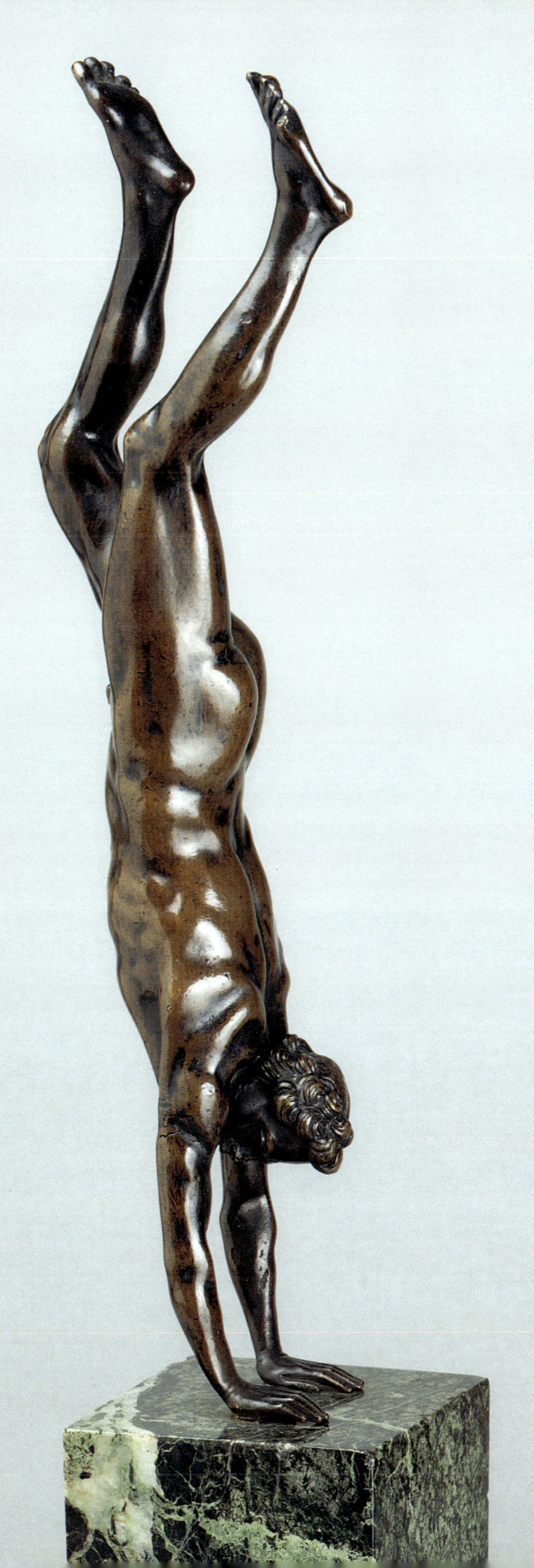

A Mother and Child

MODEL & CAST:

Attributed to Barthélemy Prieur (1536–1611), c.1600

H. (excluding plinth): 14.6 cm (5¾ in.)

Lost-wax cast with no evident flaws. Natural brown patina, with traces of translucent ruddy varnish. No integral base.
Simple ebonised-wood plinth. H.: 3.4 cm (1⅜ in.), W.: 7.7cm (3 in.), L.: 9.0 cm (3⅝ in.).

This ravishing group, one of the outstanding bronzes in the Collection, encapsulates a paradox of the Northern artistic tradition: an extremely down-to-earth subject has been rendered with meticulous care and exquisite detailing. The group represents a crouching naked young woman, who with one hand supports the head of an infant boy, dressed in a smock and holding a pear, and with the other directs his penis as he urinates. Despite the lowly theme, there is great subtlety, almost poetry, in the deliberate contrasting of detailed folds and features against expanses of smooth skin, of the directly-observed child against the idealised female: this counterpoint greatly enhances the aesthetic appeal and visual interest of the group.

The composition is related to several other statuettes of women in comparable genre poses, including a pendant of a mother teaching her child to walk. The composition of this specific model would seem to have been influenced by a rather larger statuette of *Venus Removing a Thorn from Her Foot* of the 1560s by Ponce Jacquiot (d.1570) (fig. 24). However, it is of the same scale as those bronzes now generally attributed to the workshop of Barthélemy Prieur, to whose documented work its facture seems to be much closer. The facial features of the female figure in particular may be compared with those of Prieur's allegorical figures for the Montmorency monument, executed in the 1570s (Louvre) (fig. 25). Also typical are the very small head, the braided hair, the impassive facial expression, the attenuated proportions and the smooth and curvilinear surface treatment. The Wallace Collection example is the finest of the few known casts, and indeed can claim to be one of the very finest of all the many statuettes attributed to his workshop.

In the collection of baron Boissel de Monville (1794–1873), Paris, by c.1826, and bought for 510 francs at his sale, Paris, 1861, by the 4th Marquess of Hertford.

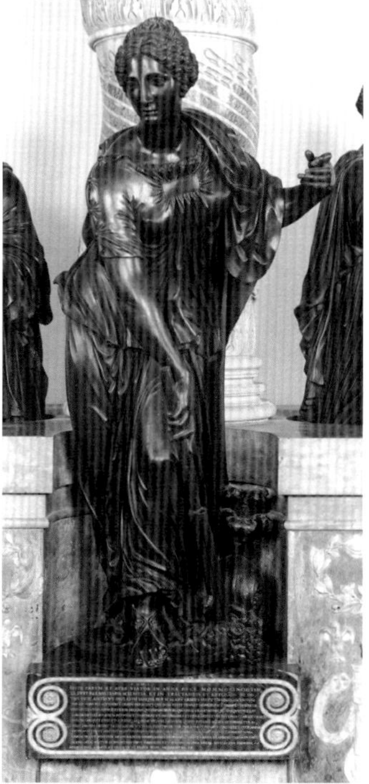

Fig. 25 *Peace* (from the *Funerary Monument to the Heart of Anne de Montmorency*), B. Prieur, 1570s, bronze, h.: 122 cm. Musée du Louvre, Paris (MR 1682)

Fig. 24 *Venus Removing a Thorn from Her Foot*, P. Jacquiot, 1560s, bronze, h.: 24.9 cm. Victoria and Albert Museum, London (A.13-1964)

S129

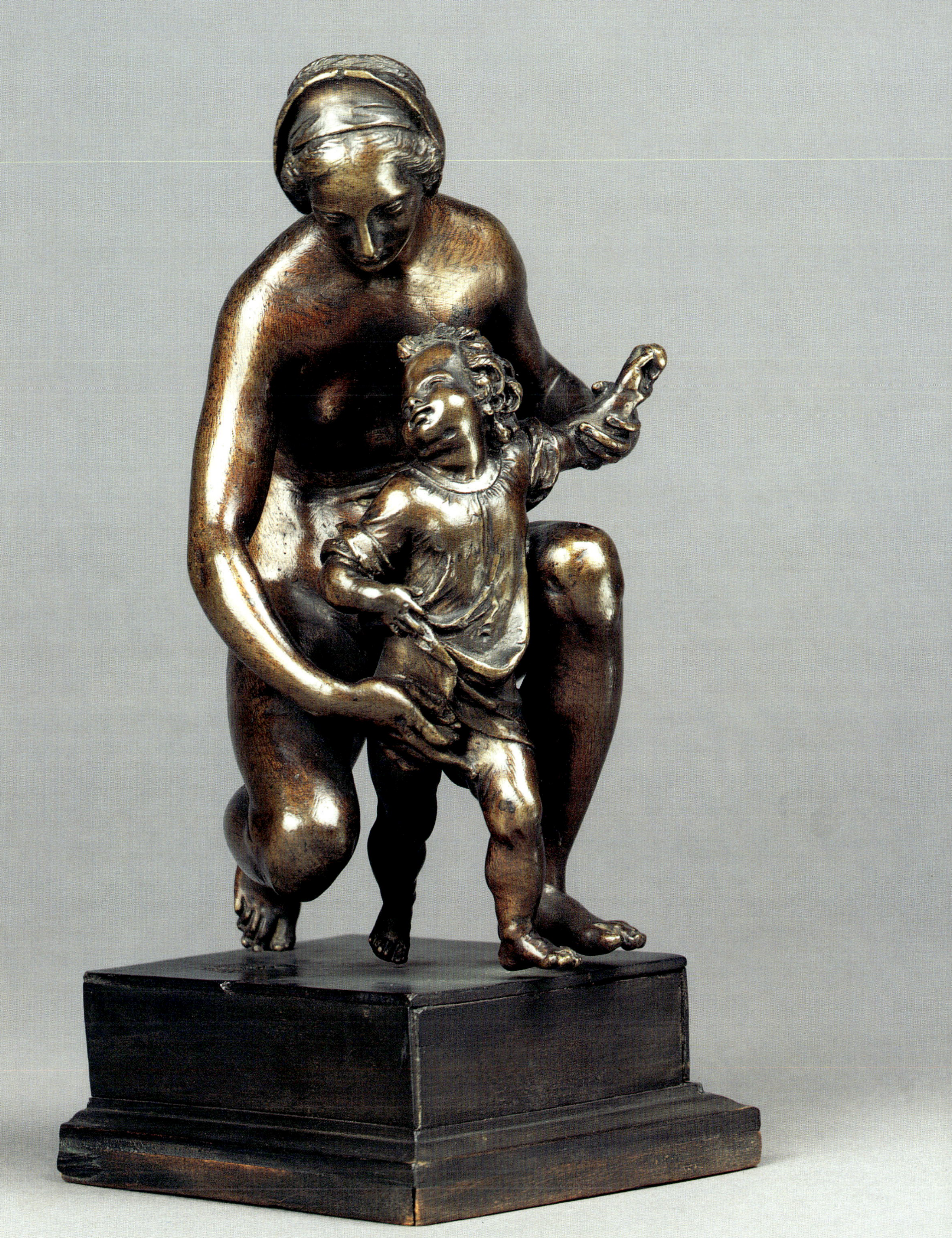

The Borghese Dancers (Les Danseuses Borghese)

MODEL:
François Anguier (1604–1669), 1641/2, after the antique

CAST:
Henri Perlan (1597–1656), 1642/3

H.: 66.6 cm (26⅜ in.), W.: 200.8 cm (79⅝ in.)

Heavy, lost-wax cast: some of the heads are solid casts. Distinctive copper alloy, with relatively small proportions of zinc and tin. Dark natural patina. Unmounted.

The antique marble sculpture known as the *Borghese Dancers* (Roman, 1st century BC– 1st century AD), now in the Louvre, was for over three hundred years one of the most famous of all classical reliefs (fig. 26). In the 18th century, the great German scholar Winckelmann described it as the most perfect example of its type. Its name originated in its acquisition in the early 17th century by Cardinal Scipio Borghese, at whose Villa in Rome it was displayed, together with a pendant of *Maidens Adorning a Candelabrum*, also now in the Louvre. The five female figures, sometimes identified as the *Horae* (Hours), solemnly dance to a measured step. They are dressed in the clinging 'wet' draperies favoured by classical artists of the period, exploited to effect a sensuous and rhythmic patterning of folds.

The most celebrated antiquities of Italy had long been of interest to French connoisseurs, and copies of the *Borghese Dancers* and its pendant were among the plaster casts of antique sculpture in Rome made for Louis XIII in 1640. Some of these, including the *Borghese Dancers* and its pendant, were intended to be set into the vault of the *grande galerie* of the Louvre, probably as versions cast in bronze.

Since the plaster cast arrived in Paris as a 'rather formless sketch', it was entrusted for reworking to François Anguier, *Sculpteur du Roi*, 'who gave it that marvellous elegance that we admire', in the words of a 17th-century writer. The casting in

bronze of this and its pendant was contracted to Henri Perlan, a specialist founder. There is little doubt that they are to be identified with the relief now in the Wallace Collection and another in the Louvre (fig. 27), which technical analysis indicates came from the same workshop.

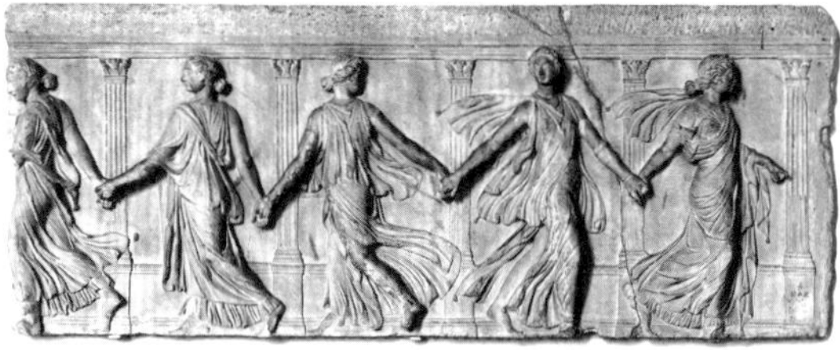

Fig. 26 *The Borghese Dancers*, Roman 1st century BC–1st century AD, marble, 72 × 188 cm. Musée du Louvre, Paris (Ma 1612)

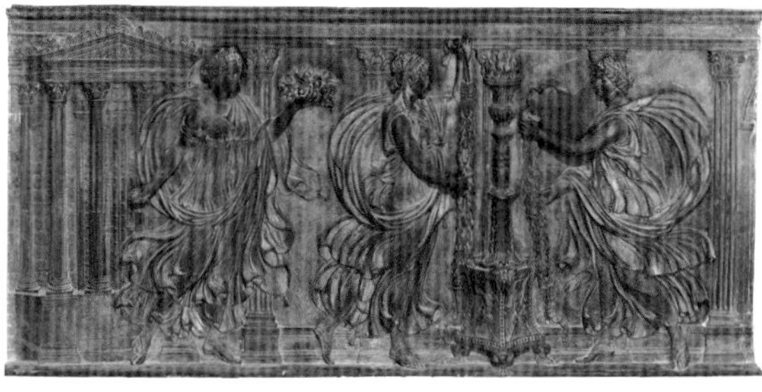

Fig. 27 *Maidens Adorning a Candelabrum, after the antique*, probably cast by H. Perlan after F. Anguier, *c*.1642, bronze, 72 × 154 cm. Musée du Louvre, Paris (MR 1709)

If it is Perlan's cast, the Wallace Collection relief was probably separated from its pendant when it was sent to Versailles for storage in 1694. It may have been acquired at auction in Paris in 1807 by the future 3rd Marquess of Hertford, but it is first certainly recorded in the Collection in the 1870 Hertford House inventory ('Mr Wallis [*sic*] Chamber: A Basrelief in Bronze: Dancing Figures').

S155

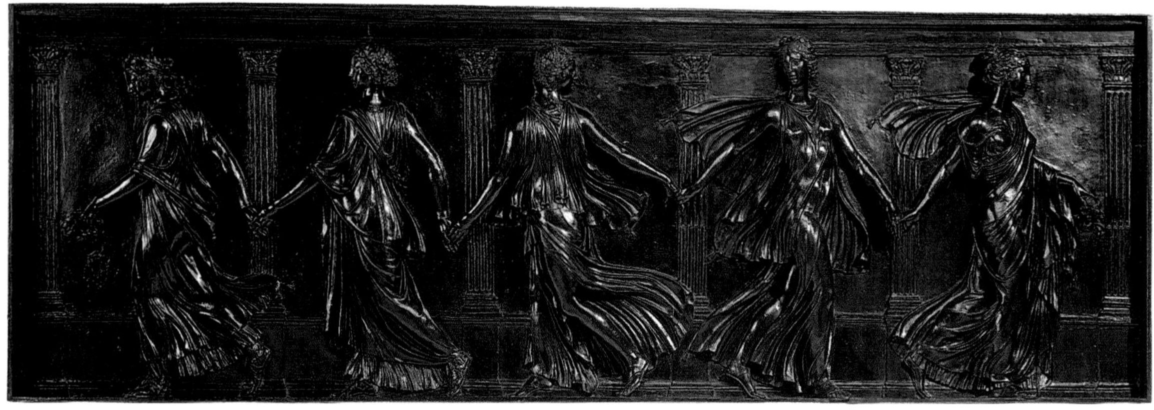

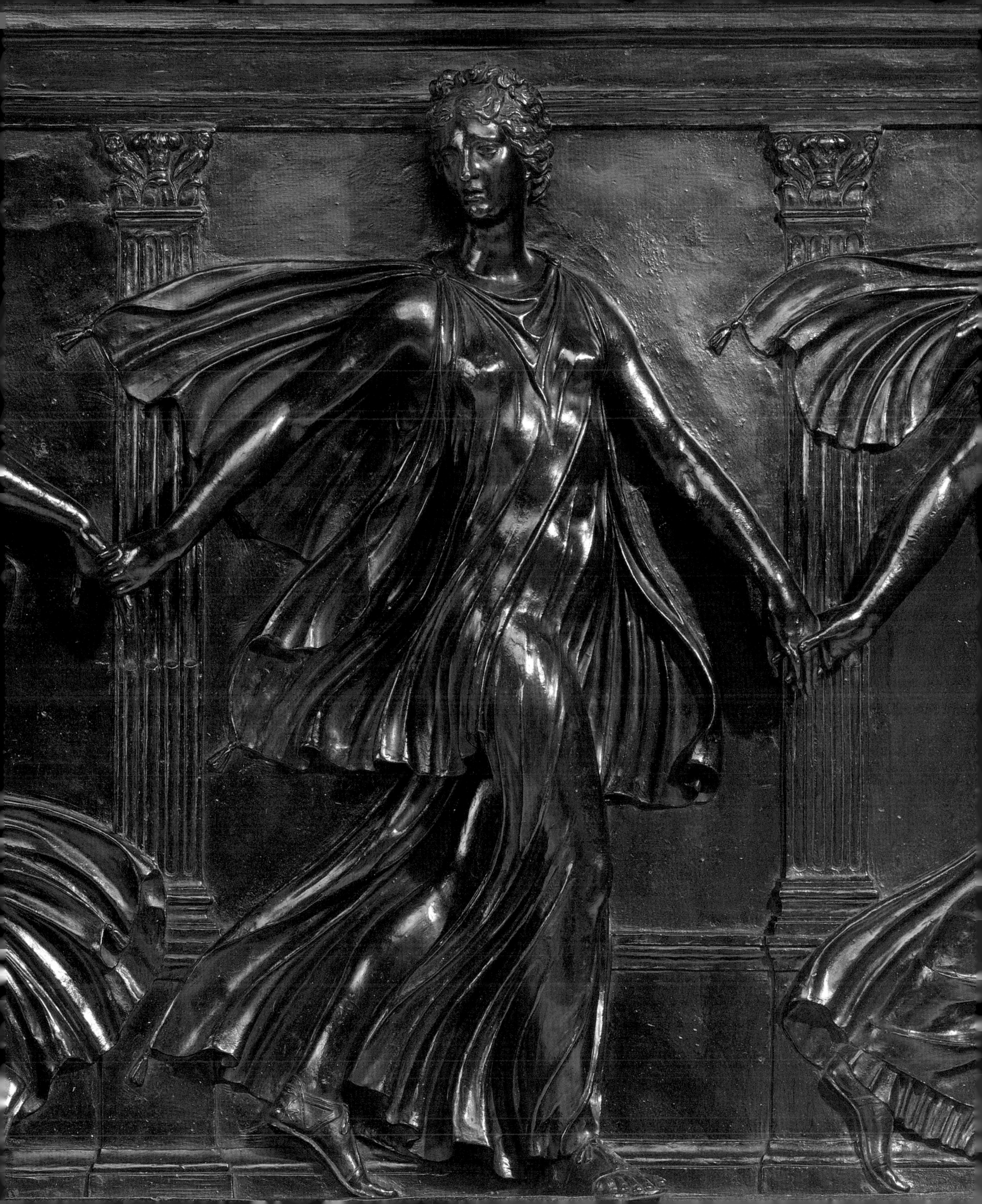

Jupiter Victorious over the Titans: 'Fire' ('Chenet de l'Algarde')

MODEL:
Alessandro Algardi (1598–1654), 1650

CAST:
probably French, c.1655–80

inscribed (base): ·N⁰·297·

H. (including base): 127.0 cm (50⅜ in.), H. (excluding base): 106.8 cm (42⅜ in.), W. (base): 58.0 cm (23 in.)

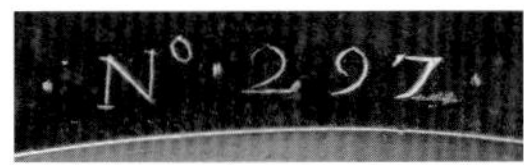

Fig. 29a Detail of *Jupiter*, showing incised inventory number.
Wallace Collection (S161)

Juno Controlling the Winds: 'Air' ('Chenet de l'Algarde')

MODEL:
Alessandro Algardi (1598–1654), 1650

CAST:
probably French, c.1655–80

H. (including base): 125.8 cm (50 in.), H. (excluding base): 105.6 cm (42 in.), W. (base): 58.0 cm (23 in.)

inscribed (base): ·N⁰·298·

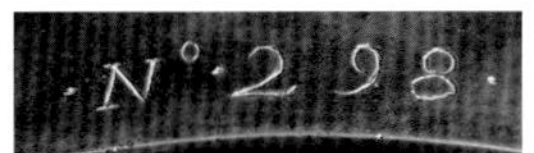

Lost-wax casts, made in sections and socketed and pinned, screwed or soldered together. Reddish to chocolate brown natural patina. Sceptre lacking from Juno's left hand.
Mounted on original quatrefoil-plan bases with concave sides, bun feet and acanthus-leaf brackets.
Associated with white marble pedestals of four fluted columns, presumably of 19th-century date (documented from 1870). H.: 100.0 cm (39⅜ in.) (not shown)

Fig. 29b Detail of *Juno*, showing incised inventory number.
Wallace Collection (S162)

Cast from superb models and beautifully finished, these magnificent bronzes also share an illustrious provenance. Their subjects, taken from Ovid's account of the creation of the world (*Metamorphoses*, Book I; *Fasti*, Book V), are suitably imposing. Jupiter sits majestically astride his attribute, the eagle; outstretched in his right hand is a thunderbolt; cowering below are three of the giant Titans, who dared to challenge the gods, and whom he has crushed under the rocks of Mounts Pelion and Ossa. Juno is shown imperiously seated on her sacred peacock, imprisoning in the cave of Aeolus three of the Winds, who would otherwise dispel the rain-bearing fourth, South Wind, sent by Jupiter to flood the earth. Between the upper and lower elements in each group is a sphere representing the inchoate world.

They are versions of bronzes, now lost, originally conceived as a pair of firedogs (*chenets*), and commissioned in 1649/50 from the Roman baroque sculptor Alessandro Algardi by Philip IV, King of Spain. It would seem that a second pair of bronzes were then ordered, although completed only after Algardi's death by pupils, which together could be taken to represent the Four Elements. Thus *Jupiter* personified Fire and *Juno*, Air; while the other two, *Neptune* and *Cybele*, stood for Water and Earth, respectively. All four, with second casts of each, were then adapted for use on a fountain,

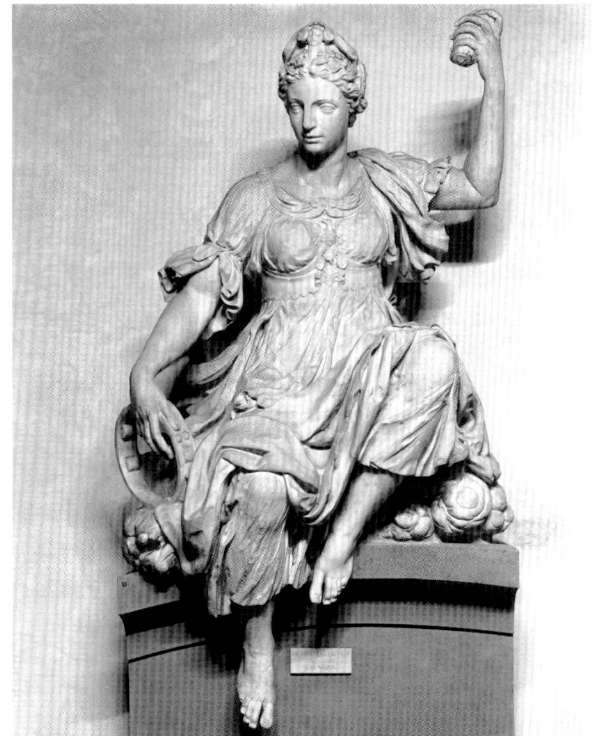

Fig. 28 *Juno*, B. Ammannati, 1556/61, marble, over life-size.
Museo Nazionale del Bargello, Florence (Inv. Dep. pag.105n5)

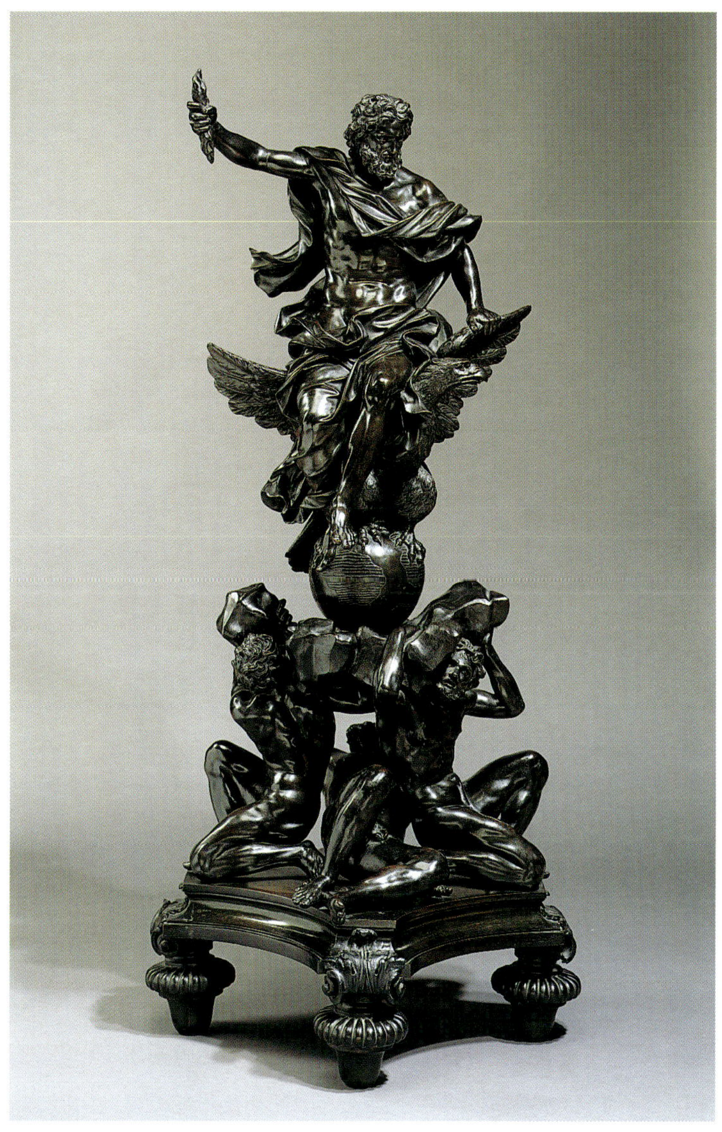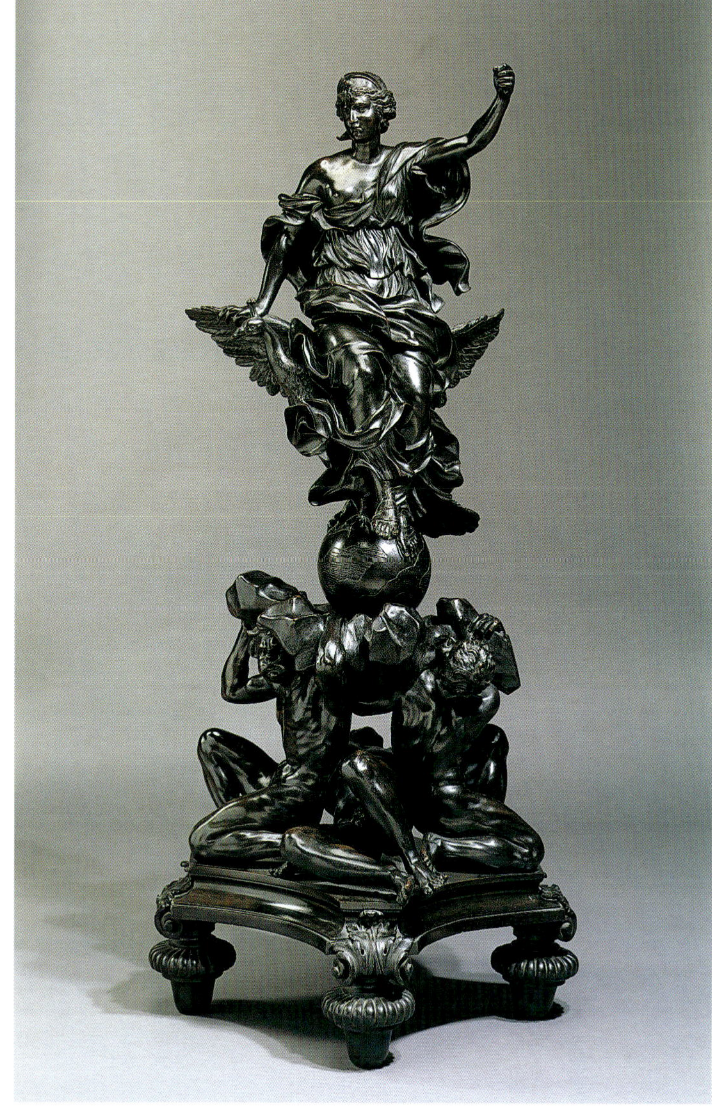

which only partially survives, in the gardens at Aranjuez, near Madrid. It would seem that the *Jupiter* and *Juno* alone were replicated in bronze and acquired by collectors, principally in France, where many, if not all of the casts were most likely made. The smoothly-polished surfaces and fine tooling of details of this pair are typical of French techniques.

Stylistically, the principal figures ultimately derive from such celebrated classical marbles as the *Giustiniani Jupiter* and the *Cesi Juno*, then in noble Roman collections. Bartolommeo Ammannati's (1511–1592) marble of *Juno* (as 'Air'), commissioned by Cosimo I de' Medici in 1555, may have served as a more immediate source for Algardi's *Juno* (fig. 28).

The finest of the four complete pairs known today, these casts can be traced back for certain to 1689, when they were inventoried in the collection of the Grand Dauphin (1661–1711). They must, however, have been acquired in or after 1681, the year Louis XIV initiated his twenty-year-old son's collection with a gift of nine

bronzes, and previously may have belonged to Cardinal Mazarin. After the Dauphin's premature death in 1711, they were claimed by the King, and passed by inheritance to Louis XVI: the incised numbers refer to their listing in the inventories of the French Royal collection (figs 29ab). They were kept at the château of Meudon until 1785, when Marie-Antoinette decided to display them in her private apartment at Versailles. At this time their patina was 'restored' and Jupiter's right arm was repaired – by no less a sculptor than Houdon. They were among the most valuable in the entire French crown collection of over 300 bronzes, but in 1796 passed as payment in kind by the new Government to a creditor, a merchant named Jacques de Chapeaurouge (1744–1805).

Inventoried in the Front State Room of Hertford House in 1870 after the death of the 4th Marquess of Hertford, who had probably acquired them in London.

S161 (Jupiter)
S162 (Juno)

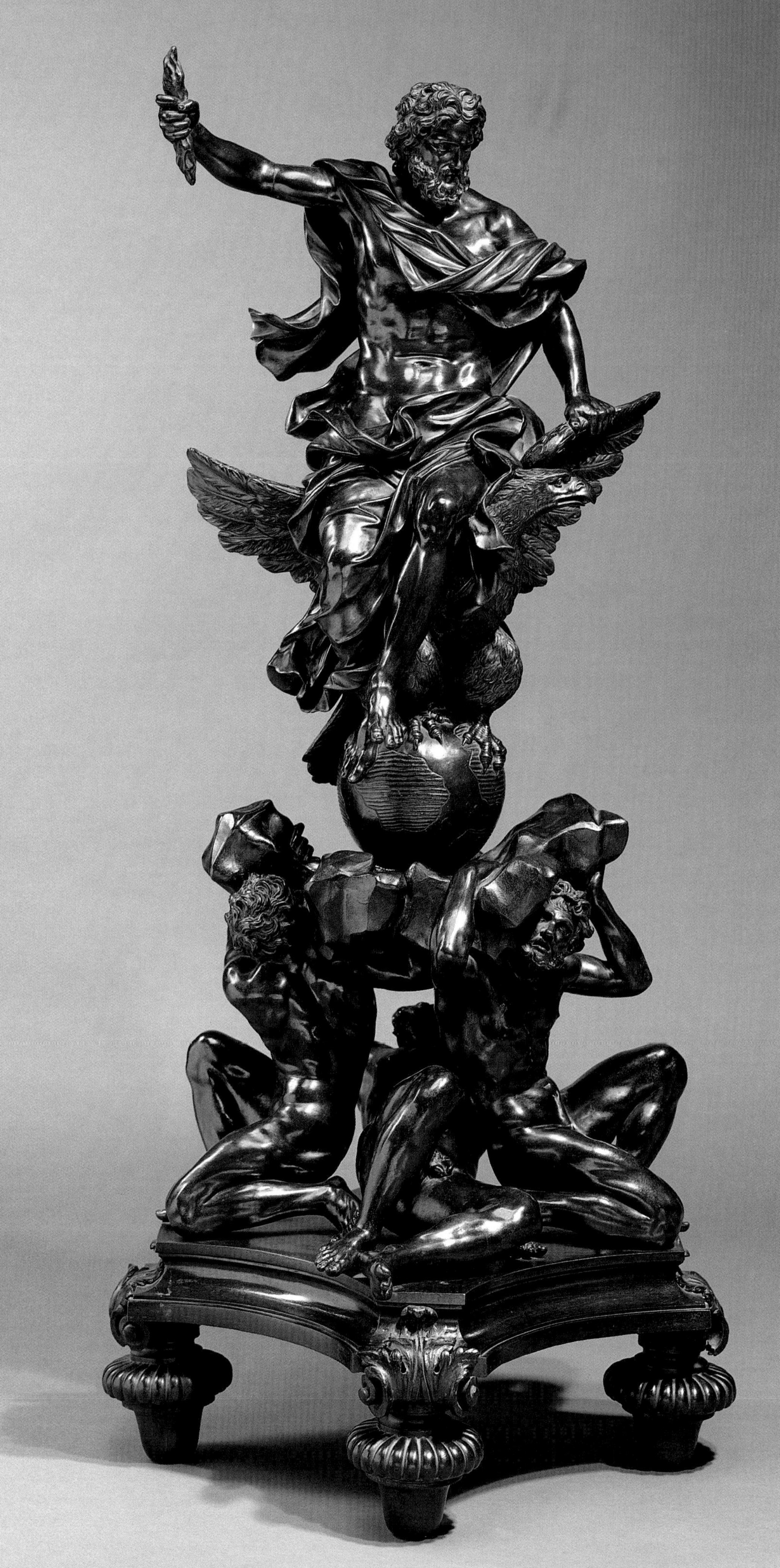

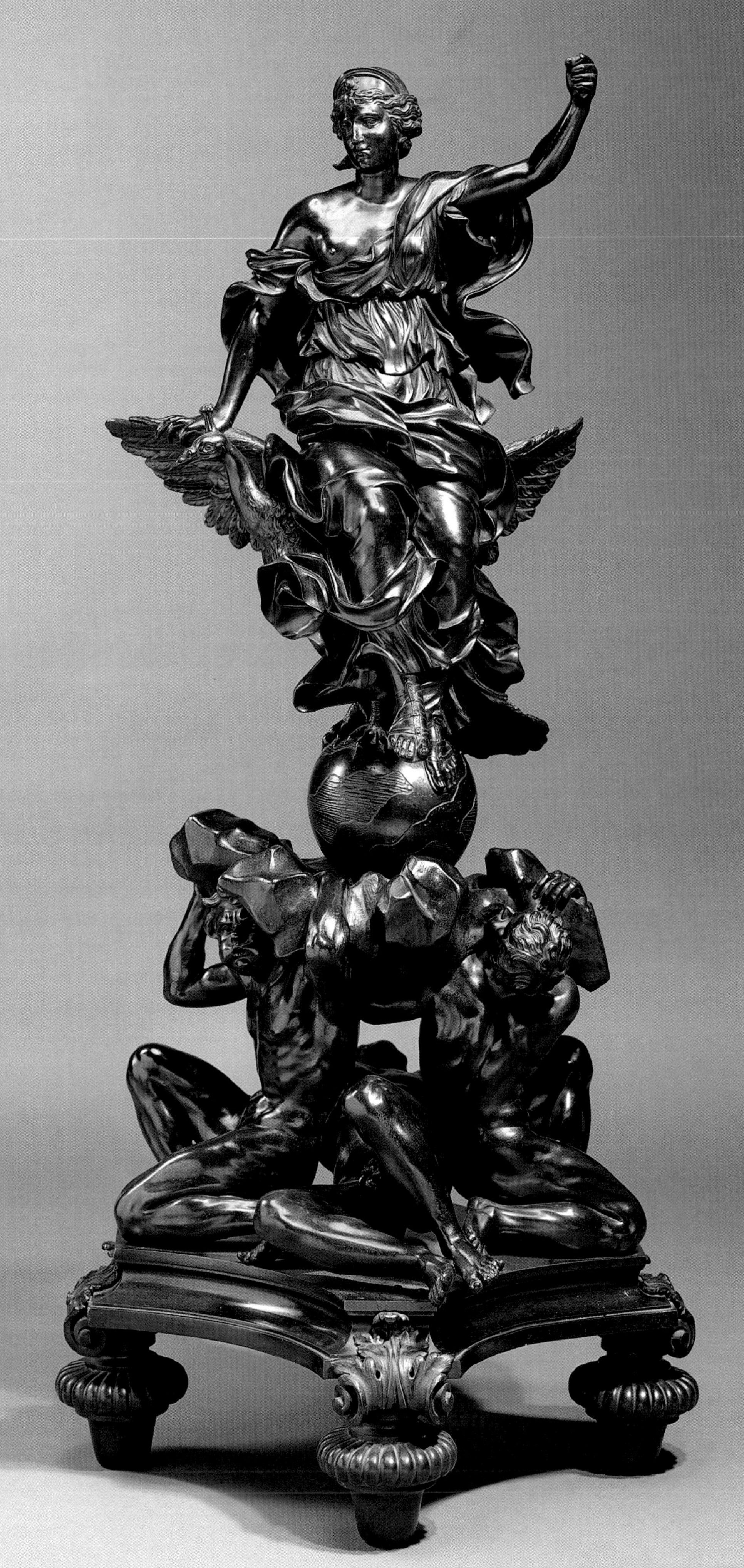

The River God Tiber and *The River God Nile*

MODELS:

Attributed to Martin Carlier (1653–1704), 1679–80, after the antique

CASTS:

French, *c*.1700–15

Tiber
H. (excluding mount): 38.0 cm (15 in.), L. (terrain base): 70.5 cm (28 in.), D. (terrain base): 30.2 cm (12⅛ in.)

Nile

H. (excluding mount): 38.0 cm (15 in.), L. (terrain base): 70.5 cm (28 in.), D. (terrain base): 30.5 cm (12⅛ in.)

Lost-wax casts, essentially cast as a whole, although defects in the casting of the Tiber *necessitated a replacement right foot for the god, and a new tip to the cornucopia; also, the upper section of the oar and one of the twins were separately cast. Mid-brown natural patina with black pooling in recesses. Integral terrains.*
Gilt-bronze mounts in the late Louis XIV style, shaped to accommodate the terrain bases. H.: 11.5cm (4½ in.).

Each of these magnificent recumbent River Gods is accompanied with identifying attributes of a local character, as well as a cornucopia symbolising the fecundity of their waters. The *Nile* is shown with the Sphinx, and the *Tiber*, who also holds an oar (to control the waters), lies beside the Wolf suckling the twins Romulus and Remus, Founders of Rome. They are reductions of very famous colossal antique marbles excavated in Rome in the early 16th century, and exhibited together in the papal collection until the end of the 18th century. The marble *Nile* (Vatican Museums, Rome) (fig. 30) is thought to be a Roman copy of a 2nd-century BC bronze original, whereas the *Tiber* (now in the Louvre) is regarded as an original work specifically created as a companion (fig. 31). Both were repeatedly drawn and engraved, and copied in various media, inevitably usually as reductions. Full-scale copies were cast in bronze for François Ier at Fontainebleau (1540–3), and carved in marble for Louis XIV at Marly (1687–92); the latter were

soon moved to the Tuileries Gardens.

Like most bronze reductions, the Wallace Collection *Nile* is represented – understandably – without the sixteen *putti* of the original (according to Pliny, these symbolised the sixteen cubits that the river rose each year at its high flood point: if it should fail to do so, the land would not be irrigated and famine would result). Less typically, the *Tiber* has been furnished with an oar that is considerably more decorative than the original. This is consistent with the exceptionally sophisticated finish of these casts, evident for instance in the careful wire-brush polishing of the bodies and limbs (see fig. 18), and with the no less superb gilt-bronze mounts.

The sculptor François Girardon (see p. 12) owned a pair of very similar bronze River Gods, apparently with comparable measurements, as illustrated in the engravings of his *Galerie* of about 1709 (although the *Tiber* was depicted with only a vestigial oar), where they were described as copied 'at Rome after the

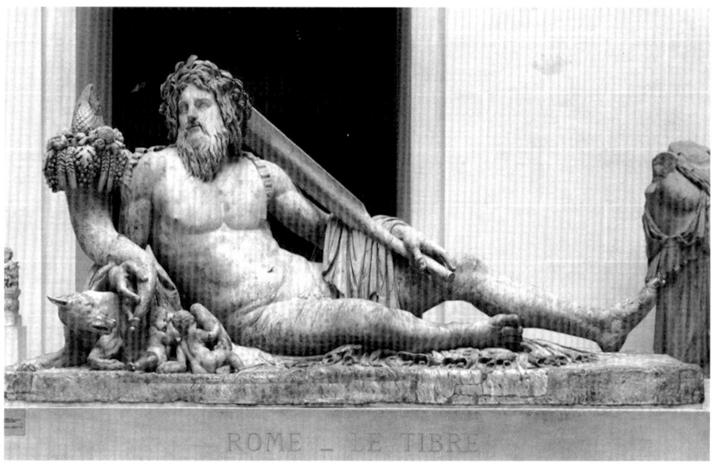

Fig. 30 *The River God Nile*, Roman probably 1st century AD, marble, l.: 310 cm. Monumenti Musei e Gallerie Pontificie, Vatican City

Fig. 31 *The River God Tiber*, Roman probably 1st century AD, marble, l.: 317 cm. Musée du Louvre, Paris (Ma 593)

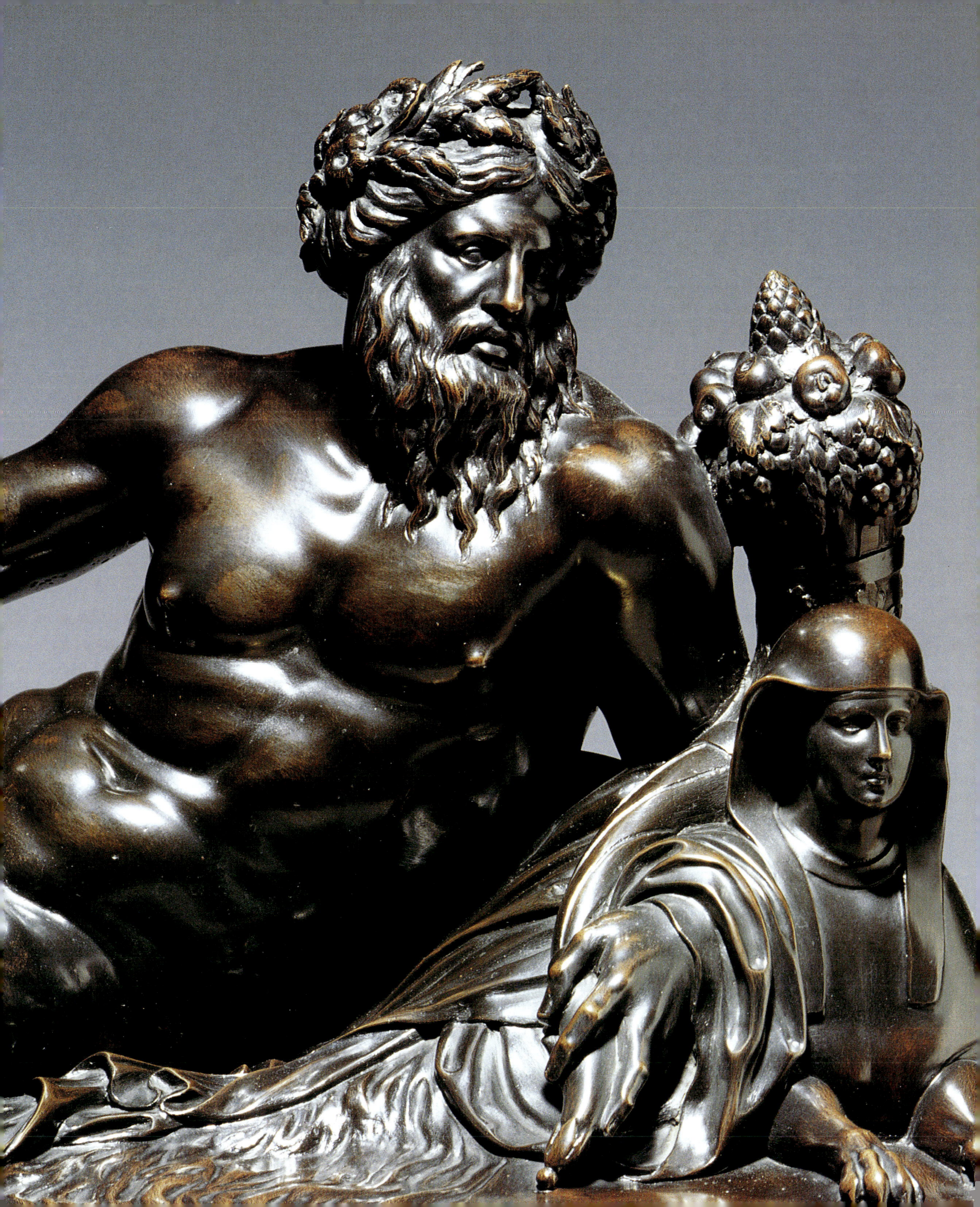

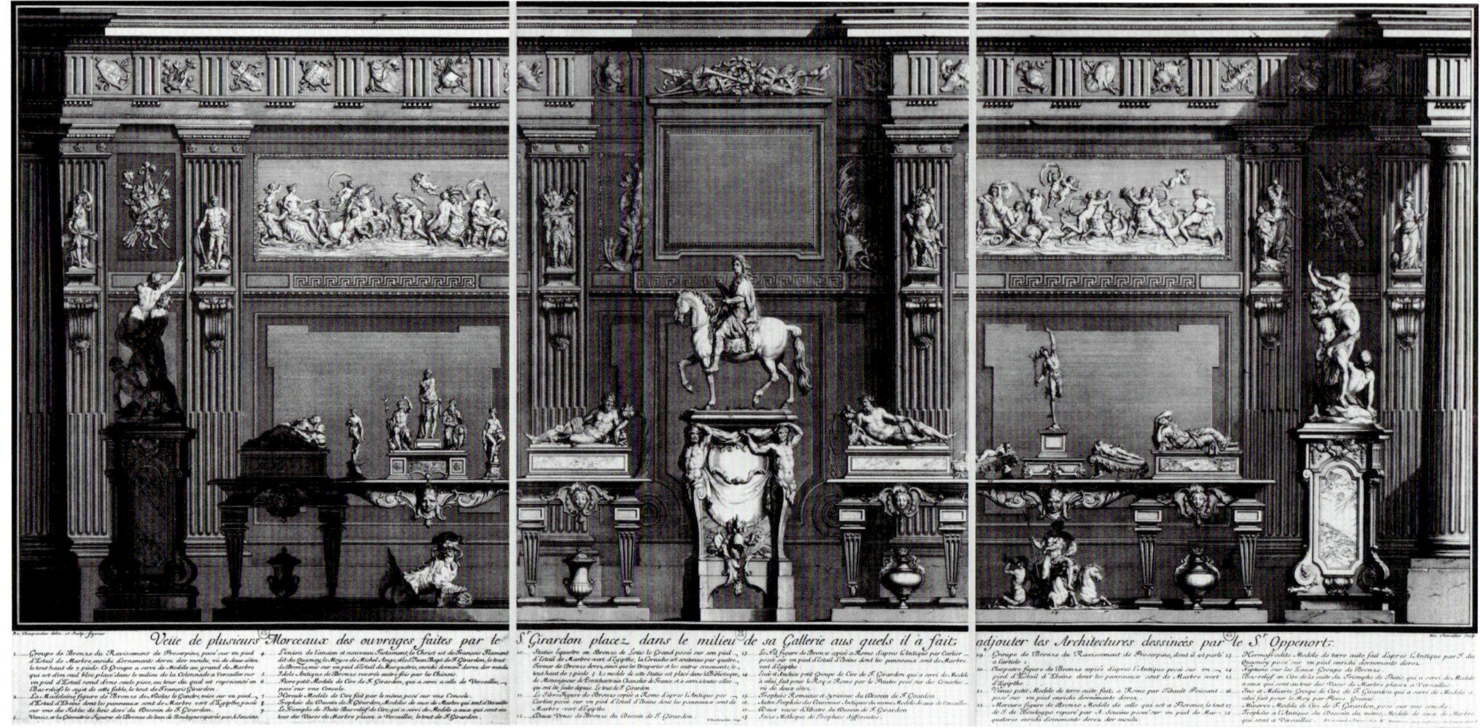

Fig. 32 *La Galerie de Girardon*, plate VI, N. Chevallier after R. Charpentier (1680–1723), *c*.1709, engraving. Bibliothèque Nationale de France, Paris

Antique by Carlier' (fig. 32; and see p. 6). Martin Carlier was a *pensionnaire* of the French Academy in Rome, 1675–80, and is documented as having made copies in 1679–80. Of similar size, but with variant details and lacking the superb finish of the Wallace Collection bronzes, is a pair in Dresden, probably acquired for Augustus the Strong of Saxony in 1715. Since the River Gods illustrated in Girardon's *Galerie* in each case combine particular details from both respective variants, it is not clear whether both or only one of the extant types should be attributed to Carlier (further variant bronze reductions were made by several other French sculptors in the late 17th century).

First recorded in the Hertford House inventory of 1870 (Large Drawing Room), and probably acquired by the 4th Marquess of Hertford.

S180 (Tiber)

S179 (Nile)

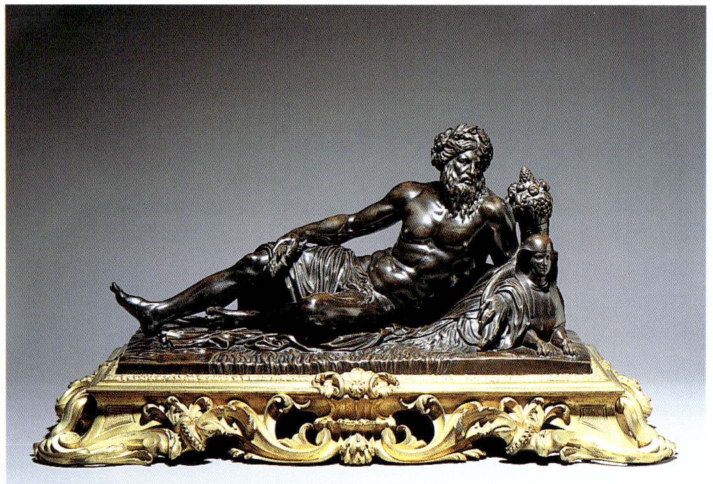

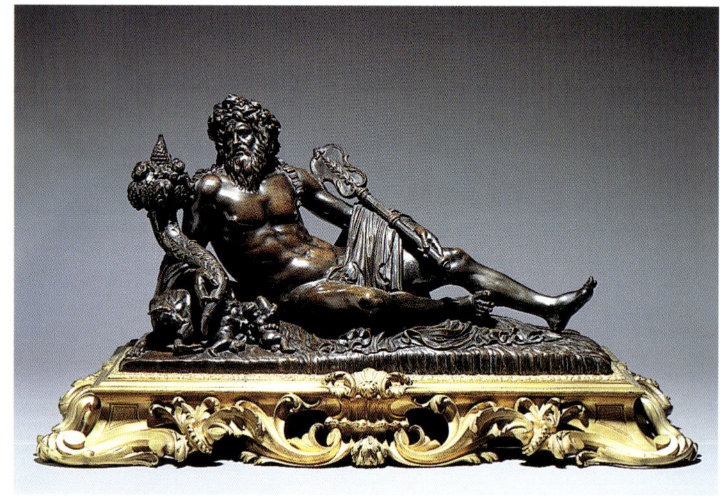

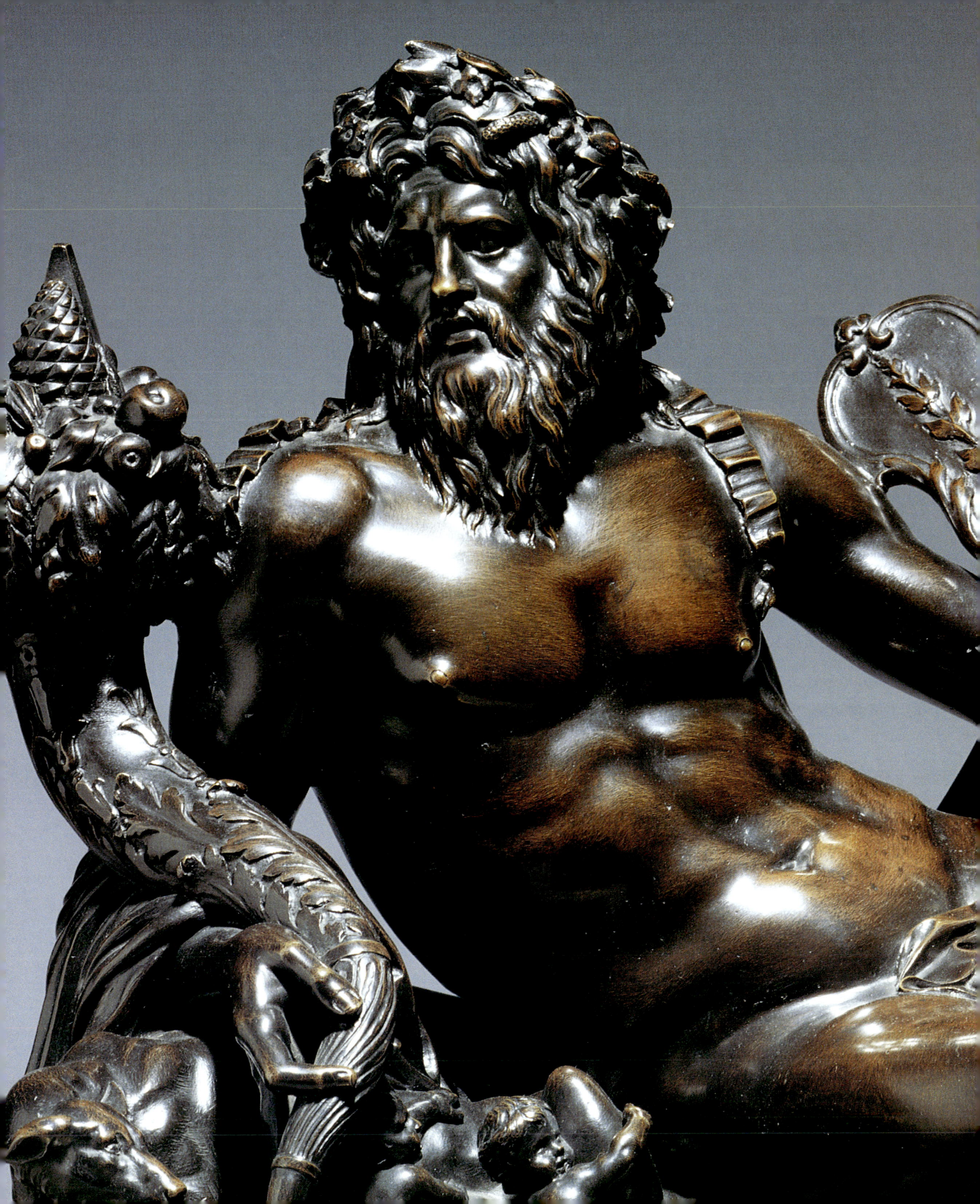

Crouching Venus

MODEL:
Antoine Coysevox (1640–1720), 1686, after the antique

CAST:
French, *c*.1700–15

H. (excluding wooden base): 33.3 cm (13¼ in.), L. (terrain base): 30.9 cm
(12¼ in.), D. (terrain base): 17.0 cm (6¾ in.)

Arrotino ('The Knifegrinder', 'Il Rotatore', 'Scythian Preparing to Flay Marsyas', etc)

MODEL:
Giovanni Battista Foggini (1652–1725), 1684, after the antique

CAST:
French, *c*.1700–15

H. (excluding wooden base): 27.9 cm (11⅛ in.), L. (terrain base): 31.2 cm
(12⅜ in.), D. (terrain base): 16.4 cm (6½ in.)

*Lost-wax casts, each limb separately cast and socketed and pinned into main torso.
Quite thick, black surface coating, degrading unevenly to reveal oxidized mid-brown
metal beneath; coppery alloy. Integral, rectangular terrain.
Louis XIV-style wood bases with gilt-bronze mounts. H.: 15.8 cm (6¼ in.).*

'The King would be most pleased to have copies made of all the
beautiful marble statues in Italy, in particular *le Rotator* or *l'Esguisseur*
which is presently in Florence'. Thus the Director of the French
Academy in Rome recorded the wishes of Louis XIV in 1684. The
King was, of course, merely partaking of the widespread
fascination of his time with classical sculpture; he was exceptional
only in the influence and wealth which he was able to use to pursue
it. It seems likely that he was especially interested in obtaining a
full-size marble copy of the *Arrotino* (the name most commonly
used today) because since 1663 he had owned, and presumably
admired, a fine Florentine bronze reduction (private collection).

The marble copy of the *Arrotino* was duly made for Louis XIV
by the Florentine sculptor Foggini (now in the Louvre) (fig. 33). It
was sent to Versailles and displayed on the steps of the *Parterre du
Nord*, where it was paired with a copy of the *Crouching Venus*,
another famous classical marble. This was executed by Coysevox in
1684–6 (also now in the Louvre) (fig. 34), but is in reality an
interpretation rather than a literal copy, with many variations, most
notably the substitution as a support of a tortoise for the original
shell. Whereas Foggini certainly copied the much-admired marble
by then in the Uffizi (and first recorded in Rome in the 1530s), it is
not clear if Coysevox's model was a version in the Villa Medici,

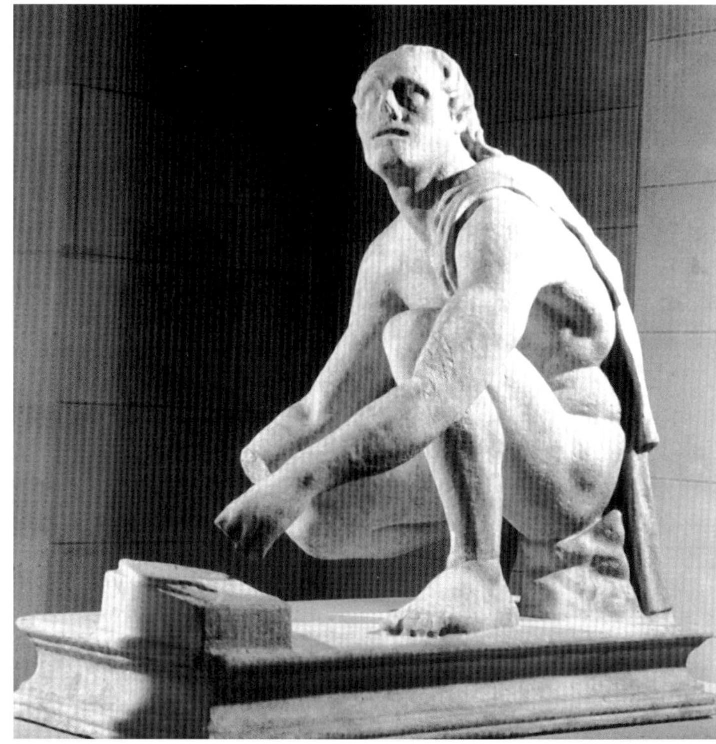

Fig. 33 *Arrotino*, after the antique, G.B. Foggini, 1684, marble, h.: *c*.105 cm.
Musée du Louvre, Paris (MR 1853)

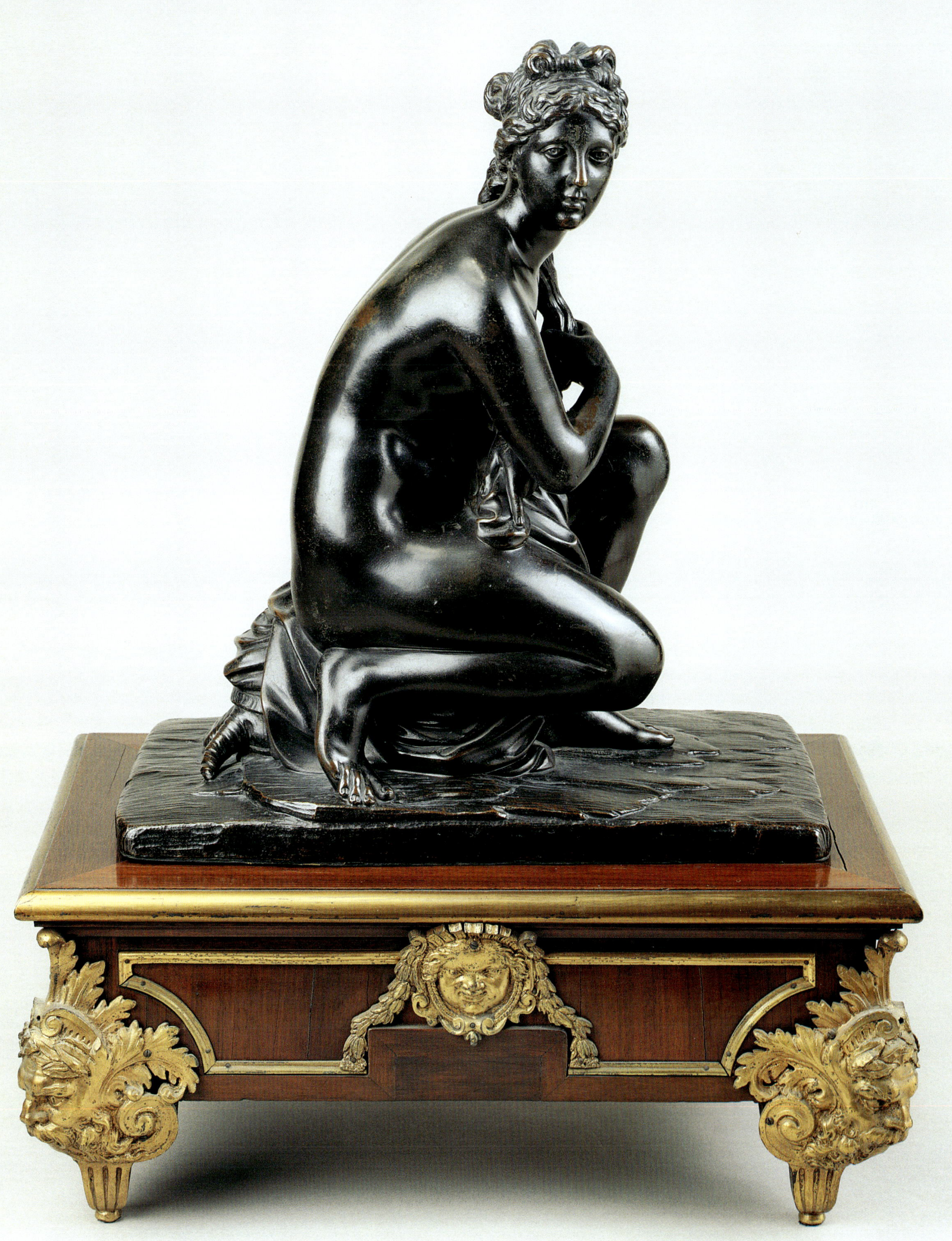

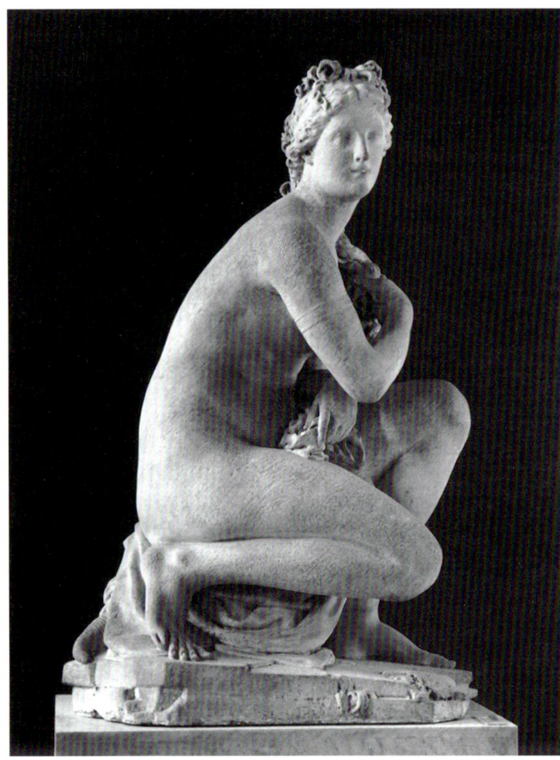

Fig. 34 *Crouching Venus*, A. Coysevox, 1684/6, marble, h.: 132.5 cm. Musée du Louvre, Paris (RF 1826)

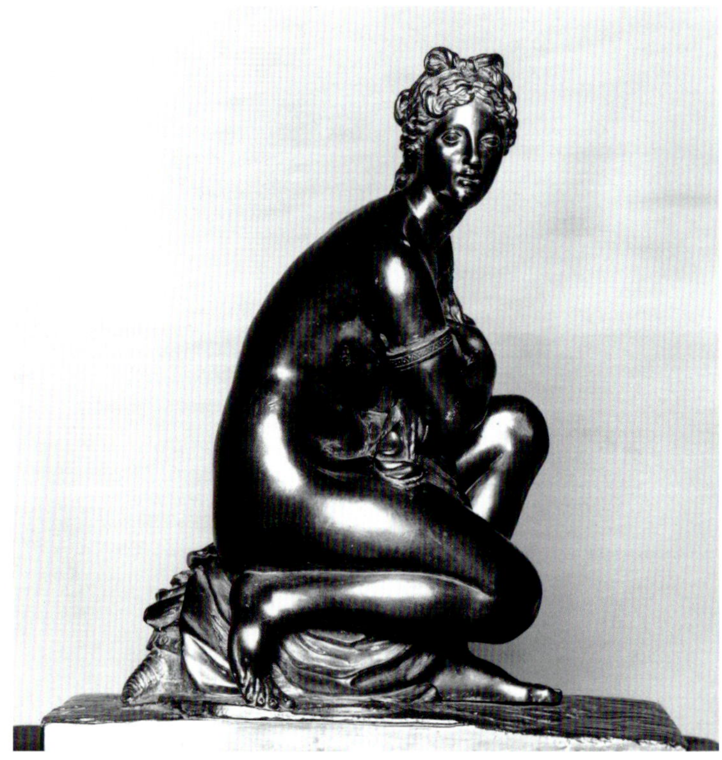

Fig. 35 *Crouching Venus*, after A. Coysevox, French *c.*1700–15, bronze, h.: 33.5 cm. Skulpturensammlung, Dresden (H⁴ 153/7)

Rome (also now in the Uffizi), or one of the several other variants then known.

The display together of these figures for the first time at Versailles undoubtedly inspired the production of copies of them as a pair for, despite their mirrored crouching postures, they were not conceived or previously shown as pendants. The subject of the *Venus* was always understood as such (even if the particular context was uncertain), but that of the *Arrotino* was much debated. In the 1680s the figure was widely believed to represent the 'Listening Slave', a servant who, while at work, overheard a plot against the State. It is now generally accepted as representing the Scythian executioner preparing to flay alive Marsyas, the hapless Satyr defeated by Apollo in a musical contest. Furthermore, although the originals are now both thought to date from the Pergamene period (3rd century BC), this was not always the case: on several occasions the *Arrotino* was even attributed to Michelangelo.

A pair of life-size bronze versions of these figures was cast by the specialist founder Joseph Vinache, *père* (1653–after 1717) in 1688–9 and displayed in the Gardens at Marly. It is possible that his foundry also cast some of the many bronze reductions, including these, which, although competent, are perhaps too 'soft' in their detailing to have been made under the direct supervision of a sculptor such as Coysevox. Their methods of construction and pattern of terrains are similar or identical to those of the *Crouching*

Venus in Dresden (fig. 35) which, with its pendant (since lost) formed part of the consignment of bronzes acquired in Paris for Augustus the Strong of Saxony in 1715.

Displayed on 'marble stands' in the Principal Drawing Room at Dorchester House in 1842, as inventoried after the death of the 3rd Marquess of Hertford (by whom they were presumably acquired).

S188 (Crouching Venus)
S189 (Arrotino)

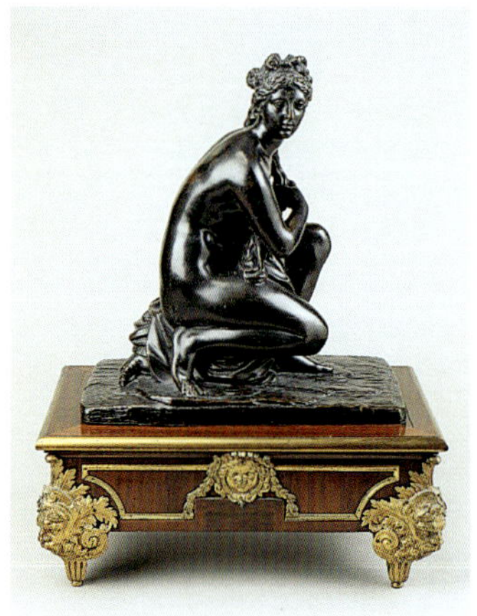
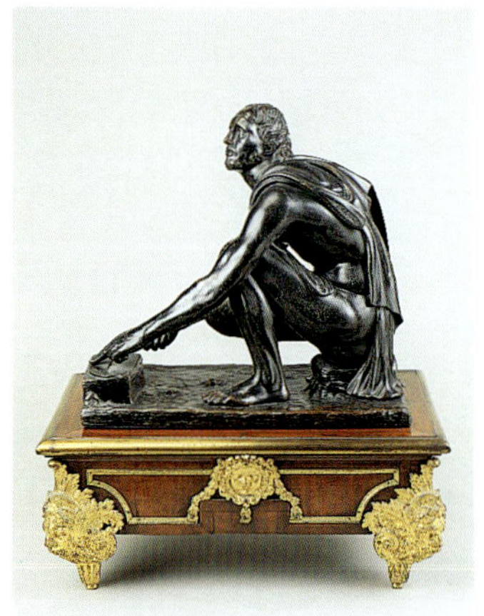

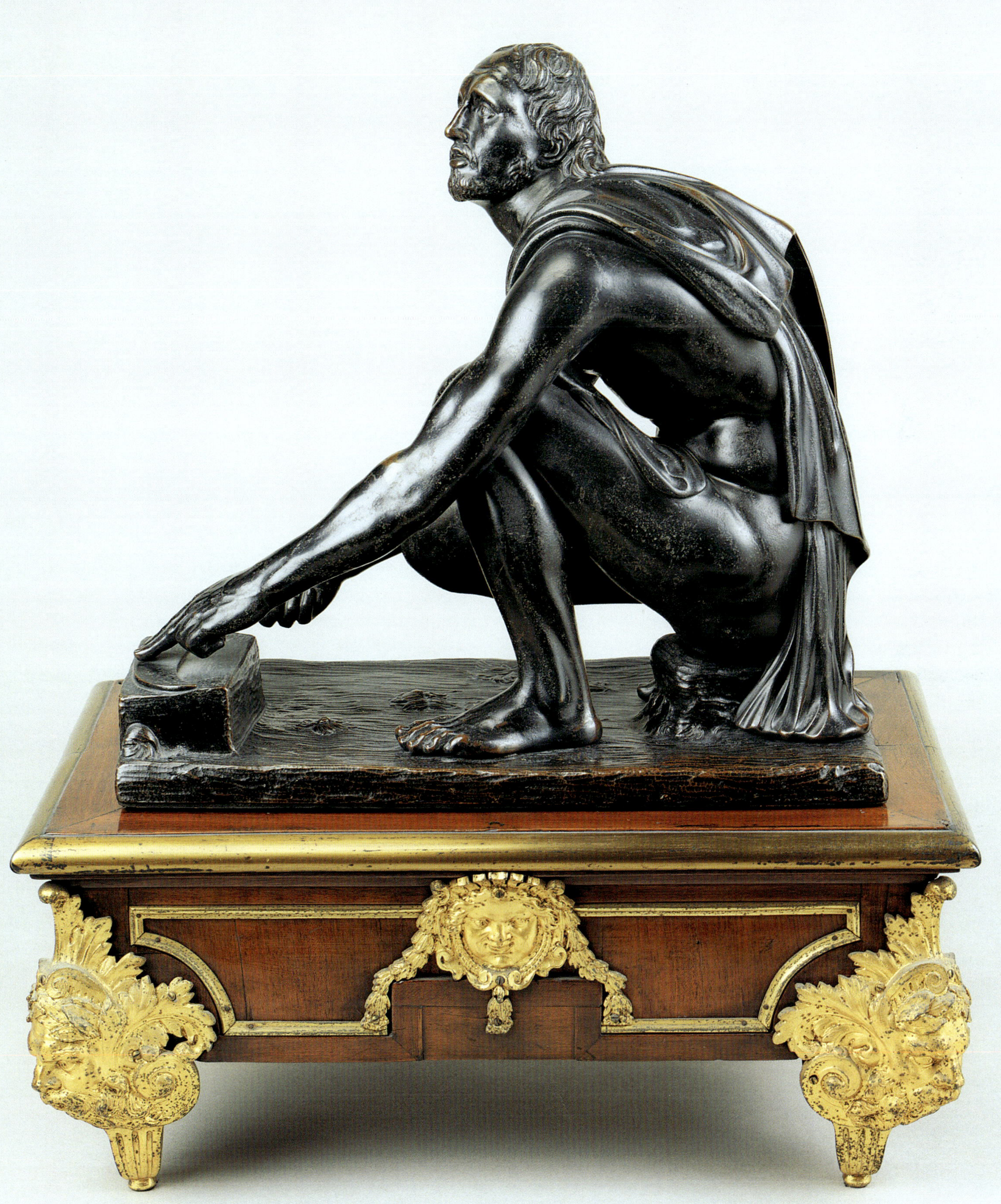

Nessus Abducting Deianira

MODEL:
French, *c.*1700–15, after a variant by Antonio Susini (*fl.*1572–1624) of a
model of *c.*1575 by Giambologna (1524–1608)

CAST:
French, perhaps *c.*1725–50

H. (excluding mount): 43.8 cm (17⅜ in.), L. (terrain base): 23.3 cm (9¼ in.)

'Rape of a Sabine Woman by a Roman Horseman'

MODEL:
French, *c.*1700–15

CAST:
French, perhaps *c.*1725–50

H. (excluding mount): 40.0 cm (15⅞ in.), L. (terrain base): 23.3 cm (9¼ in.)

*Light, lost-wax casts, made in sections and sleeve-joined. Polished dark brown patina.
The hind legs of the equine element are attached to a separately-cast patinated-bronze
terrain, of broadly oval form, sloping up towards the rear.
Louis XV-style openwork gilt-bronze mounts of scrolls and leaf-sprigs. H.: 6.9 cm
(2¾ in.).*

The Nessus group captures a dramatic moment from the life of
Hercules as recounted in the Roman poet Ovid's *Metamorphoses*. It
represents the centaur Nessus abducting Deianira, the wife of
Hercules, who had entrusted Nessus to carry her across a river. For
his treachery, Nessus would be shot dead by Hercules with an
arrow (for which episode see pp. 62–3).

The earliest known bronze of this composition was made in
1575/6 by Giambologna in Florence, but a distinct variant was made
by his assistant Antonio Susini, probably after 1600. Authentic
casts of this variant are rare – perhaps four are known – although
two examples may have been in France by the early 18th century.
One, now in the Louvre, was in the collection of Louis XIV,
possibly by 1693, while the sculptor Girardon believed he had
another (untraced), almost certainly acquired from the collection of
Cardinal Richelieu (1585–1642) (see fig. 36). A further variant of the
Nessus group, of which this bronze is an example, copies the
figurative elements of the Susini version fairly closely, but casts of it
have the landscaped bases (or terrains) typical of French bronzes of
the late-17th and early 18th centuries, and display a generally less
refined finish. Moreover, they are frequently associated, as here,
with a group of a galloping horseman carrying off a woman,
usually identified as 'The Rape of a Sabine Woman', a subject drawn
from classical history. The composition was evidently an entirely
new invention, even if inspired by Giambologna's work.

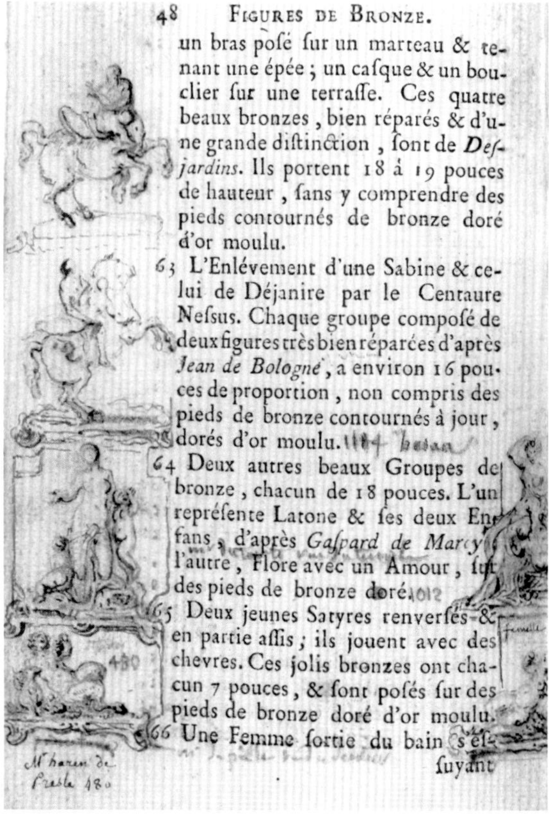

Fig. 37 Detail of Gaignat sale catalogue, 1768/9, p. 48, with sketches
by Gabriel de Saint-Aubin (1724–1780). Petit Palais, Paris (L Dut 1171)

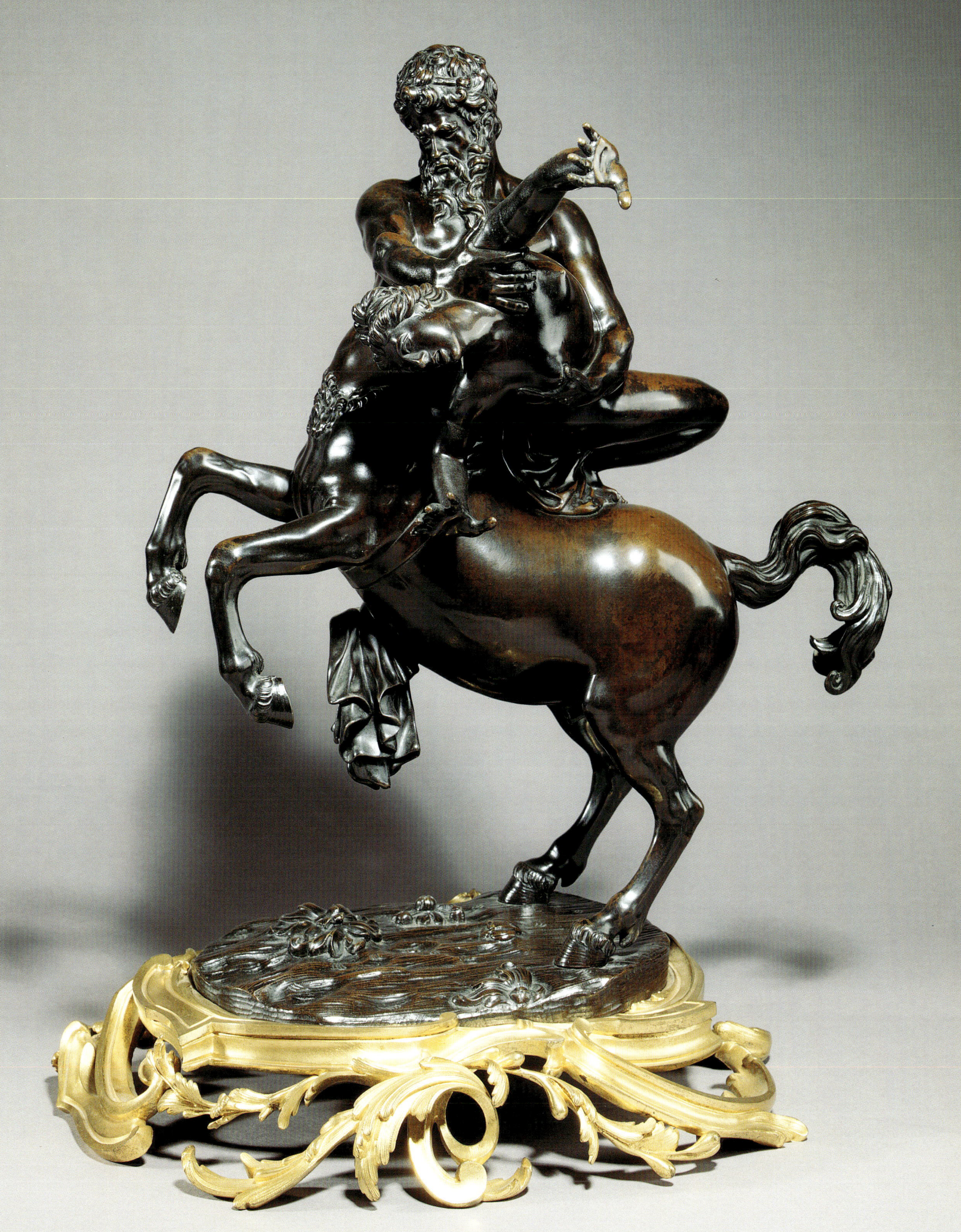

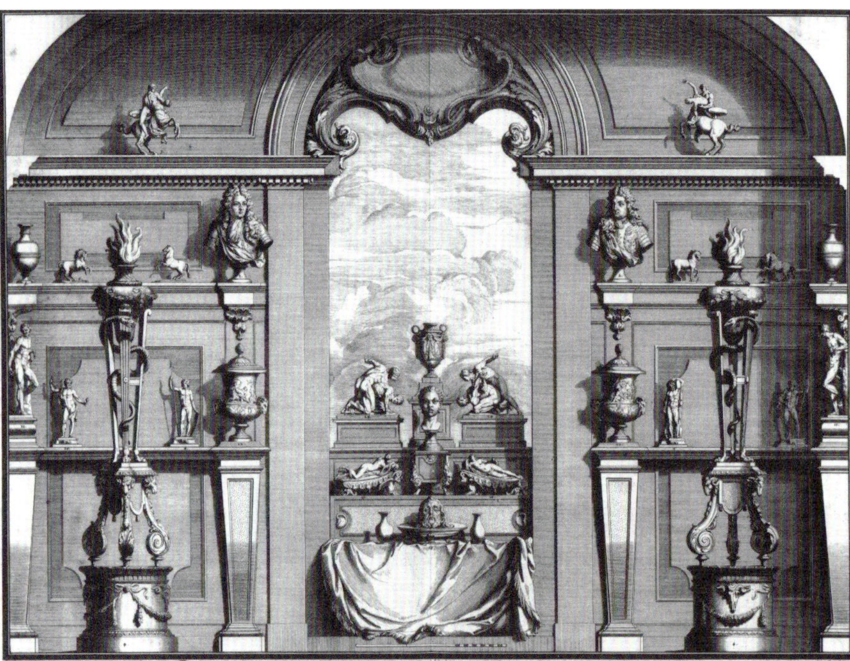

Fig. 36 *La Galerie de Girardon*, plate II, N. Chevallier after R. Charpentier (1680–1723), *c.*1709, engraving. Bibliothèque Nationale de France, Paris

The models and the many known casts of both bronzes of these types are generally accepted as French. The earliest documented example of the Sabine group, in Dresden, was mentioned, without the Nessus group, in a list of 1715, recording bronzes acquired in Paris for Augustus the Strong of Saxony. The absence of this model from his earlier purchase list of 1699 may indicate a *terminus post quem* for its conception. The Sabine group may have been a pastiche, perhaps invented for the market by a dealer specifically as a pendant to the Nessus group. It is a sculpturally weaker composition, not least because the protagonists' heads face in opposite directions and so the group lacks a satisfactory single viewing point. Also, the two compositions are not symmetrically balanced, since when looked at side by side from the 'front' the equine elements face the same direction. In the engravings of Girardon's collection (*c.*1709), a single Nessus group is shown from different sides to provide the illusion of balanced pendants (fig. 36). Augustus ultimately owned two near-identical pairs of each model, and perhaps intended to display them similarly. The sloping bases present on the Dresden and Wallace Collection examples could suggest that they also were intended to be seen from below.

Numerous other pairs are known, variously with oval, shaped or rectangular bases (an example of the latter, for a solitary Nessus group, is in the Wallace Collection (S115)). A pair in the Gaignat sale, Paris, 1768/9 is known from a contemporary sketch to have had gilt-bronze Louis XV-style openwork *rocaille* mounts similar to those of the Wallace Collection pair (fig. 37). If these mounts are co-eval with the casts, the groups could be dated to *c.*1725–50, a proposition supported by the presence of a 'crowned-C' tax mark (in use between 1745–9 only: see pp. 74–5) on the similar mounts of another pair currently on the art market. Given the numbers that survive, it is quite possible that examples of the pendants were produced by more than one workshop, and over an extended period of years.

Acquired by the 4th Marquess of Hertford, almost certainly at the prince de Beauvau sale, Paris, 1865 (for the large sum of 12,000 francs).

S116 (Nessus group)
S132 (Sabine group)

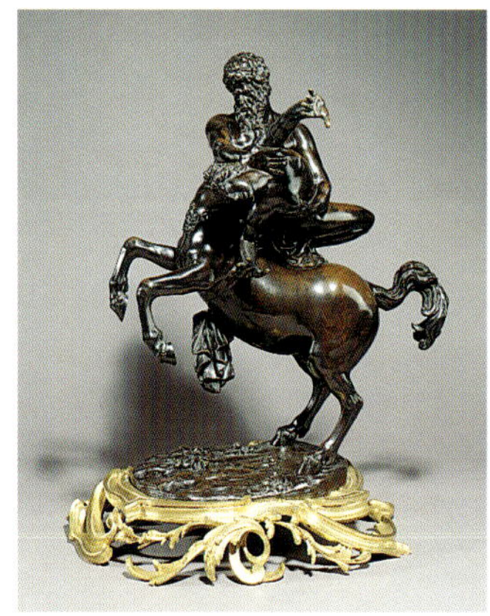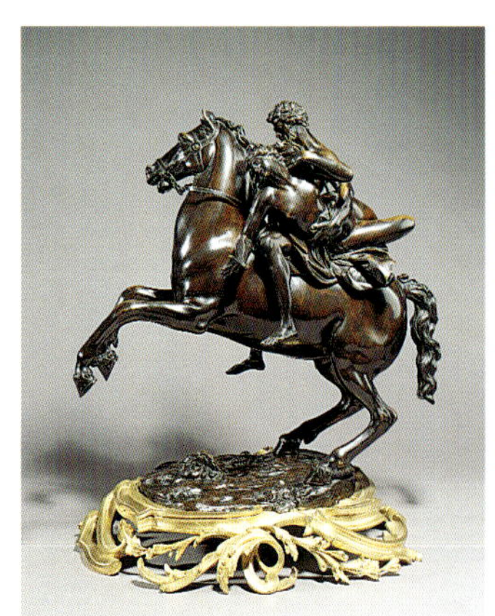

48

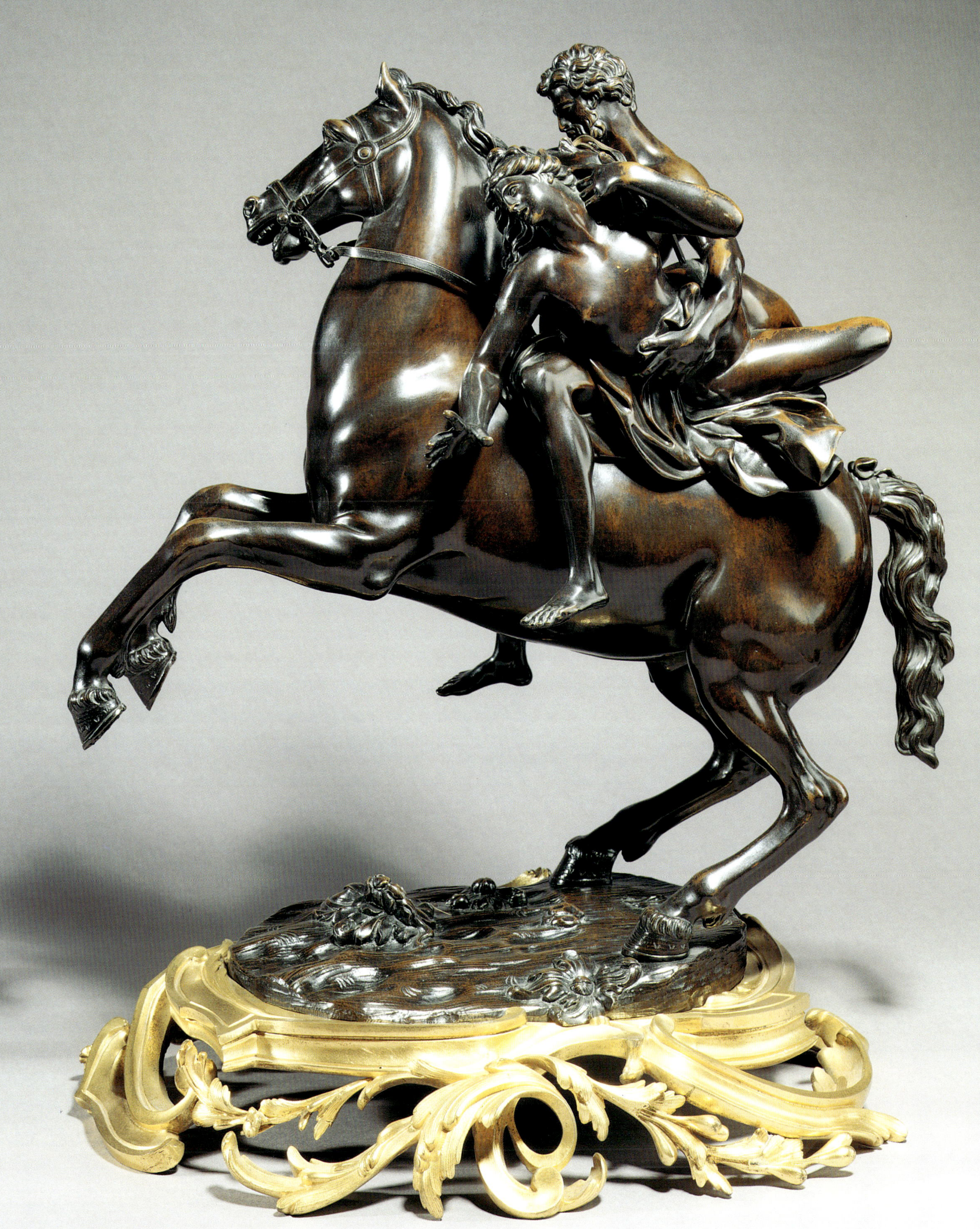

Louis XIV (1638–1715), King of France

MODEL:
Martin van den Bogaert, called Desjardins (1637–1694), c.1688/91

CAST:
Attributed to Roger Scabol, called Roger (c.1656–after 1714), c.1700–05

H. (excluding socle):43.5cm (17¼ in.), L. (maximum): 37.8cm (15 in.)

Light, thin-walled lost-wax cast. Tail, sword, reins, bit and chains separately cast, as is right arm (to elbow) with baton, and left rear leg of horse (at the hock; possibly a repair). Light-brown natural patina, with a deep burgundy varnish, turning blackish; high points worn to reveal brassier-coloured metal.
No terrain; set onto a contemporary patinated-bronze socle, with gilt-bronze escutcheons with royal arms and crown on short sides, and cartouches back and front bearing inscriptions:
(front): Ludovicus XIIII franciae et Navarrae Rex
(back): Louis XIIII Roy de france et de Navarre
H.: 12.5 cm (5 in.), L.: 39.5 cm (15⅝ in.), D.: 19.8 cm (7⅞ in.)

The image of a ruler on horseback stretches back to antiquity, most famously exemplified in the monument to Marcus Aurelius in Rome, and was traditionally regarded as the most dignified and exalted representation of authority. In 1685, when Louis XIV was at the height of his powers, an official propaganda campaign was launched to stamp his authority on the most-recently absorbed outlying regions of France. Under a central directive, *intendants* were to request of their Provinces that as an expression of their

hommage and loyalty they erect monuments to Louis 'le Grand'. These were to be of bronze, the noblest of materials, and centred in new squares, *'les place royales'*, where they would be the focal point of popular celebrations and official events.

One of the ten equestrian statues of Louis XIV begun at this time was for the place Bellecour, Lyons, formally commissioned in May 1688. The initial conception of the monument by Jules Hardouin-Mansart (1646–1708), *Premier Architecte des Bâtiments du*

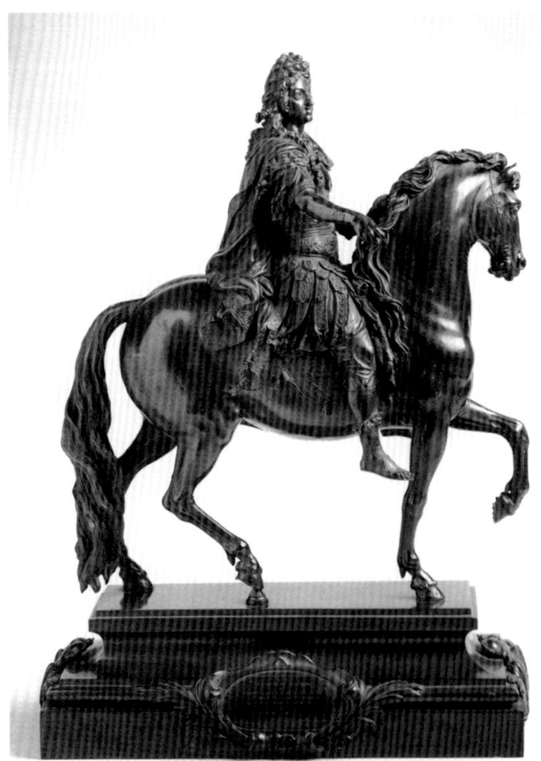

Fig. 39 *Elector Max Emanuel of Bavaria on Horseback*, R. Scabol, 1699, bronze, h.: 45.5 cm. Germanische Nationalmuseum, Nuremberg (Pl 3139)

Fig. 38 *La Statue Équestre de Louis XIV, Place Bellecour, Lyons*, Benoît Audran (1661–1721) and Jean Audran (1667–1756), 1720, engraving. Bibliothèque Nationale de France, Paris

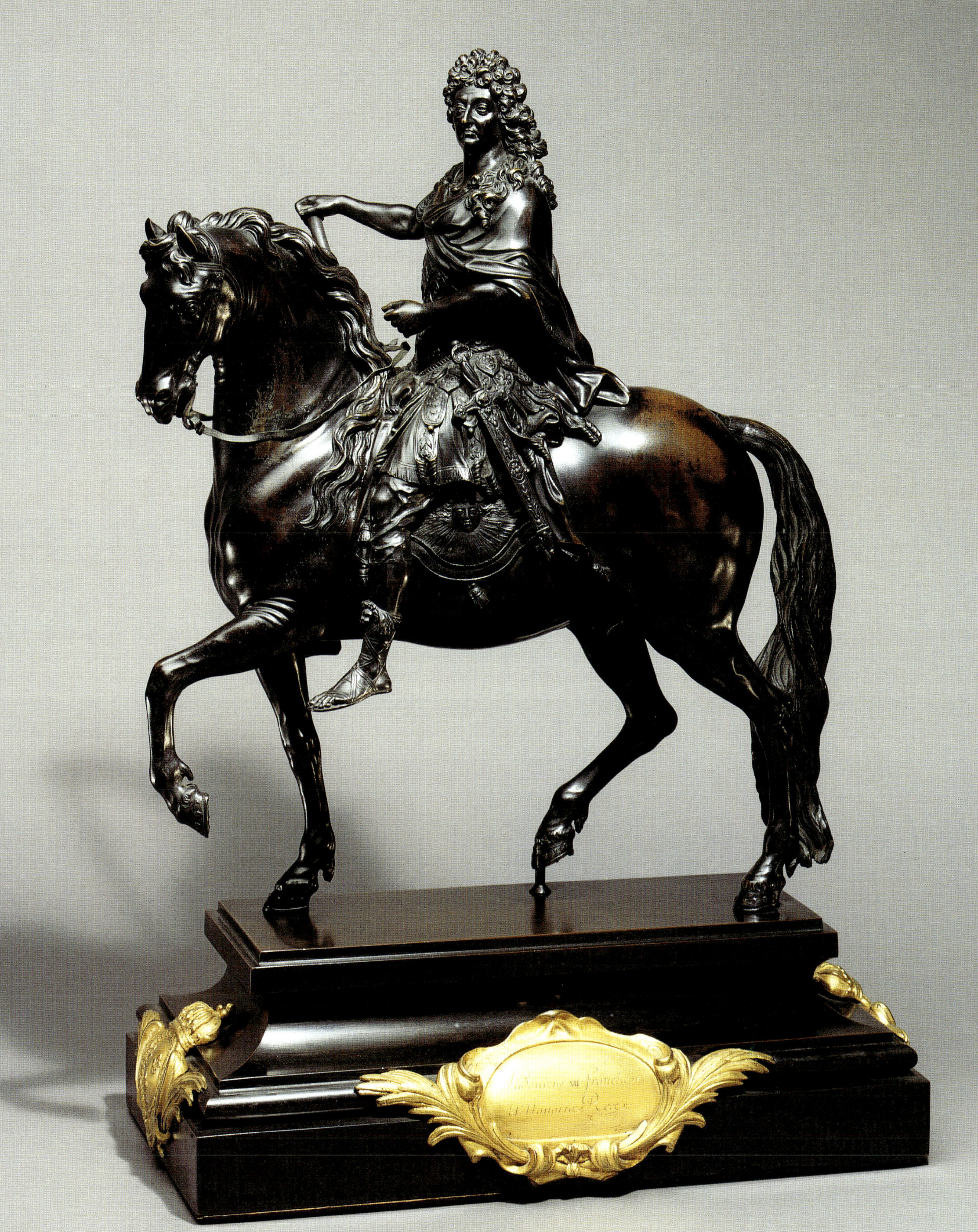
Ludovicus XIIII Franciae
et Navarrae Rex

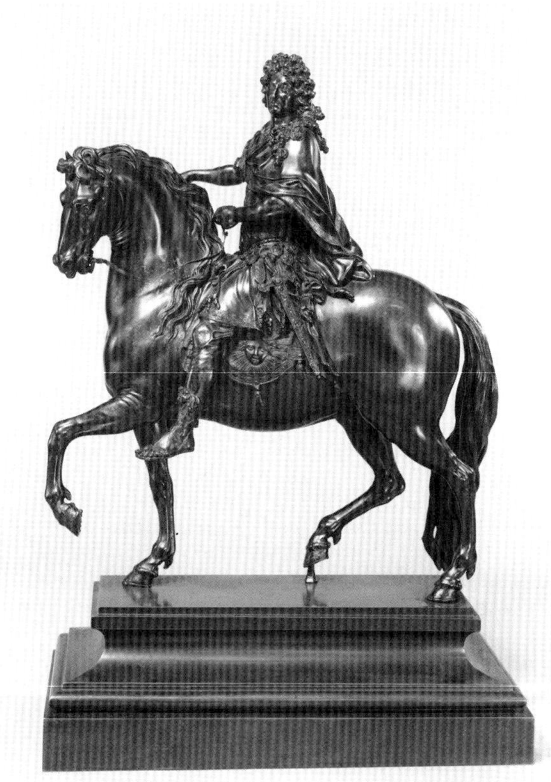

fig. 40 *Louis XIV on Horseback*, attributed to R. Scabol, after M. Desjardins, c.1698/9, bronze, h.: 44.9 cm. National Gallery of Art, Washington, Andrew W. Mellon Fund (A-1742)

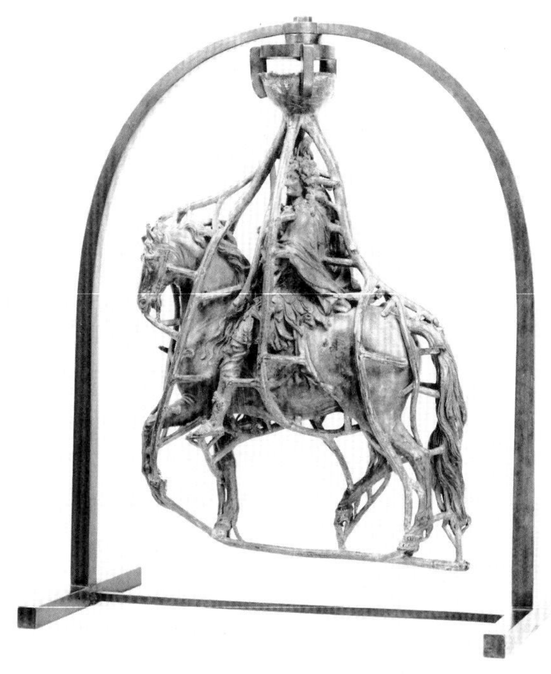

Fig. 41 *Louis XIV on Horseback*, R. Scabol after M. Desjardins, unchased cast, c.1700, bronze, h.: c.45 cm. Statens Museum for Kunst, Copenhagen (KMS5403)

Roi, was closely based on the Marcus Aurelian prototype, representing the rider without stirrups and in armour *à l'antique*, but with a contemporary peruke. This design was subtly adapted by the sculptor, Martin Desjardins, who, for instance, exchanged the lion skin of the original for a saddlecloth with the personal motif of a *rayonnant* sun. The monument was cast by the specialist founder Roger Scabol, and completed only after the death of the sculptor in 1694. It took seven years for Lyons to pay for and effect the transport of their monument from Paris, and another twelve to complete its erection (1713). The pedestal was completed even later, in 1714–20 (fig. 38) – after Louis XIV's death – only for the whole monument to be destroyed during the Revolution.

The success of the equestrian group is reflected in the large number of surviving small-scale replicas – indeed, after that by Girardon it was the most reproduced of all the Louis XIV equestrian monuments. Reductions of Desjardin's monument fall into two main categories: those from his own studio, probably cast by his nephew, Jacques (1671–1737); and those by Scabol, which portray a rather more solemn image. Technically Scabol's bronzes are distinguished for being fine, thin-walled sectional casts, meticulously finished. Such qualities induced the Elector Max Emanuel of Bavaria to buy seven bronzes by Scabol from a Brussels jeweller in 1701. It was presumably the Elector, or a member of his

entourage, who acquired from Scabol a variant bronze of the Louis XIV equestrian group in which his own features were substituted (Nuremberg) (fig. 39). This is signed and dated 1699, and has the same distinctive bronze socle as the Wallace Collection *Louis XIV*. Identical socles appear on the paired groups of *Louis XIV* (fig. 40) and the *Grand Dauphin* in Washington, and another *Louis XIV* on the art market, all believed to have been cast by Scabol. A remarkable unchased version of this model, with casting vents and ducts uncut, is in Copenhagen (fig. 41).

The approximate dating of these casts can be estimated by the facial features of Louis XIV, in which respect the sculptor took care to be up to date, and thus the imperious face of the King in the Washington cast appears to have been modified from that conceived for the original monument. Moreover, its pendant *Grand Dauphin*, with which it is presumably co-eval, has been dated to 1698/9, on the basis that the heir briefly enjoyed two quasi-sovereign governorships in those years. The Wallace Collection version is probably later still, for it shows the King's mouth drawn and sunken, indicating the loss of teeth that occurred in his final years.

Bought by the 4th Marquess of Hertford in 1869 from Delaroche, Paris, for 11,500 francs.

S166

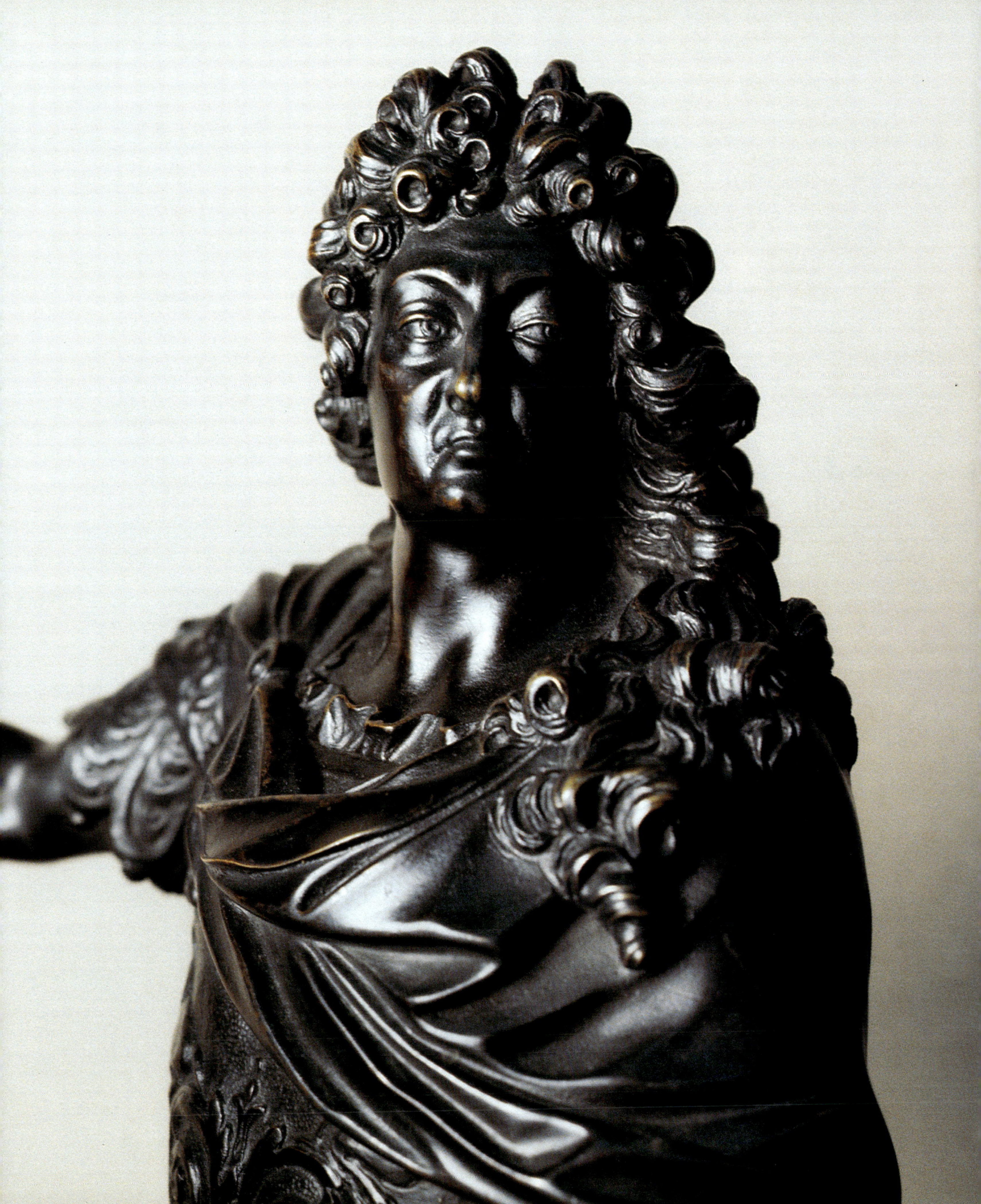

Pluto Abducting Proserpine: 'Fire'

MODEL:
François Girardon (1628–1715), *c*.1699

CAST:
French, *c*.1700–25

H. (excluding mount): 54.6 cm (21⅝ in.), W. (terrain base): 21.1 cm (8⅜ in.),
D. (terrain base): 21.1 cm (8⅜ in.)

Boreas Abducting Orithyia: 'Air'

MODEL:
Gaspard Marsy (1624/5–1681) and Anselme Flamen (1647–1717), *c*.1687

CAST:
French, *c*.1700–25

H. (excluding mount): 54.6 cm (21⅝ in.), W. (terrain base): 21.1 cm (8⅜ in.),
D. (terrain base): 21.1 cm (8⅜ in.)

Lost-wax casts, made in sections and sleeve-joined; upper figures socketed into lower figure and terrain, and secured with pins. Yellowish, brassy metal, with natural patina, varying from olive to chestnut, darkened (or wax-coated) to blackish colour in several areas. Square-sectioned integral terrain.
Gilt-bronze bases in the Louis XV style. H.: 10.7 cm (4¼ in.).

Pluto, god of the underworld, chanced upon Proserpine, the young daughter of Jupiter and Ceres, picking flowers by a Sicilian lake and immediately fell in love with and abducted her (Ovid, *Metamorphoses*, Bk V). She is represented struggling and calling out for help. Below lies Cyane, a local water-nymph who in vain implored Pluto to release her. The companion bronze, taken from the same source (Bk VI), is of winged Boreas, the violent North Wind of Thrace, abducting Orithyia, the daughter of the King Erechtheus of Athens, while trampling on his rival, perhaps Zephyr, the gentle South Wind.

Each bronze is a reduction of a life-size marble group conceived for one of the corners of the *Parterre d'Eau* at Versailles, part of Colbert's 'Grand Commande' of 1674 for populating the gardens with sculpture. There were originally to be four such groups, each a three-figure abduction scene taken from Ovidian mythology, and each further allegorising one of the Four Elements. To hasten progress each was commissioned from a different sculptor, although they were all based on designs supplied by Charles Le Brun, *Premier Peintre du Roi*. However, of the other two groups, *Neptune and Coronis* ('Water') by J.-B. Tuby seems not to have progressed beyond the small model stage, while *Saturn and Cybele* ('Earth') by T. Regnaudin (now in the Louvre) never achieved the prominence of the other two, which were probably conceived as a discrete pair within the quartet.

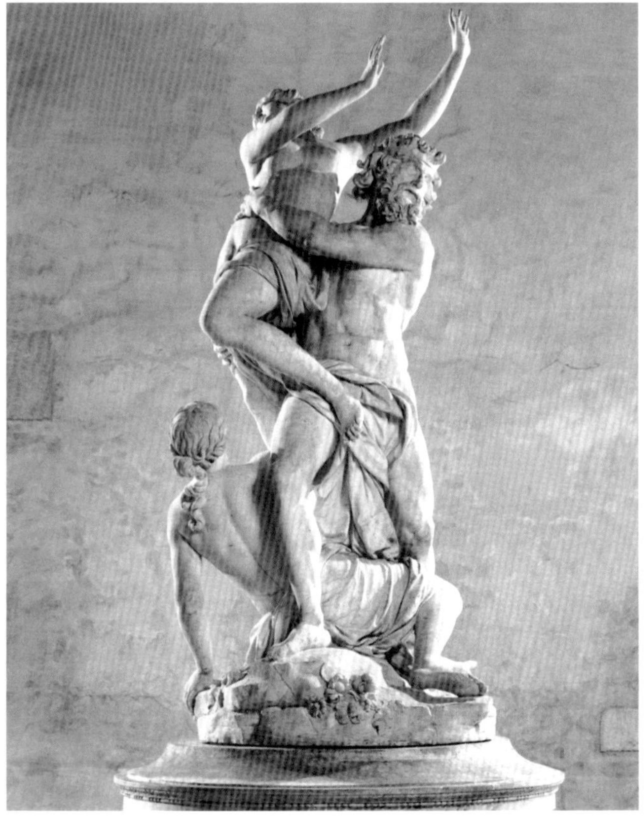

Fig. 43 *Pluto Abducting Proserpine*, F. Girardon, *c*.1699, marble, h.: 260 cm. Châteaux de Versailles et de Trianon (MV 8952)

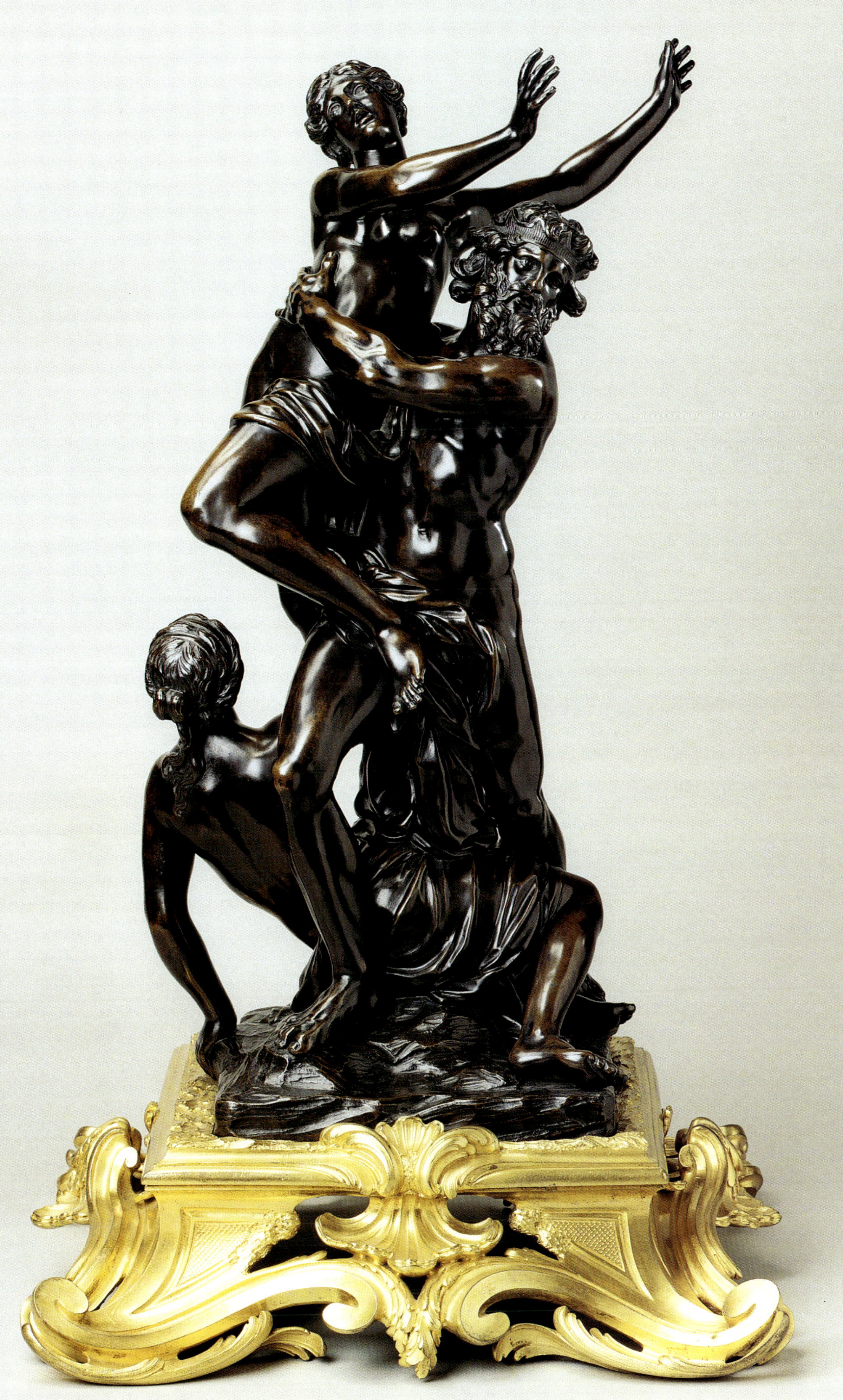

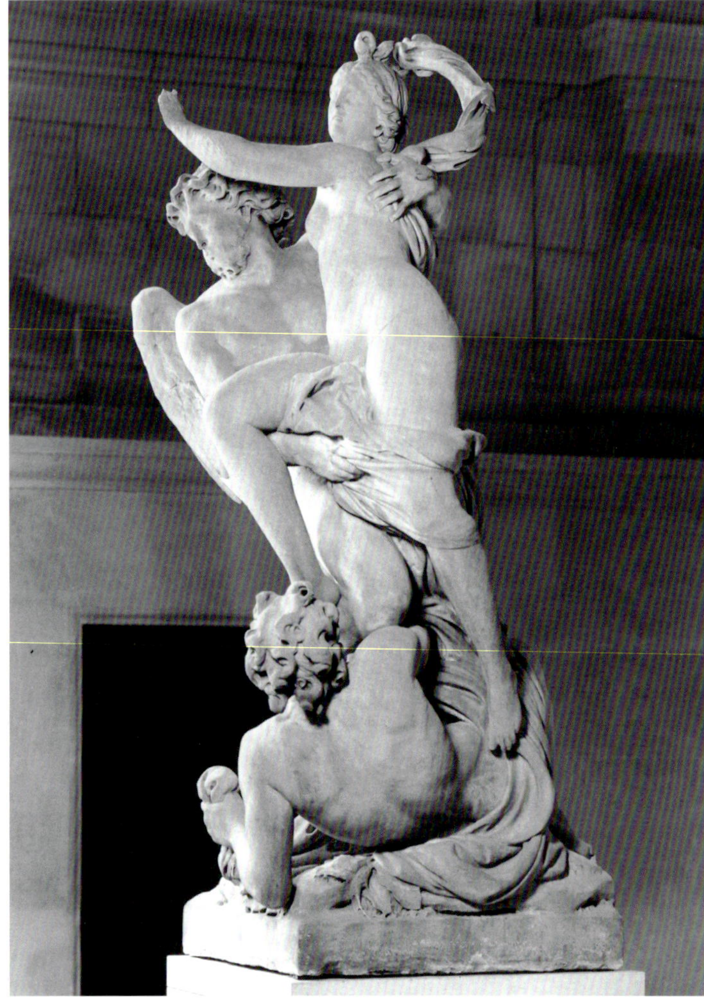

Fig. 42 *Boreas Abducting Orithyia*, G. Marsy and A. Flamen, *c.*1687, marble, h.: 260 cm. Musée du Louvre, Paris (MR 1844)

Marsy had completed his model by 1681, but it was carved after his death by his pupil, Flamen, and set up in the Orangery at Versailles in 1687. It was moved to the Tuileries in 1716, and is now in the Louvre (fig. 42). Girardon's marble (fig. 43), completed as late as 1699, was set up on its own at the centre of the Colonnade at Versailles (original now in the Musée de l'Œuvre, Versailles). Whereas the frontal composition of Marsy's group betrays its origins in a two-dimensional drawing, Girardon's group is more fully modelled 'in the round', albeit owing much to celebrated antecedents by Giambologna and Bernini.

The earliest bronze reductions of Girardon's group predate the marble and are all about twice the height of this example. One example was delivered to Versailles in 1693, when it was probably first paired with a reduction of the Marsy/Flamen *Abduction*. Both were displayed in the *Salon Ovale* in 1707, together with casts of the Algardi firedogs (see pp. 34–7). The enormous popularity to collectors of these pendant models is confirmed by their regular appearance in French 18th-century sales, and by the numerous

examples that survive today, usually of this smaller size. Unlike the larger pairs, these follow the final marbles closely, and tend to have squarish terrain bases, which promote a single, frontal viewpoint. One of the smaller pairs owned by Augustus the Strong of Saxony was acquired in Paris in 1715, which provides a *terminus ante quem* for them. Who made such casts is unclear, although a pair sold at the Le Marié sale, Paris, 1776, was described as 'after the reductions by Duplessis', presumably the designer J.-C. Duplessis, *père* (*c.*1695–1774). The Wallace Collection bronzes, despite their superb gilt-bronze mounts of the Louis XV period, would seem to be of a quality and method of facture consistent with French bronzes of the early 18th century.

Probably either the 'Pluto & Proserpine' and 'Eolus [*sic*] – companion' stored at the Pantechnicon, London, in 1846 (the property of the 3rd Marquess of Hertford), or the '2 *groupes en bronzes Enlèvements Louis XIV*' bought from the Countess Catherine Koucheleff (1811–after 1867), St Petersburg, for the 4th Marquess of Hetford in 1867. Not certainly recorded until lent by Sir Richard Wallace to the Bethnal Green Museum exhibition, 1872–5.

S170 (Pluto)

S169 (Boreas)

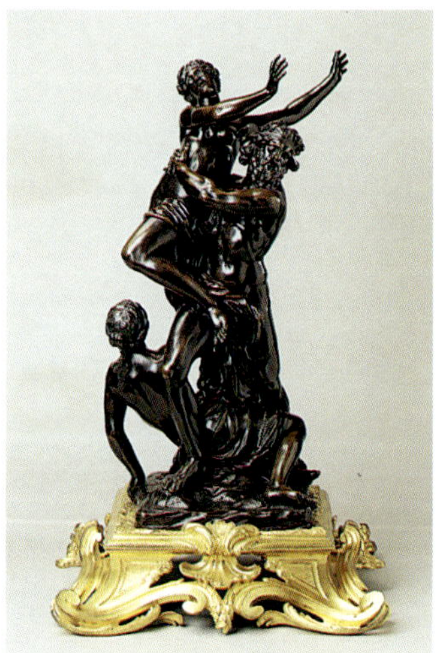

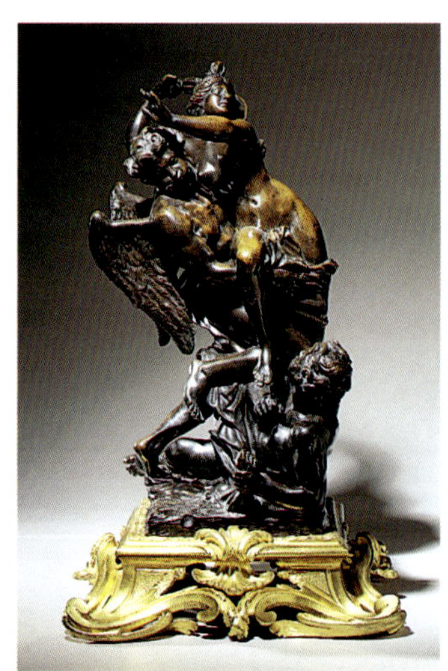

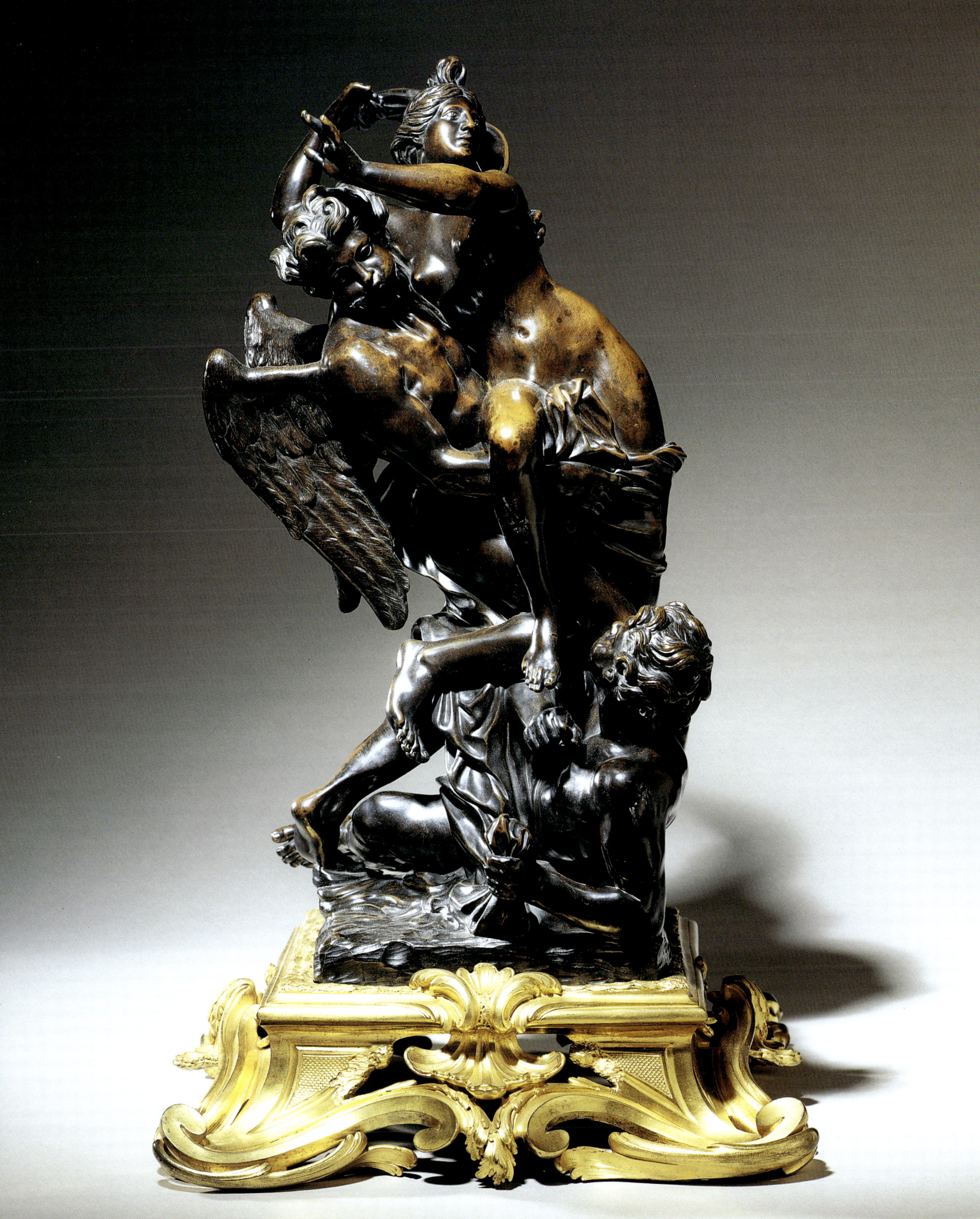

The Triumph of Thetis

MODELS:

François Girardon (1628–1715), c.1683

CASTS:

French, probably 18th century

H.: 44.4 cm (17⅝ in.), Diam. (maximum): 35.3 cm (14 in.)

Heavy, thick casts, apparently directly from the wax model. Dark brown patina. Unmounted and lacking lids.

These vases depict the triumph of Thetis, a Nereid (sea-nymph) of classical mythology who was the mother of the Greek hero Achilles. She is accompanied by her followers: fellow Nereids, Tritons, hippocampi (marine centaurs), a capricorn (marine goat), dolphins and amoretti. Thetis herself, oddly, is somewhat obscurely placed above the left-hand goat's-head handle of the left-hand vase, seated in a chariot with paddle-wheels, drawn by two sea-horses. The sketchy finish of these bronzes can be explained by the fact that they are very probably casts taken directly from Girardon's original wax preparatory models for large-scale marble vases completed in 1683 for the gardens at Versailles, probably those now in the Louvre (figs 44,45), from which they differ in significant details (see also the wax reliefs in a *Galerie de Girardon* engraving: fig. 32, nos. 9,25). As such, they are rare and valuable records of the sculptor's initial compositional ideas and, if indirectly, of his skill at modelling in the more spontaneous medium of wax. Indeed, the relationship of the figures is perhaps better resolved and the facial expressions and execution more lively than in the marble versions.

A pair of bronze vases described as models for the Versailles

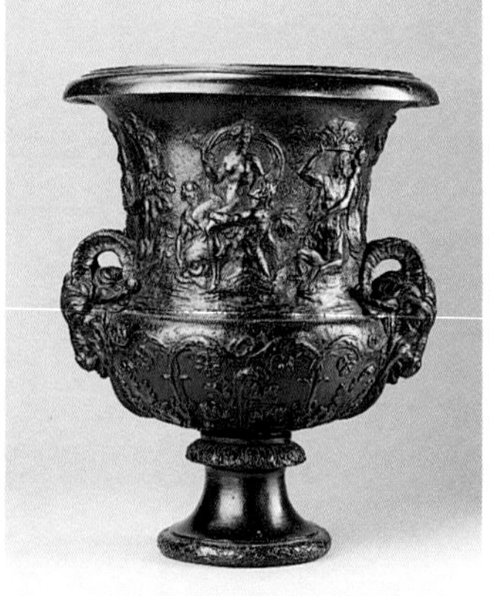

S167

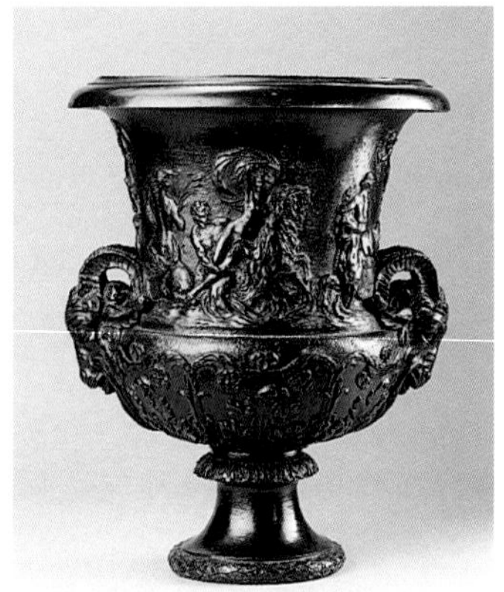

S168

marble versions were exhibited by Girardon at the Salons of 1699 and 1704; they were inventoried in his studio after his death and later appeared in the posthumous sale of C.-A. Coypel (1694–1752), *Premier Peintre du Roi*, Paris, April 1753. However, to judge from their depiction in another *Galerie de Girardon* engraving (fig. 36, no. 12), although of the same height (without lids) as the Wallace Collection vases, these seem to have been meticulously finished and are shown with spiral fluting on their feet. It is not easy to determine when the Wallace Collection vases were cast although, given the perishable nature of the wax models, it is perhaps more likely to have been in the 18th century than in the early 19th. The waxes were last recorded at the same Coypel sale, where they were bought by the celebrated collector A.-L. La Live de Jully (1725–1779).

Acquired by the 4th Marquess of Hertford at the Fould sale, Paris, 1860, for 6000 francs.

S167 (Triumph of Thetis)
S168 (Followers of Thetis)

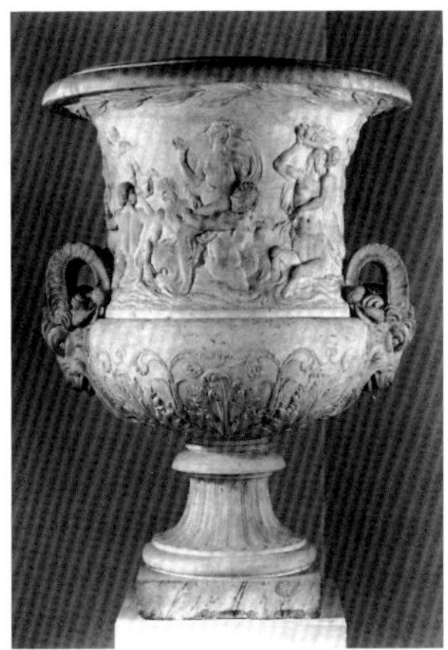

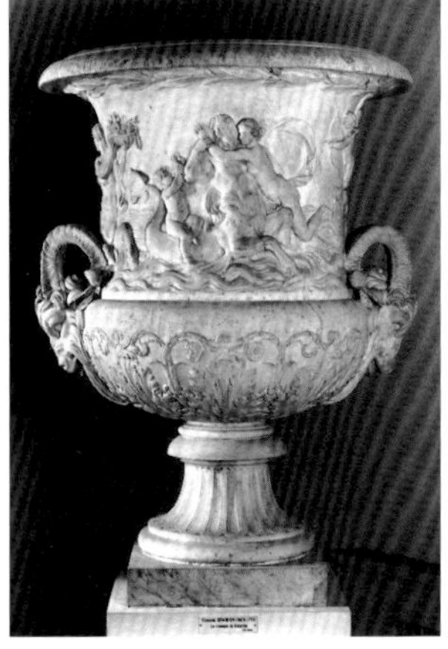

Fig. 44 Vase with Relief of the *Triumph of Thetis* (or of 'Amphitrite'), F. Girardon, 1683, marble, h.: 105 cm. Musée du Louvre, Paris (MR 3003)

Fig. 45 Vase with Relief of the *Followers of Thetis* (or 'The Triumph of Galatea') (reverse), F. Girardon, 1683, marble, h.: 105 cm. Musée du Louvre, Paris (MR 3004)

opposite: detail of S168

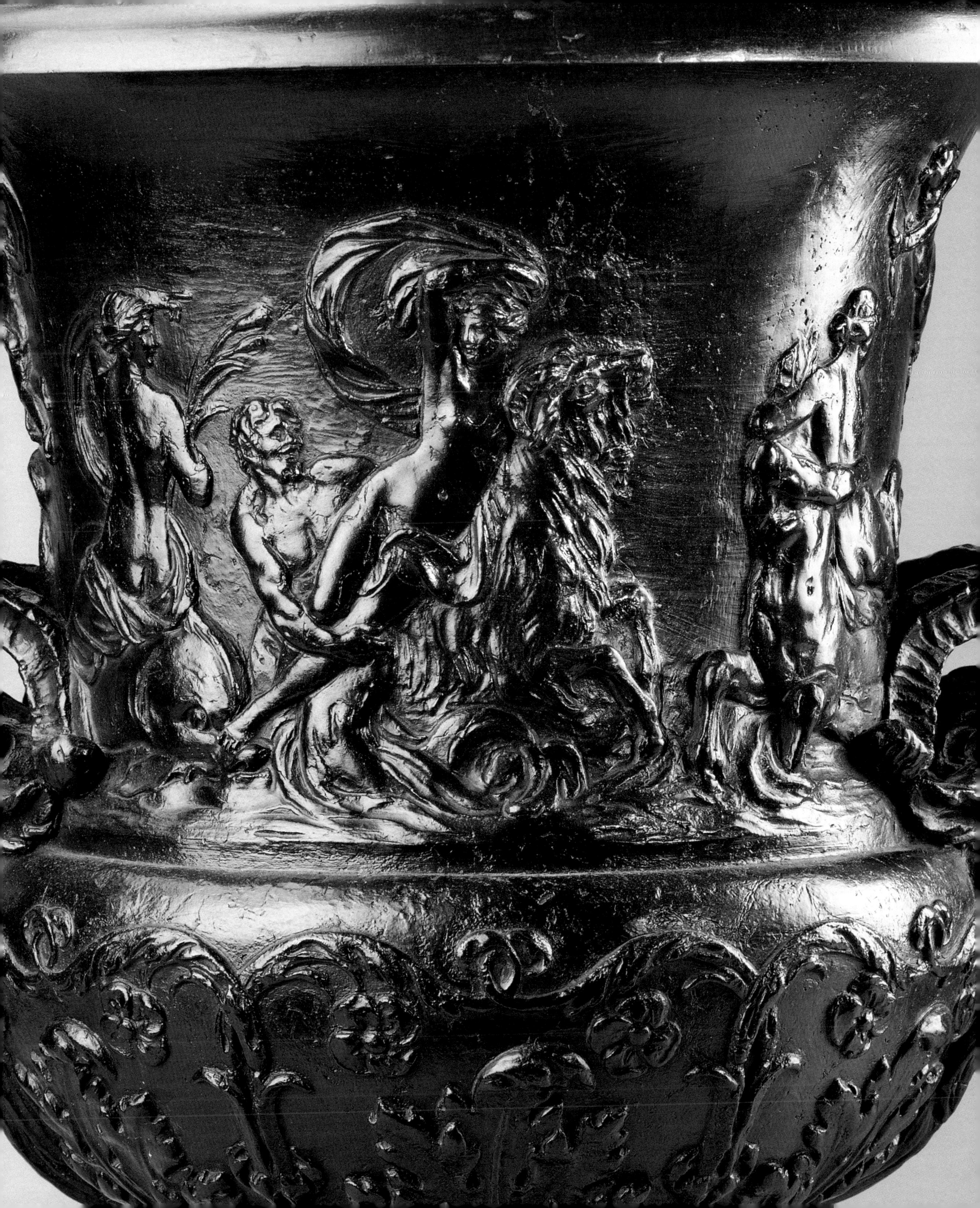

Angels of the Eucharist

MODELS & CASTS:
French (possibly Flemish or Dutch), c.1650–1700

Angel with the wheat-sheaves
H.: 83.7 cm (33¼ in)

Angel with the grapes
H: 85.0 cm (33¾ in.)

Heavy, thick lost-wax casts, cast in small pin-joined sections. Broadly modelled and summarily chased and finished. Dark brown-black surfaces. Each figure stands on an irregularly-shaped fragment of a base, of the same alloy and finish.

Each angel is represented as a standing boy 5–6 years old with feathered wings. One carries wheat-sheaves and looks to his left, the other holds a bunch of grapes, extends his right hand and turns to his right. They stand on irregularly-shaped bases which perhaps are intended to represent clouds. Previously assumed to represent two of the Seasons (Summer and Autumn, respectively), their wings identify these figures as angels or cherubs rather than secular *putti*. Furthermore, their attributes of wheat and grapes traditionally symbolised the bread and wine of the Eucharist. The fragmentary nature of the bases, when considered with the gestural relationship of the two figures and the iconography of their attributes, suggest that these companions, which are unique casts, were originally part of a larger group. The exact nature of this group has yet to be determined, but a religious, or quasi-religious context (such as a monument) is perhaps the most likely. Both figures look inwards, and the grape-bearer stretches towards whatever was the focus of their attention, perhaps a representation of Christ on the Cross.

The figure types themselves are strongly influenced by mid- to late 17th century Italian baroque models. A comparison may be made with the Calvary-group *Angels* in the Wallace Collection of c.1649 by the Florentine sculptor Ferdinando Tacca (1619–1686) (figs 46ab), although the sculptured infants by François Duquesnoy (see also pp. 82–3) provide closer parallels. The gentle *contrapposto* of the figures and their fluttering drapery and hair indicate a date in the second half of the 17th century. Their facture would appear to be French or, possibly, Flemish or Dutch.

First recorded in the Hertford House inventory of 1870 (Entrance Hall), at the death of the 4th Marquess of Hertford, who presumably acquired them.

S156 (Angel with the wheat-sheaves)
S157 (Angel with the grapes)

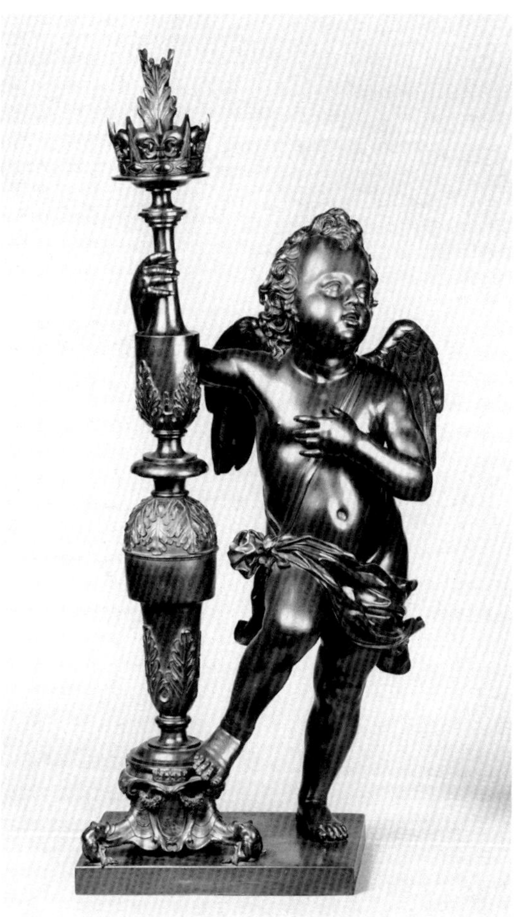
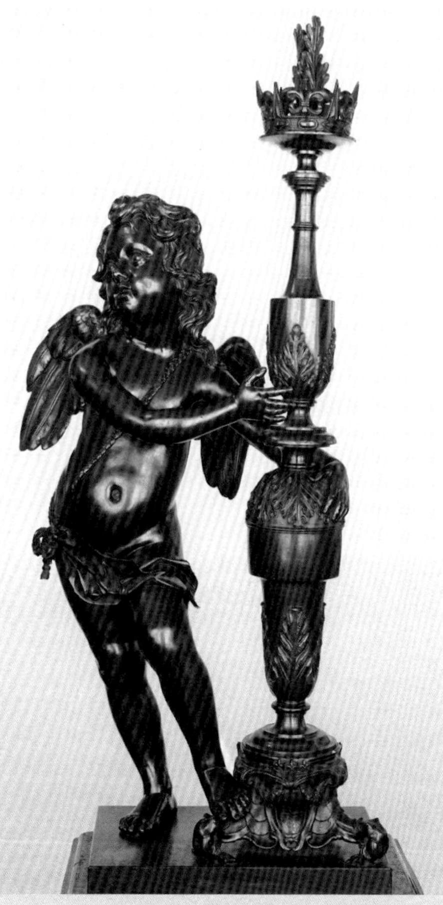

Figs 46ab Pair of *Angels with Candelabrum*, F. Tacca, c.1649, bronze, h.: 104.1 cm. Wallace Collection (S138, S139)

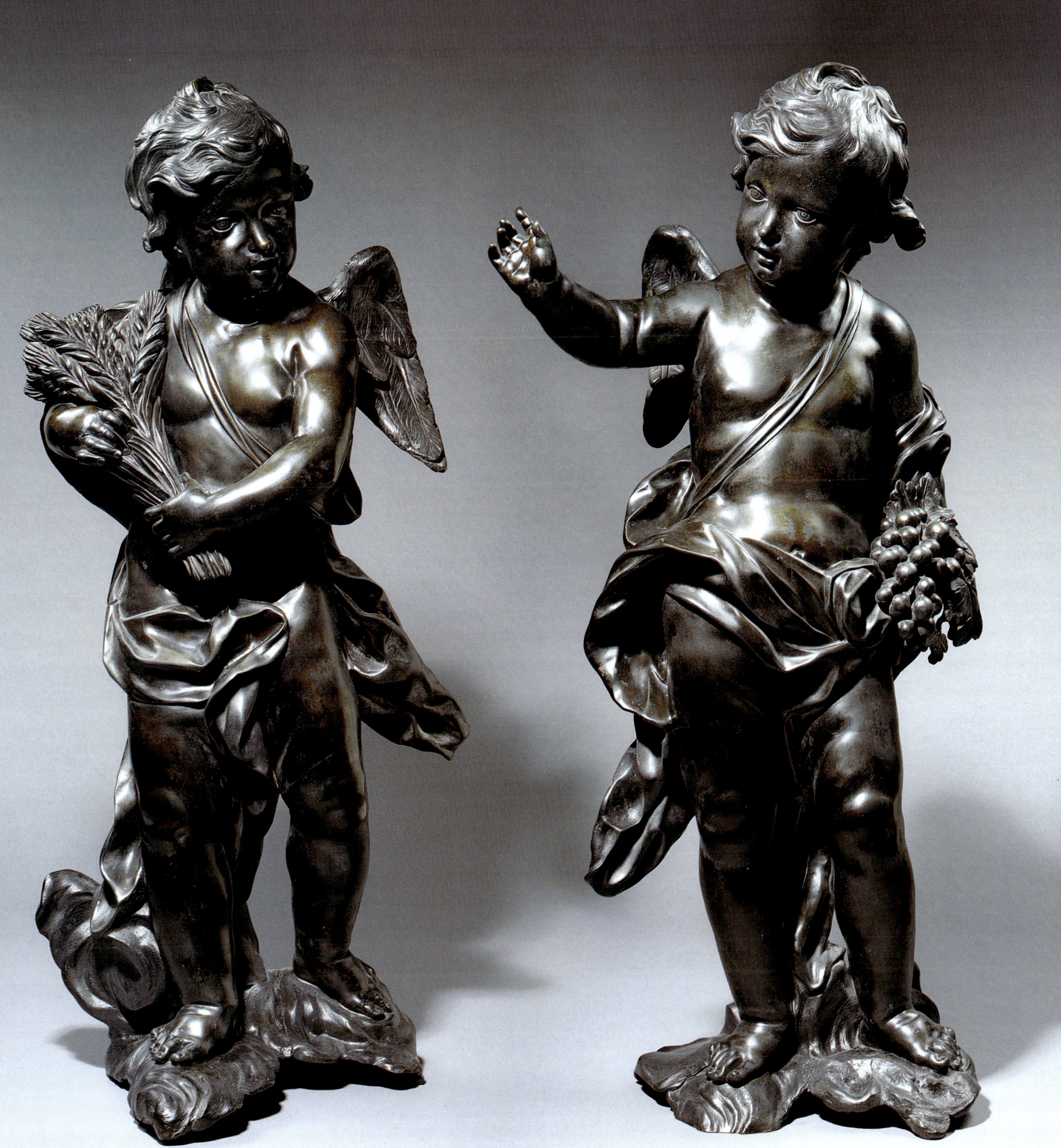

Nessus and Deianira

MODEL & CAST:
French, c.1690–99

H. (excluding mounted base): 19.6 cm (7¾ in.), L. (terrain base): 21.1 cm (8⅜ in.)

Lost-wax cast of several parts, the separate limbs joined to the main group, which is bolted to the terrain. Coppery alloy with extensive traces of a reddish-gold varnish, sometimes mottled to deep brown, especially on body of centaur; other parts much chipped, scratched and worn.
Thin, rectangular terrain; set in a plain, rectangular dark-grey marble base with a gilt-bronze Louis XVI-style mount with lion's-paw feet. H.: 11.2 cm (4½ in.).

This episode of the story of the centaur Nessus forms a sequel to that told in the group conceived by Giambologna (see pp. 46–9). It represents him collapsing to the ground in torment, struggling in vain to remove the fatal arrow shot by his rival, Hercules. He still grasps around her waist his captive Deianira, the wife of Hercules, who seems to be shown about to strike her abductor with a weapon (now missing).

The model bears no stylistic relationship to Giambologna's group, and the composition is visually unsatisfactory to the extent that there is no single ideal viewpoint that reveals the faces of both protagonists. The existence of a 'pendant' bronze, representing *Europa and the Bull*, could suggest that the two groups were meant to be seen side by side in a balanced display. However, the *Europa* group seems to have been modelled by another hand, and may have been adapted from a more complex composition to serve as a

pendant. It is perhaps more likely that the *Nessus* group was originally intended to be shown on its own on a central table or pedestal, visible from all sides. Its compact composition may derive from a group carved on the front of a classical sarcophagus or pediment, where the architectural surround would tend to constrain the figures.

It is generally accepted that the model and all authentic individual casts were executed in France. Of the six known early casts of the *Nessus* group in public collections, the one in Stockholm, together with its pendant *Europa*, was purchased by Count Carl Gustav Tessin in Paris before 1740, while two more in Dresden (one only also with a pendant), had been part of a purchase of bronzes made in Paris for the Elector of Saxony in 1699 (figs 47,48). Furthermore, two bronzes of '*l'Europe enlevée par Jupiter*' and '*le Santor* [sic] *et Déjanire*', presumably a pair of the same models, appeared as successive entries in the 1700 inventory of André Le Nôtre's collection. Thus the model and casts are now generally regarded as French, 1690s.

Inventoried in the Breakfast Room at Hertford House in 1870 ('An [old French bronze of] Nessus Wounded'), having probably previously been acquired by the 4th Marquess of Hertford.

S187

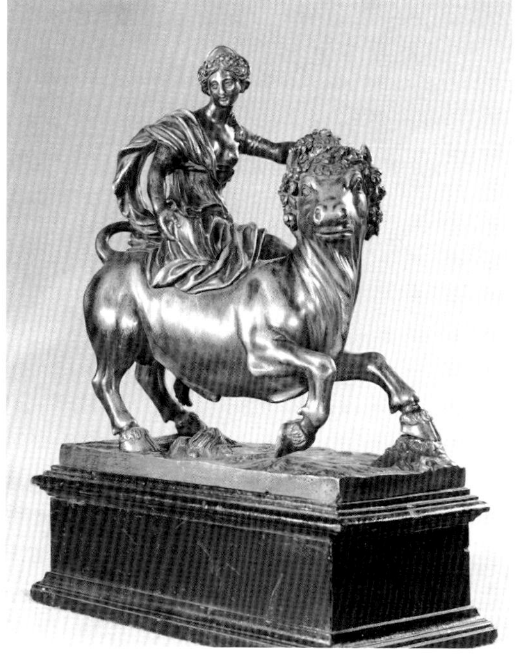

Fig. 47 *Nessus and Deianira*, French c.1699, bronze, h.: 22 cm. Grünes Gewölbe, Dresden (IX.63)

Fig. 48 *Europa and the Bull*, French c.1699, bronze, h.: 24.5 cm. Grünes Gewölbe, Dresden (IX.45)

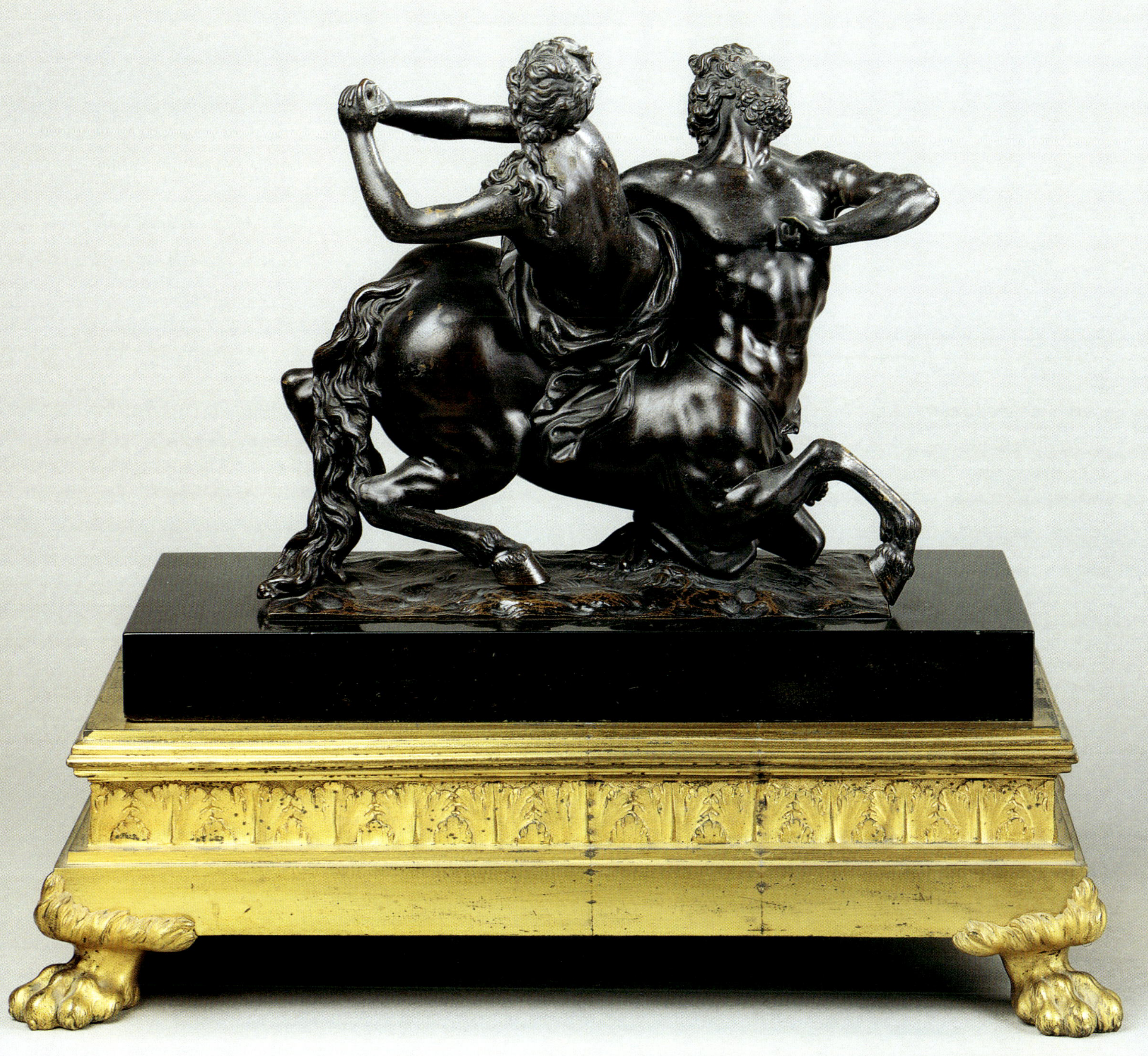

Louis XIV (1638–1715), King of France

MODEL & CAST:

Antoine Coysevox (1640–1720), c.1699

H. (excluding socle): 74.9 cm (29¾ in.), W. (maximum): 71.8 cm (28½ in.)

Lost-wax cast, open at the back. Cleaning in 1982 removed a layer of waxed black paint to reveal the worn remains of the original gilt-bronze surface, coppery-brown in colour; the high points of the nose have been rubbed to a deep brown.
On an octagonal-section brownish-white marble socle. H.: 15.8 cm (6¼ in.).

This magnificent sculpted portrait brilliantly conveys the imperious quality of the *Grand Monarque* by successfully combining compositional verve with acute observation in a virtuoso technical performance. The lively posture is achieved by the twist of the shoulders, the alert turn of the head, the swaggering swing of the cascading peruke, and the pronounced diagonal sweep of the sash across the chest. Allied to the baroque drama of the composition,

which owes much to Bernini's famous marble bust of the King of 1665 (Versailles), is Coysevox's sense of the majesty of his subject. This is conveyed less by such details as the armour with its *fleurs de lis*, as by the haughty arrogance of the monarch's demeanour. Although the very essence of a formal state portrait, the characterisation does not evade realism in its literal depiction of the heavy jowls and sagging flesh of late middle age. The impact of the image is greatly enhanced by the skilful modelling and finishing of the bust, which is especially remarkable in such details as the abundant curls of the free-flowing peruke and the intricacies of the fluttering lace cravat.

In most respects the bronze is a repetition by Coysevox of a marble bust executed for the Parliament of Burgundy in 1680 for its new *Salle des États* (Musée des Beaux-Arts, Dijon) (fig. 49). However, the facial features have been modified to show the King at a significantly more advanced age, close to that of the equestrian group after Desjardins in the Wallace Collection (see pp. 50–3). The only known cast of this model, it may be identifiable as the bronze bust of the monarch exhibited by Coysevox in the Salon of 1699, when the King was aged sixty-one.

Possibly identical with a bust of Louis XIV in the Beckford sale, London, 1823, and acquired from this source by the 3rd Marquess of Hertford (although not inventoried in his possession). Exhibited by the 4th Marquess of Hertford at the 'Musée Rétrospectif', Paris, 1865.

S165

Fig. 49 *Bust of Louis XIV*, A. Coysevox, 1680, marble, h.: 89 cm.
Musée des Beaux-Arts, Dijon (CA 1023)

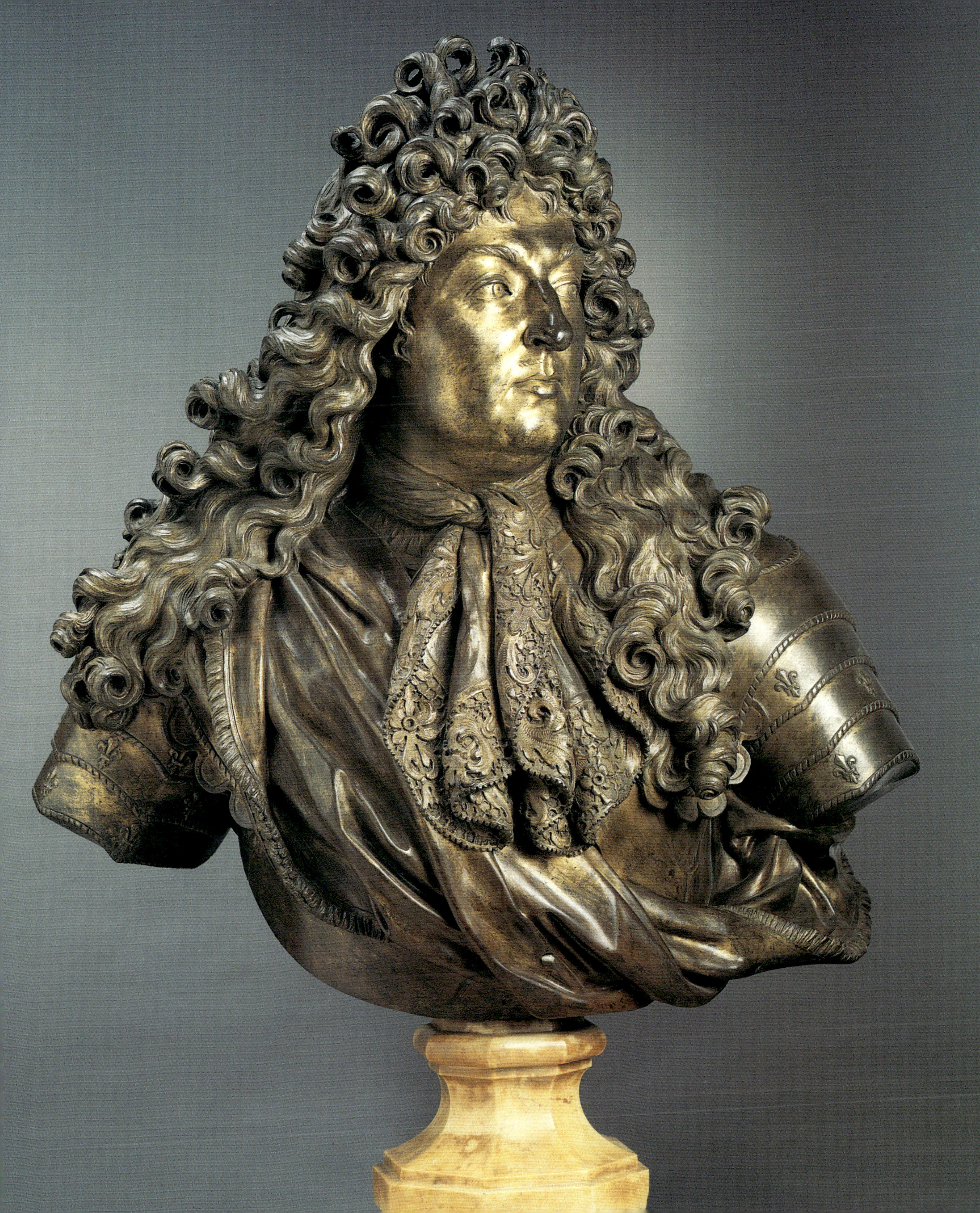

The Birth of Venus

MODEL & CAST:

Attributed to the circle of Philippe Bertrand (1663–1724), c.1700–1720

H.: 66.7 cm (26½ in.)

Lost-wax cast. Zephyr and Cupid are separately cast, each attached to the cloud-form base by a single rivet. Brassy-yellow alloy with a near-black surface. Integral square base with plain sides.

The sensuous figure of Venus, goddess of love, stands naked on a foam-borne scallop shell, holding a length of loose drapery between her legs and behind her back. Zephyr (the benign West Wind), held aloft on a pillar of swirling clouds, blows into a triangular section of this drapery, so forming a concave sail. To the right of Venus' legs is suspended the winged infant Cupid, and by her feet is an infant mermaid who proffers a bivalve shell.

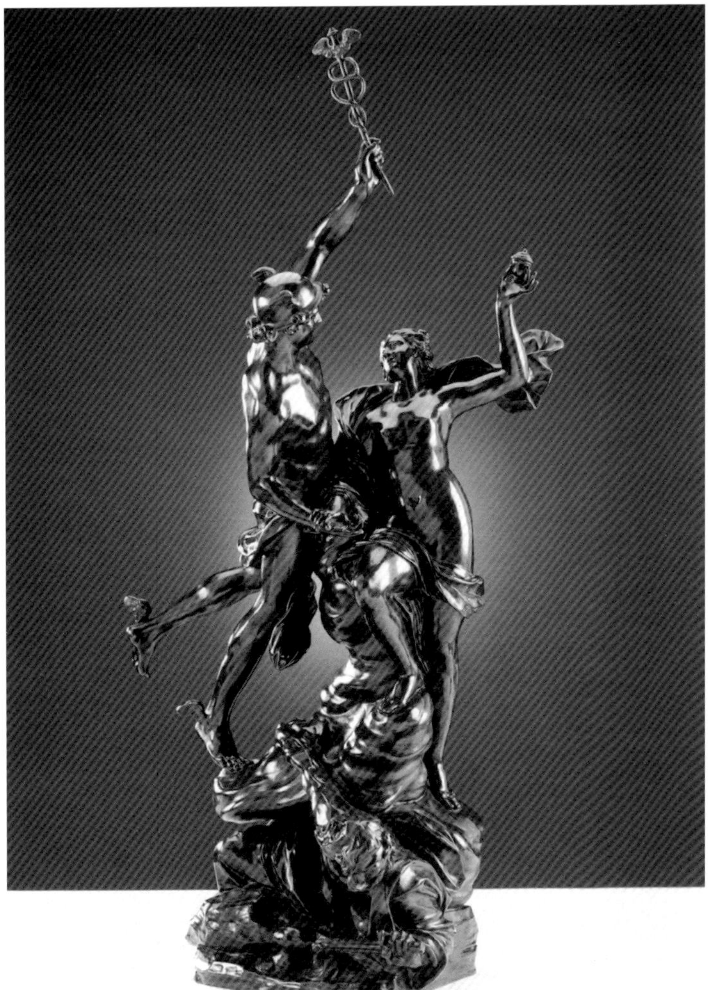

According to Hesiod (8th century BC), Venus (Gk: *Aphrodite*) sprang from the foam (Gk: *aphros*) of the sea that gathered around the severed genitals of Uranus (the Sky) when he was castrated by his son Cronus – at the instigation of the latter's mother, Ge (the Earth). She was then wafted ashore on a scallop shell. Undoubtedly the most famous post-classical image of this subject, like this bronze complete with a puff-cheeked Zephyr, is the celebrated painting of c.1486 by Sandro Botticelli (1445–1510) in the Uffizi, Florence. The few obvious sculptural precedents for this composition mostly represent the distinct scene of Venus rising from the waves ('Venus Anadyomene').

The stylistic homogeneity of the period tends to preclude the easy attribution of undocumented French bronzes to specific sculptors. Similarities of detail or style may be seen in the work of several early-18th century French sculptors, including Robert Le Lorrain and Corneille Van Clève (see pp. 72–5). However, this group relates most closely to the bronzes of Philippe Bertrand. His *Abduction of Psyche*, exhibited in 1704, is almost a mirror composition in its deployment of figures (fig. 50). Comparisons also can be made with various figures and details in the four bronzes of the *Seasons*, c.1715–20, attributed to Bertrand (Royal Collection), and with other documented works. The black patina may date from the late-18th century, when such surface finishes were especially fashionable.

Apparently listed in the 1870 inventory of Hertford House (North State Room), taken after the death of the 4th Marquess of Hertford, although not certainly recorded until exhibited by Sir Richard Wallace at the Bethnal Green Museum, 1872–5.

S195

Fig. 50 *Abduction of Psyche*, P. Bertrand, c.1704, bronze, h.: 61.6 cm. The Royal Collection (RCIN 21641)

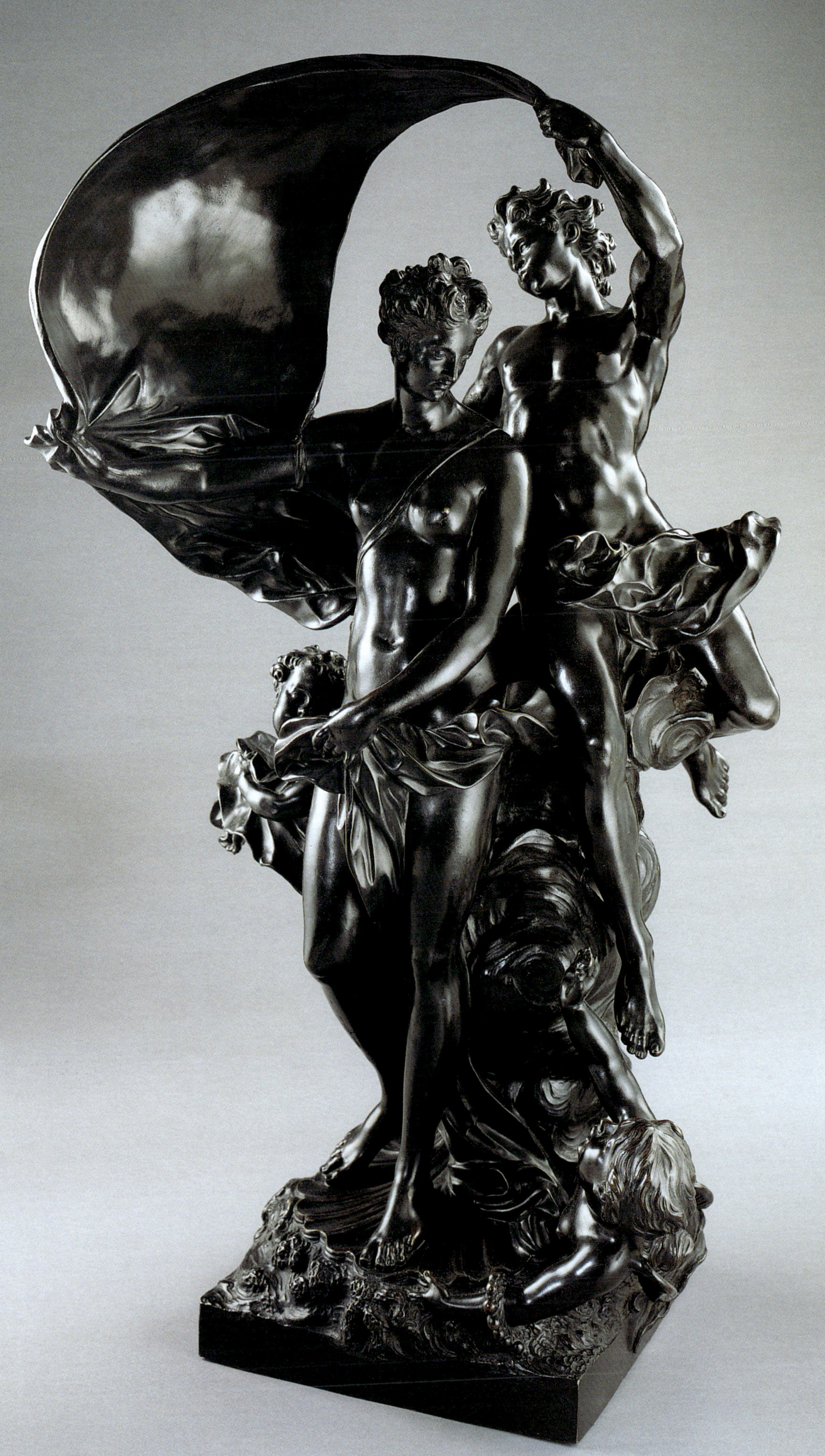

Venus Disarming Cupid

MODEL & CAST:
French, *c.*1700–30

H. (excluding plinth): 43.8 cm (17⅜ in.), L. (terrain base): 23.3 cm (9¼ in.),
W. (terrain base): 19.2 cm (7⅝ in.)

Lost-wax cast of several parts, sleeve-joined or plugged into the main body. Light-mid brown surface, brassy yellow alloy beneath. On an integral rectangular terrain, the upper surface striated with punchmarks.
Associated with a low rectangular plinth of ebonised wood and gilt-bronze mounts, including, on each face, medallion busts in the Louis XIV style. H.: 9.5 cm (3¾ in.).

The elegant figure of Venus, seated in her cloud-borne chariot, teasingly holds aloft Cupid's bow, while he vainly protests. That she is the goddess of love is clear from such details as the wreath of rose blossoms and laurel in her hair, the billing doves at her feet, and the scallop shell (she was born in the sea) that terminates the yoke of her chariot, the back of which is engraved with a flaming heart motif. Also visible from the back is the particularly beautiful detail of her tumbling hair (fig. 51).

The subject of Venus disarming Cupid is a variant on the frequently-depicted theme of the 'Punishment of Cupid', in which Cupid is chastised for the mischief his arrows have caused. In other interpretations, Venus confiscates, breaks or burns his arrows, clips his wings, or beats him with a bunch of her roses. Jean-Antoine Watteau's (1684–1721) *Cupid Disarmed* (Musée Condé, Chantilly), a similar composition painted *c.*1715–20, may share with this model a common prototype in various 16th-century Italian representations of the subject. An even more direct influence would seem to be certain small bronzes associated with the Florentine Massimiliano Soldani-Benzi (1656–1740), variously dated *c.*1695–1730.

In the context of contemporary French sculpture, this group relates most closely to an impressive but unattributed bronze thought to represent the *Abduction of Helen* (Louvre) (fig. 52). The respective figures of Venus and Helen are related in pose and very similar as types, as are the two Cupids. The Louvre group, which derives from versions of the same subject by Pierre Puget (1620–1694), has, like this bronze, been associated with Philippe Bertrand (see pp. 70–1). Although there are undoubted parallels with his work, his own bronze of the *Abduction of Helen* (1701; Fontainebleau) is quite distinct. There are also affinities with works by other early-18th century French sculptors, especially René Frémin, Le Lorrain and Van Clève (see pp. 72–7).

Possibly bought by the 4th Marquess of Hertford at the Soret sale, Paris, 1863, and certainly lent by him to the Palais de Trianon exhibition, Paris, 1867.

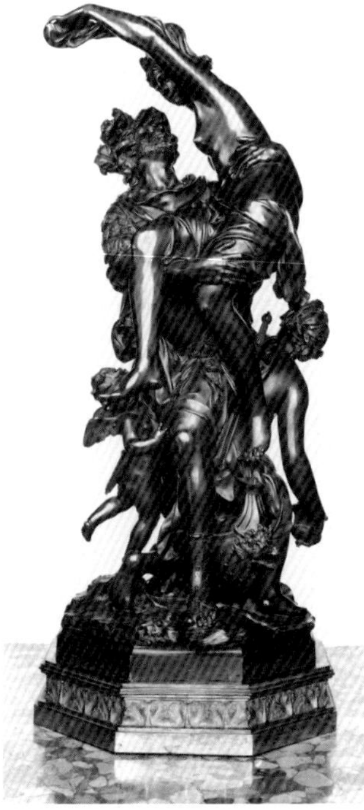

Fig. 52 *Abduction of Helen*, French, early 18th century, bronze, h.: 79 cm. Musée du Louvre, Paris (OA 7339)

Fig. 51 *Venus Disarming Cupid*, detail from back. Wallace Collection (S194)

S194

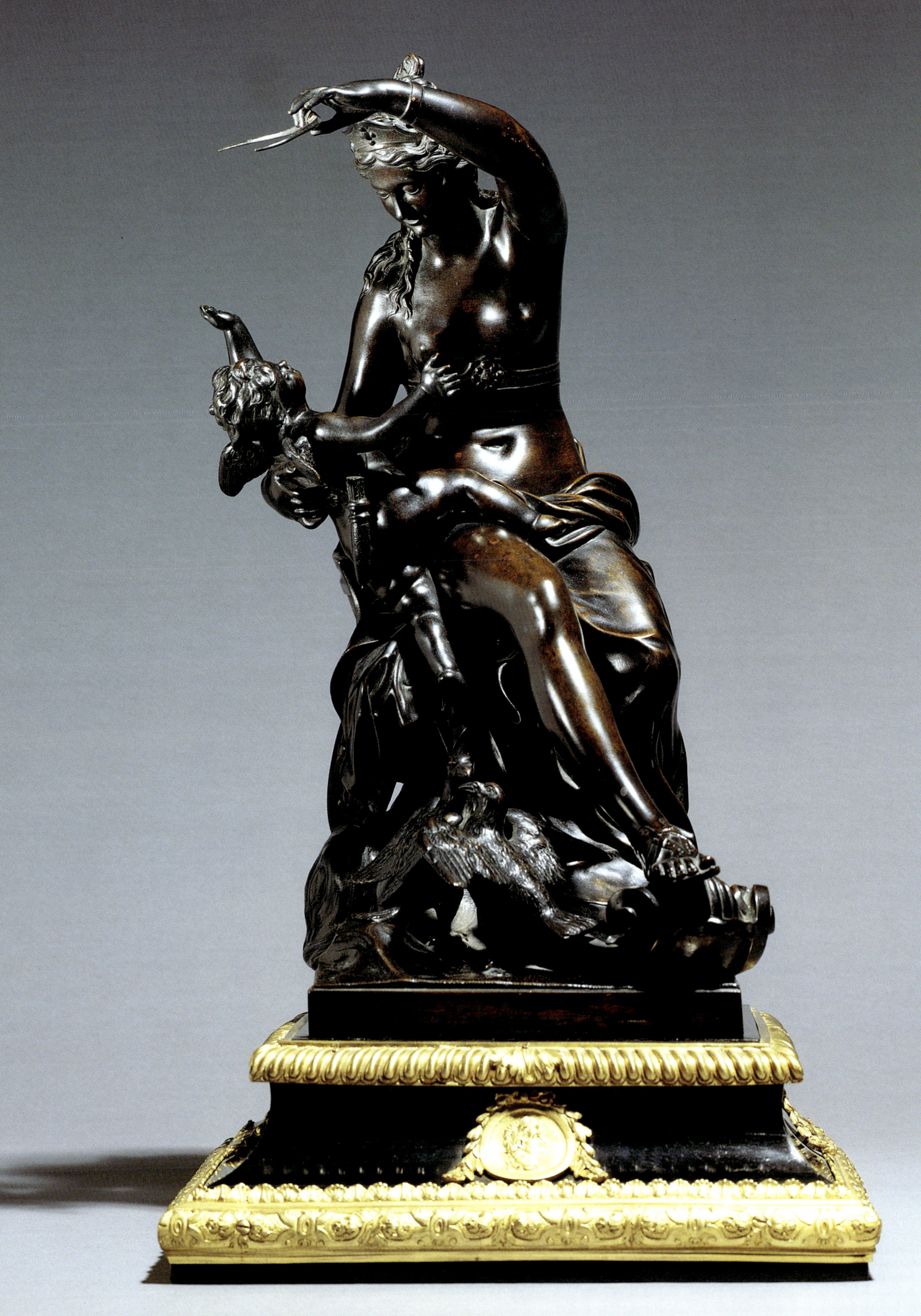

Allegory Commemorating the Accomplishment of the Vow of Louis XIII

MODEL & CAST:

Philippe Bertrand (1663–1724), 1714

signed (inscribed, terrain, front): *Philip Bertrand, Sculp. du Roy* (fig. 55)
inscribed (brass cartouche, mounted on back of marble base): *Prix de Poësie donné extraordinairement/ Par l'Academie Françoise, le 25 jour d'Aoust 1714[…]Ce Prix a esté remporté par M. l'Abbé du Jarry.* (fig. 53)

Medals:

I (held by Religion) by Thomas Bernard (1650–1713)
II (held by Piety) by Jérôme Roussel (1663–1713) (aftercast)

III (held by the angel) by Jean Mauger (1648–1722), 1672

H. (excluding marble base): 46.9 cm (18⅝ in.)

Lost-wax cast, with the parts of each figure separately cast and joined. Religion has lost her attribute (?a cross), originally held to her chest, and her nose is damaged. Blackish surface layer over olive/mushroom oxidised metal, worn to brassy-yellow at high points.
On a polygonal white marble and brass base. H.: 9.3 cm (3¾ in.), W.: 43.2 cm (17⅛ in.).

The *Allegory* is an imposing group of particular interest on several counts: as a rare signed and dated French bronze of the period; as an unusual example of a French bronze in the Wallace Collection with a religious aspect; and, not least, as the documented prize for a competition for which one of the greatest writers of the century was an entrant.

The circumstances of the prize, which dictated its subject matter, are encapsulated in a long inscription on the back of the base (fig. 53). In 1638, when Louis XIII hoped for the birth of a son, he made a vow pledging the redecoration of the Choir of Notre-Dame, Paris. Under that son, Louis XIV, the Vow was fulfilled with the installation of a new altar and sculptural elements, completed in April 1714. The French Academy decided to offer a poetry prize in honour of this event, which they awarded on 25 August 1714, the Feast of St Louis. The bronze group represents the allegorical figures of Religion (left), Piety (right), Fame ('*La Magnificence du Roi*'), and an angel. Cloud-borne Fame trumpets the achievement with her gilded instrument, while the other figures support medals bearing the busts of the two kings (obverses) and images relating to the making and completion of the Vow (figs 54ab), and to the Academy itself (reverses). The winner of this prize was the now utterly forgotten abbé du Jarry (1658–1730). The runner-up was the young Voltaire (1694–1778), who exacted his revenge by ridiculing du Jarry's work. But he never again entered a literary competition.

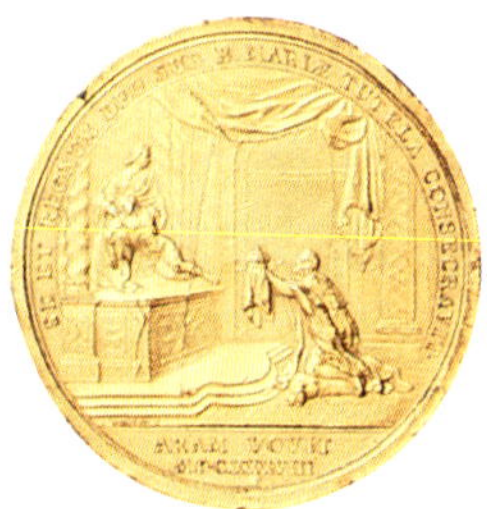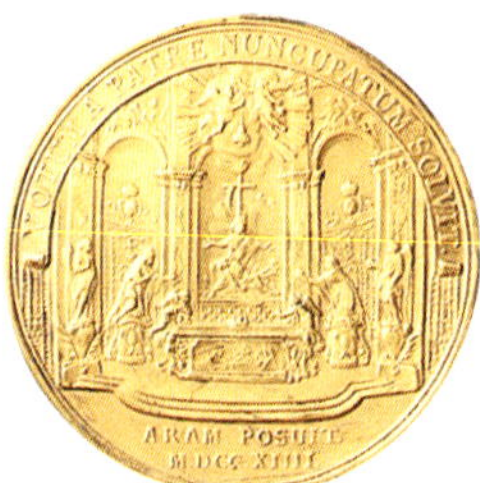

Figs 54ab (left) Reverse of medal by T. Bernard: *Louis XIII Kneeling before an Altar*, gilt-bronze, diam.: 6.9 cm. (right) Reverse of (aftercast from) medal by J. Roussel: *Louis XIII and Louis XIV Kneeling before the Altar of Nôtre-Dame, Paris*, gilt-bronze, diam.: 6.8 cm. Wallace Collection (S176). photo: Alastair Johnson

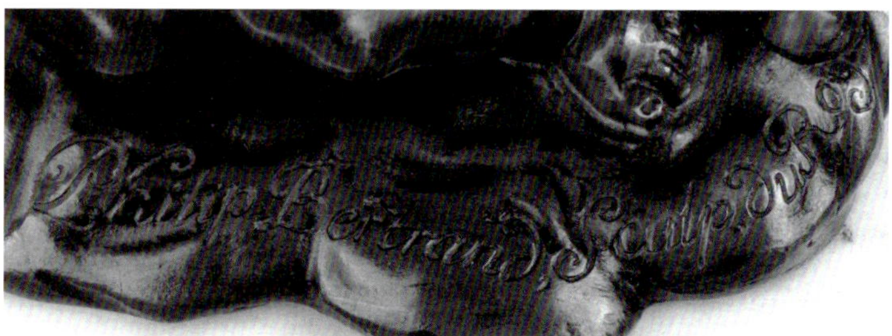

Fig. 55 *Vow of Louis XIII*, detail of signature. Wallace Collection (S176)

The group is proudly signed and dated by Philippe Bertrand (fig. 55), who presumably received the commission as one of the sculptors who had worked on the extensive redecoration at Notre-Dame. In sculptural terms, his bronze impresses for the balanced, pyramidal massing of its intersecting triangular elements. However, the rather lifeless drapery folds make for a dull composition, of which the details are not especially delicately modelled or finished.

This unique cast was in the marquis d'Arcambal sale, Paris, 1776; it was lent to the Palais de Trianon exhibition, Paris, 1867 by the 4th Marquess of Hertford, who had presumably acquired it in Paris.

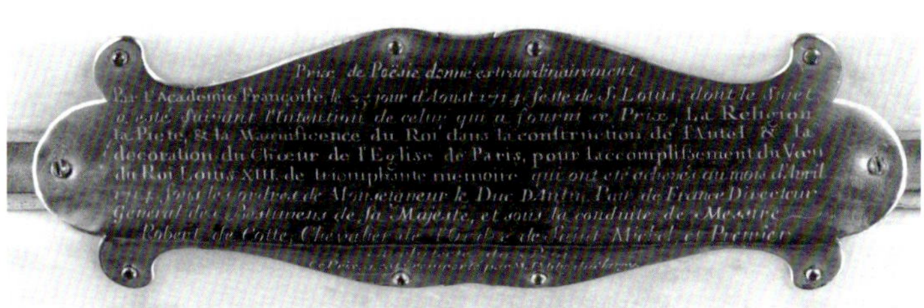

Fig. 53 *Vow of Louis XIII*, detail of inscription. Wallace Collection (S176)

S176

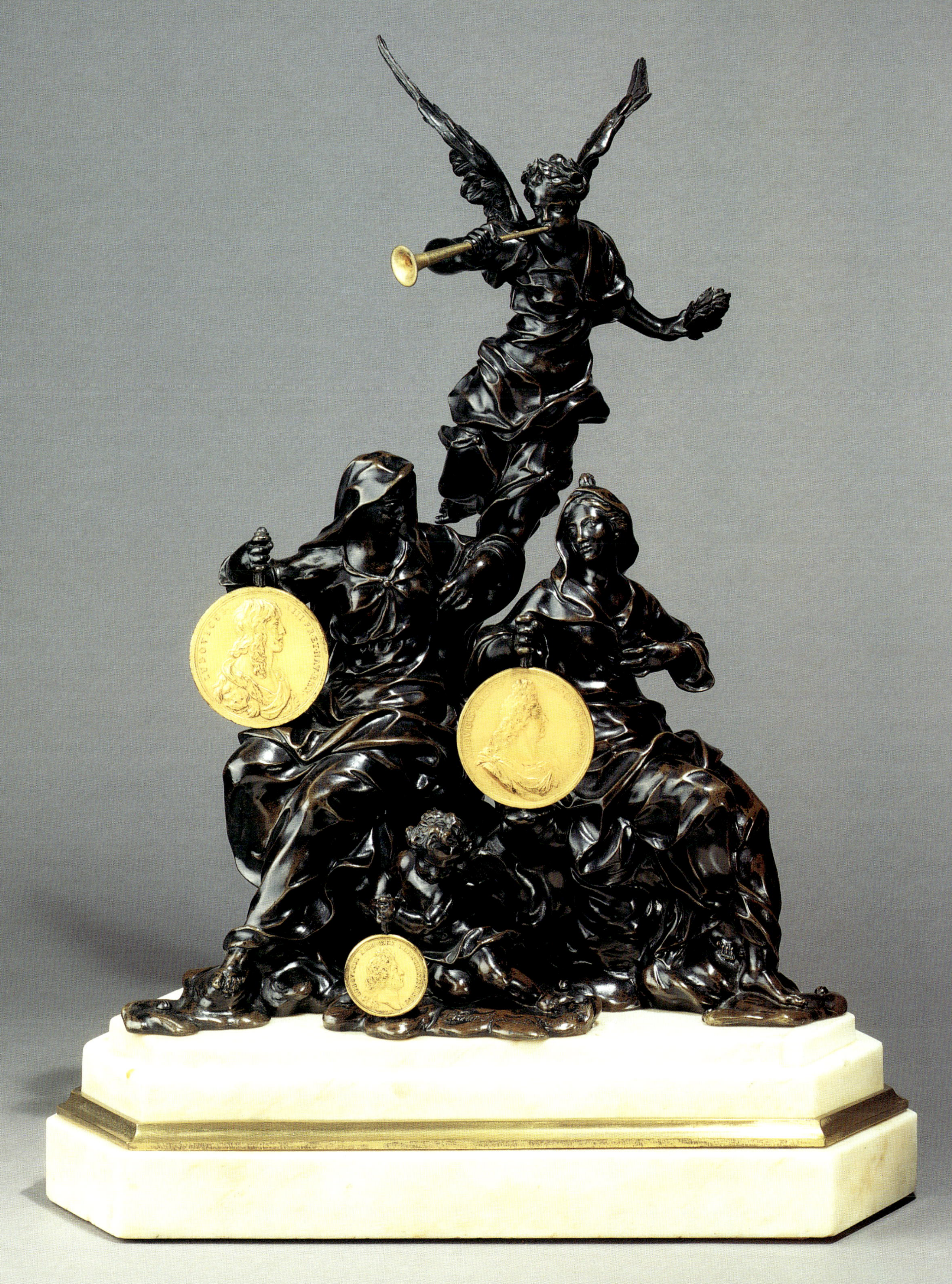

Venus and Adonis

MODEL:
Attributed to Robert Le Lorrain (1666–1743), c.1704

CAST:
Perhaps workshop of Le Lorrain, c.1705–25

H. (including mount): 55.5 cm (22 in.)

Lost-wax cast, cast in sleeve-joined sections. Thickish near-black coating (?wax), now partly chipped and scratched; some traces of natural brown patina beneath; brassy yellow alloy visible at digits.
High-sided integral circular terrain. Diam.: c.23.0 cm (9⅛ in.). To this subsequently has been attached a thin, naturalistic patinated-bronze mount, of approximately square section. H.: c.10.4cm (4⅛ in.).

Venus, by accident grazed with one of Cupid's arrows, fell helplessly in love with Adonis, a youth of surpassing beauty. As he indicates his path ahead she, fearful for his safety lest he encounter wild animals, implores him to forebear hunting – in which pursuit he would, indeed, meet his death. The story, taken from Ovid's *Metamorphoses* (Book X), had long been a very popular one with artists and writers, who often chose to represent this pivotal moment.

In a series of prominent mid-18th century Paris sales, a bronze identifiable with this model appeared as a pendant to a group featuring another pair of youthful Ovidian lovers, *Vertumnus and Pomona* (fig. 56), itself first recorded when exhibited at the 1704 Salon by Le Lorrain. A pair appeared in the Selle sale of 1761: according to the catalogue, the 'author' 'under whose eyes' the bronzes 'allegedly' were executed was 'Robert Le Lorain' [*sic*]. The attribution of this group is confirmed by the similarities between Venus's physiognomy and body type with those of other idealised female figures in sculptures by, or firmly attributed to Le Lorrain, datable to c.1695–1701. The elegant and expressive composition, which may derive from earlier Florentine bronzes of the same subject, is typical of the emerging style of the first quarter of the 18th century. The light and charming subjects of this model and its pendant, and their very production as a pair, are symptoms of their essentially decorative function.

Even while studying in Rome (1692–4), Le Lorrain sent models to Paris for casting in bronze and then private sale. The gently erotic character and refined finishing of his bronzes was carefully targeted at his market, but evidently they were made in small numbers. Only four authentic casts of *Vertumnus and Pomona* are known, and just one other of *Venus and Adonis* (Elysée Palace, Paris). The latter is virtually complete, unlike this cast, from which are missing the figure of Cupid, originally behind Venus, and Adonis's dog, formerly between his feet. Furthermore, its surface has been dulled by a later repatination.

First recorded in the inventory of Hertford House (Front State Room) taken in 1870 after the death of the 4th Marquess of Hertford, by whom it was presumably acquired.

S185

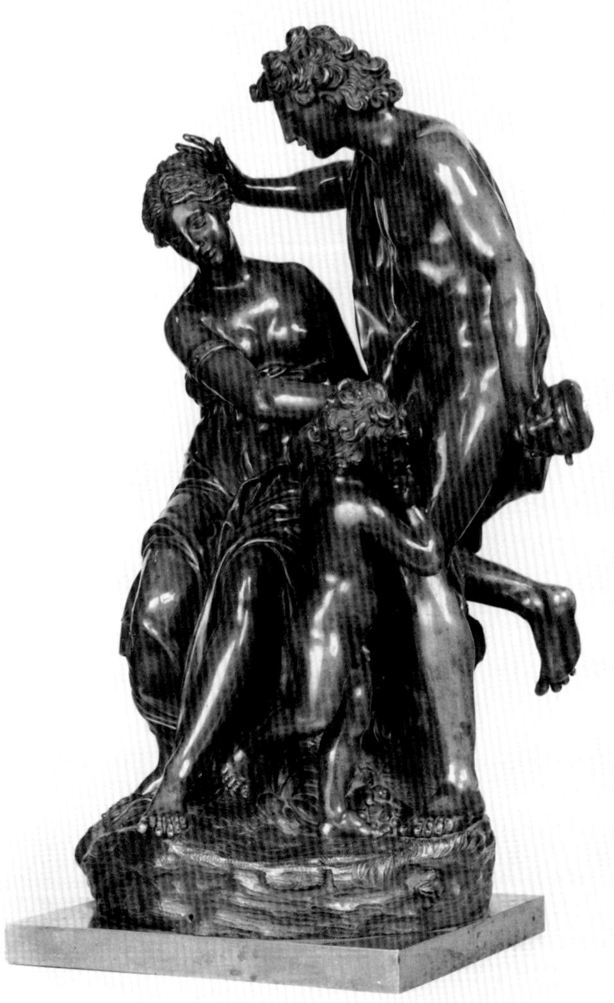

Fig. 56 *Vertumnus and Pomona*, attributed to Robert Le Lorrain, c.1704, bronze, h.: 47 cm. State Hermitage Museum, St Petersburg (H.ck.1844)

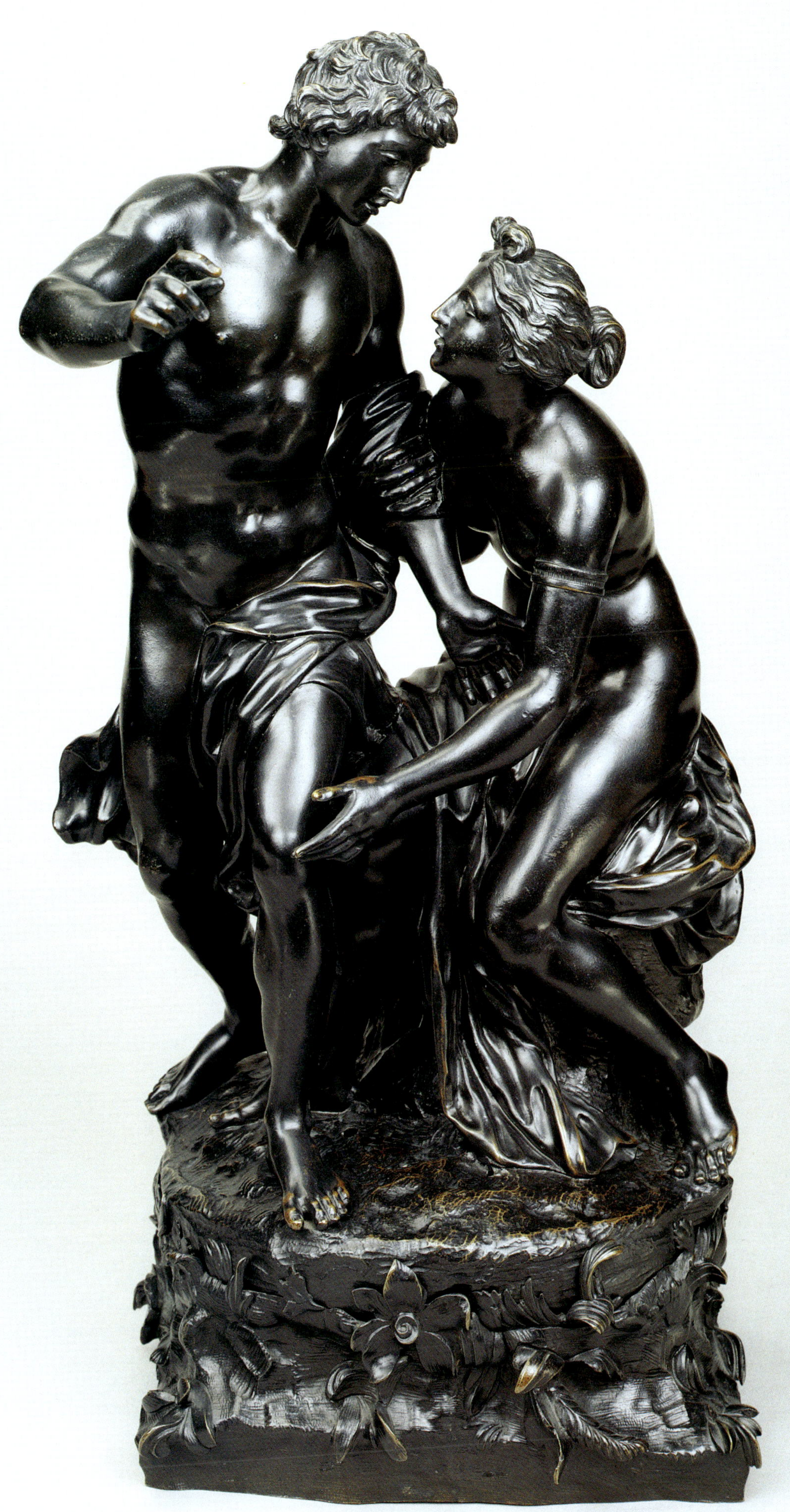

Psyche Discovering Cupid

MODEL & CAST:

Attributed to the circle of Corneille Van Clève (1645–1732), *c.*1715–20

stamped (I, on fold of drapery on terrain; II, beneath foot of lamp): 'crowned-C' copper-tax mark (applied to goods with a copper content made for or on the Paris market between 1745–9)

H. (excluding mount [not shown]) : 45.7 cm (18⅛ in.)

Lost-wax cast, cast in sleeve-joined sections (oil-lamp probably sand-cast). Yellow brassy alloy with rich reddish-gold varnish, somewhat darkened, especially visible on Psyche's torso.
Integral terrain. Formerly mounted on a gilt-bronze base of the Louis XV style (not shown).

The romantic story of Psyche, a beautiful princess, and Cupid, who fell in love with her, was hugely popular in the 17th and 18th centuries. Originally told by the 2nd-century AD Roman writer Apuleius, it was better known in France in La Fontaine's version (1669). This bronze represents the episode when Psyche, hitherto prevented from discovering the identity of her lover, crept up on him as he slept but, in her excitement, spilt burning oil from her lamp. He is shown still half-asleep, scowling in pain as the oil drips across his forehead. Moments later he will take flight, and Psyche suffer the torment of long, lonely years in search of him, before their ultimate reconciliation. The tale could be read as an allegory of the earthly voyages of the soul (Gk: *psyche*) and its final union with the divine, but here it would seem to be little more than a pretext to represent the naked female form in a charming narrative context.

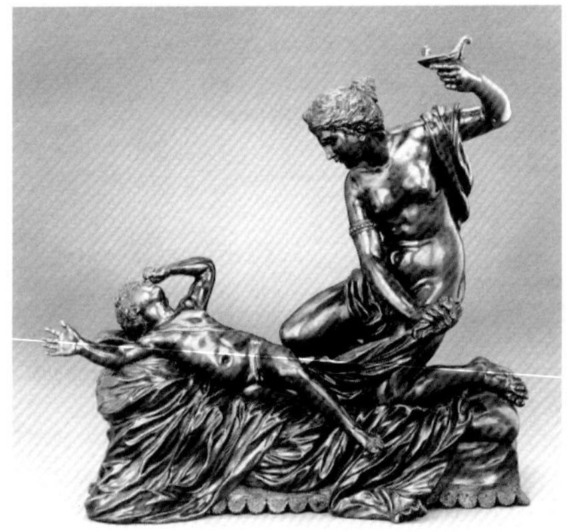

Fig. 58 *Cupid and Psyche*, G.B. Foggini, *c.*1710, bronze, h.: 34 cm. Detroit Institute of Arts, Founders Society Purchase, Robert H. Tannahill Foundation Fund (81.695)

Most of the dozen surviving examples are paired with a bronze unrelated in subject, *Venus Disarming Cupid* (fig. 57). Until recently, these were attributed to Van Clève by comparison with his documented work. However, neither model is mentioned in his posthumous inventory, nor is a sculptor's name given in any of the 18th-century sale descriptions of the pair. They perhaps also lack the invention and refinement of his securely attributed bronzes, although it remains possible that they were largely workshop products intended for a less wealthy market. There are parallels with contemporary Florentine bronzes, in particular here with a *Cupid and Psyche* of *c.*1710 by Foggini (fig. 58).

The earliest documented pair of *Cupid* groups is that in Dresden, acquired for Augustus the Strong of Saxony in 1723. They were bought in Rome, which may indicate they were made by a French sculptor studying there, or simply reflect the popularity and dispersal of casts. The finish and facture of the Wallace Collection cast, stamped with a tax-mark only used 1745–9, is closely comparable to the Dresden example, but with a much better-preserved surface.

First certainly recorded when lent by Sir Richard Wallace to the Bethnal Green Museum exhibition, 1872–5.

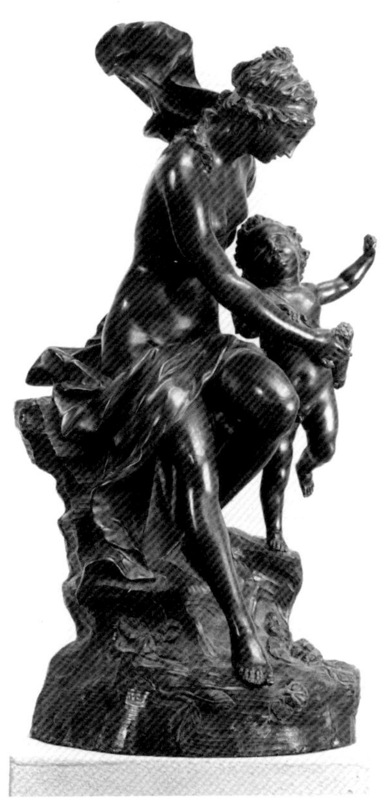

Fig. 57 *Venus Disarming Cupid*, attributed to the circle of C. Van Clève, *c.*1715–20, bronze, h.: 48.6 cm. Skulpturensammlung, Dresden (H⁴ 153/3)

S186

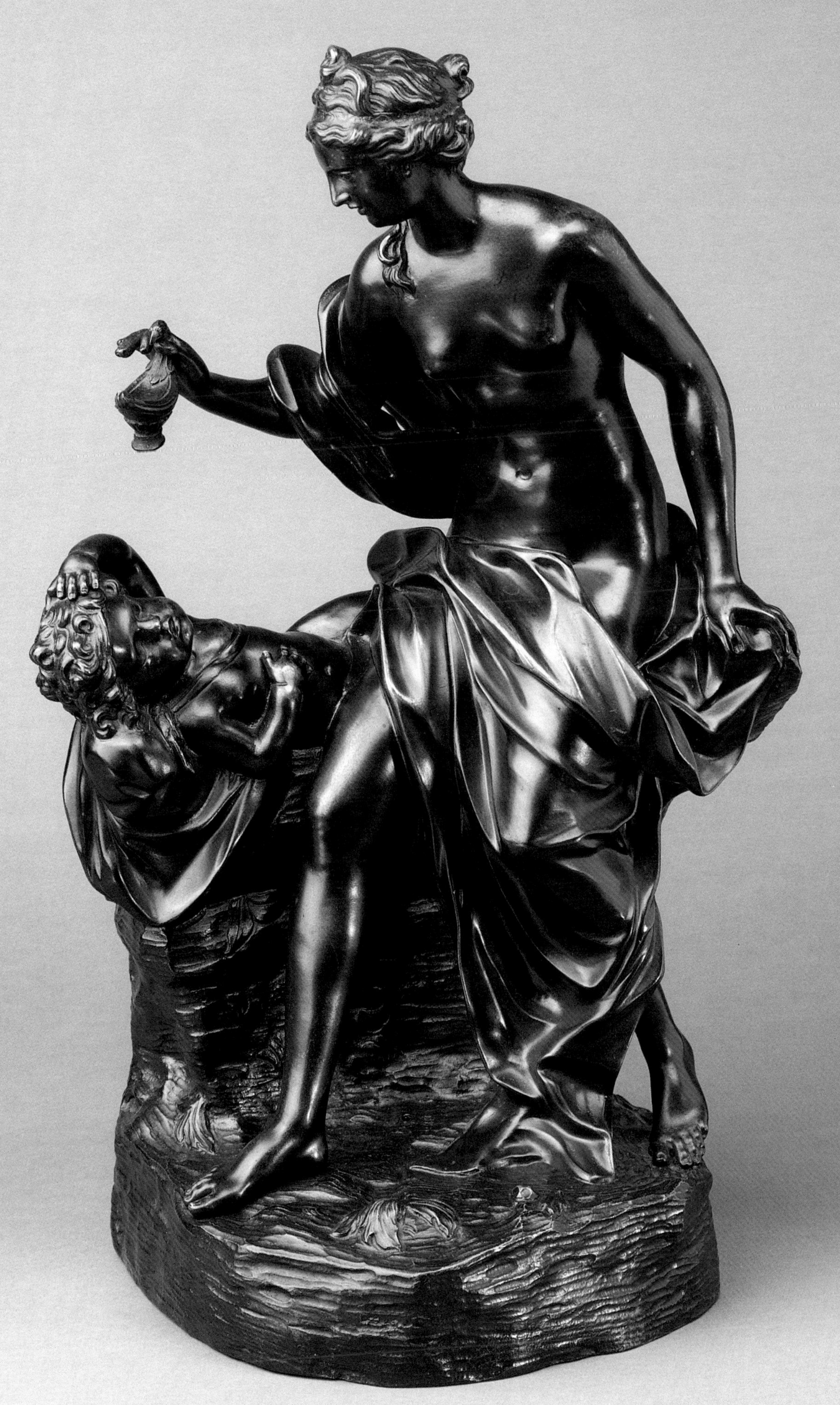

Allegory of Time Witnessing the Triumph of Honour, Probity and Prudence over Vice

MODEL:
French, *c.*1700

CAST:
French, perhaps *c.*1720

H.: 74.8 cm (29⅝ in.), W. (base): 29.3 cm (11⅝ in.), D. (base): 28.0 cm (11⅛ in.)

Lost-wax cast; each figure separately cast and screwed into main section. Blackish surface over natural (lightish chocolate-brown) patina, worn to brassier metal in a few places.
Integral square base, from which springs a naturalistic terrain. No socle.

Although the cartouche of this enigmatic bronze has been left blank, helpfully the figures are identified on that of the only other known cast (private collection) (fig. 59). At the apex is Time, scythe and hourglass in hand. Vice cringes below in his lair, grasping the mask of Deceit, and shaking his fist in frustration (fig. 60). Laurel-crowned Honour stands proudly in the centre, a cornucopia of fruit, medals, gold chains and laudatory scrolls spilling out before him. Probity rests on a cubic block with a triangle in her hand (for four-square honesty), disdaining the symbols of wealth and war (or love) by her feet. Finally, Prudence holds the mirror of self-knowledge entwined with the snake of wisdom.

We remain ignorant of what occasioned this allegory and of its full meaning. In the late 19th century, it was said to represent 'Louis XV protecting Religion and Truth from Falsehood' and explained as a commemoration of the King's escape from an assassination attempt in 1757. This must be incorrect because of the misidentification of the figures. Moreover, a bronze of similar description had already appeared for sale in Paris in 1744.

Stylistically the group belongs to the period *c.*1690–*c.*1730, when such complex tableaux-like scenes of theatrically gesturing figures were fashionable. Examples include bronzes attributed to François Lespingola (1644–1705) dated to the late 1690s, and an unattributed bronze of *Dido on the Funeral Pyre*, in existence by at least 1726 (fig. 61). Like those, this group was probably influenced by both contemporary French historical paintings and prints and Florentine bronzes. Arguably more convincing parallels can be drawn with the work of René Frémin (1672–1744), specifically his various fountain groups executed for the gardens of La Granja Palace (near Segovia) in 1721–8. Frémin also exhibited small bronzes with comparable subjects in the 1704 Salon.

First recorded after the death of the 4th Marquess of Hertford in the 'Grande Galerie' of his Paris *hôtel*, 2 rue Laffitte (inventoried 1871).

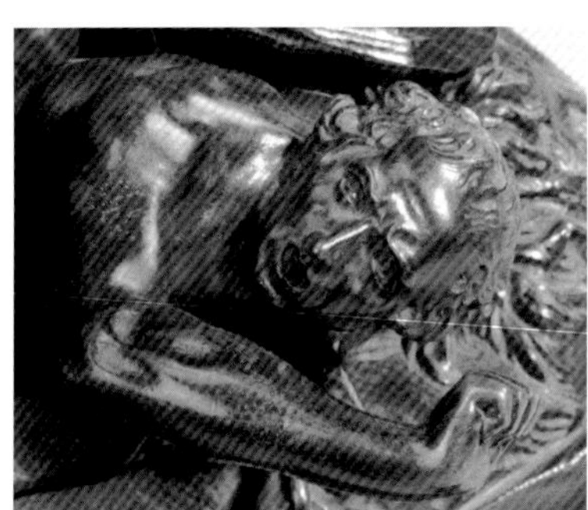

Fig. 60 *Allegory*, French *c.*1720, detail of Vice. Wallace Collection (S190)

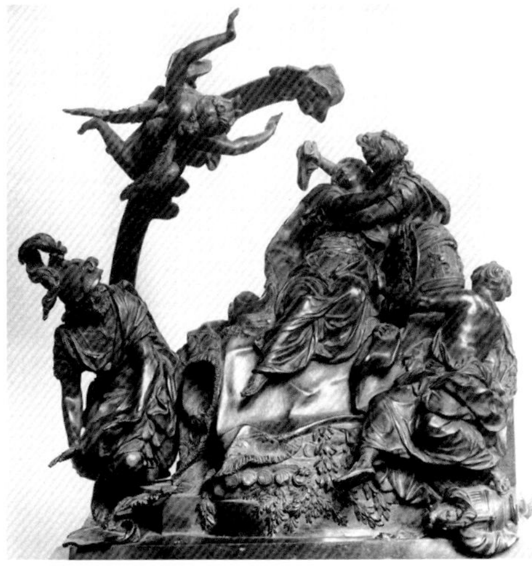

Fig. 61 *Dido on the Funeral Pyre*, French *c.*1720, bronze, h.: 59.7 cm. Skulpturensammlung, Dresden (H⁴154/15)

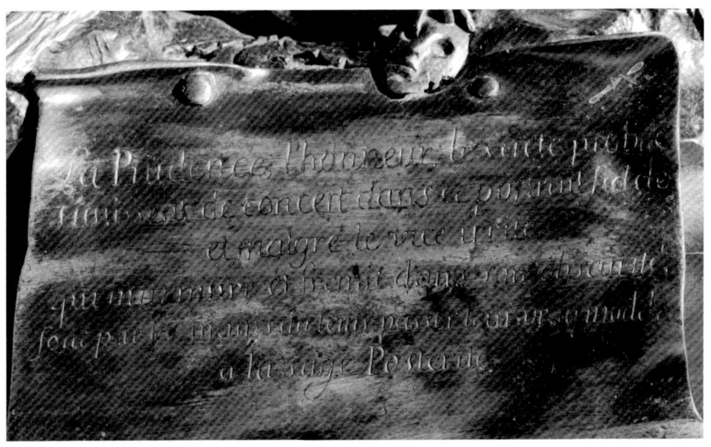

Fig. 59 *Allegory*, French *c.*1700, detail of inscription. Private Collection

S190

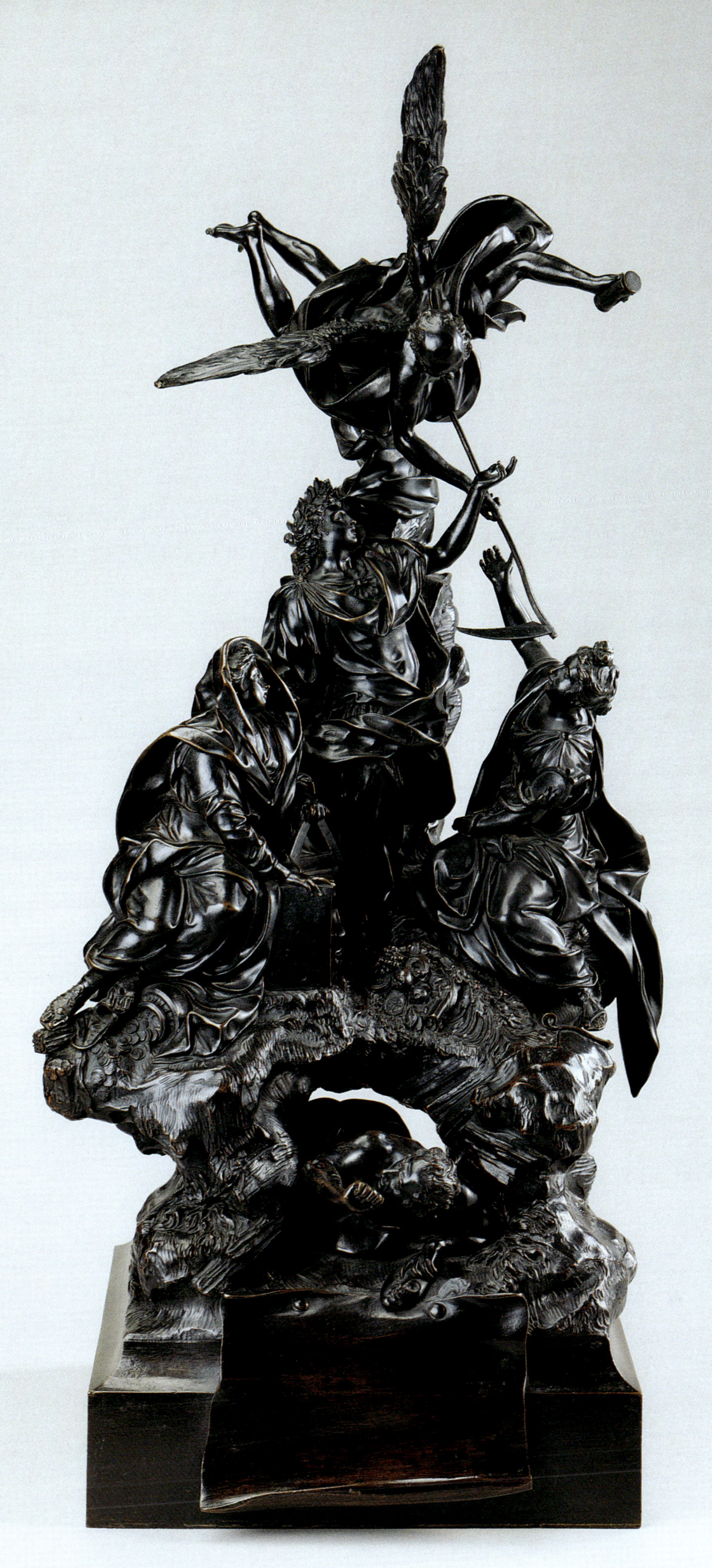

Drunken Silenus with Bacchante and Satyr

MODEL:
Probably French, *c.*1700, after designs by Peter Paul Rubens (1577–1640)

CAST:
French, early 18th century

H. (excluding base): 19.2 cm (7⅝ in.)

Thick, heavy, lost-wax cast; cast in sections and joined in the metal. Greenish patina, worn to brassy-yellow metal; darkish brown-black in recesses. Integral terrain. Gilt-bronze base. H.: 5.4 cm (2⅛ in.).

In classical mythology, Silenus was a rural satyr-like god, one of the more dissolute followers of Bacchus (Gk: *Dionysus*), and usually characterised as a fat old drunkard (albeit endowed with wisdom, prophetic powers and musical skills). As such, he was a natural subject for artists of the Northern tradition, unconstrained by classical tenets of decorum.

The composition of this group originated in various paintings and drawings of related subjects executed in the late-1610s by the celebrated Flemish artist Peter Paul Rubens, who himself was inspired by a classical marble of the subject (Dresden). Rubens's images spawned countless copies and variants across Europe in both two and three dimensions. Georg Petel (?1601/2–*c.*1634), a Bavarian sculptor who was friendly with Rubens, made several versions in ivory of the *Drunken Silenus* group both as reliefs and as independent figures, in the years around 1630. Lucas Faydherbe (1617–1697), who trained under Rubens, or his workshop also made various terracotta reliefs of the *Drunken Silenus* group in the 1630s

and 1640s (fig. 62).

It seems likely that it was from such sculptural sources, rather than directly from Rubens's work, that the model for this bronze was derived, although it remains uncertain exactly when and by whom. Casts of the bronze are rare – only five are known – and each varies somewhat in its details, particularly in the heads of the two attendants. Two are to be found in Paris museums, while those in Stockholm and Braunschweig (first inventoried in 1753) were probably acquired in Paris. This may imply an origin for the bronze group in Paris in the early 18th century. This is consistent with the facture and finish of the Wallace Collection cast, perhaps the finest known; with the huge interest in Rubens's art in France in this period; and with the existence of a pendant group (another bacchic trio), sold as such in the Beringhen sale, Paris, 1770.

Acquired by the 4th Marquess of Hertford at the Fould sale, Paris, 1860.

S213

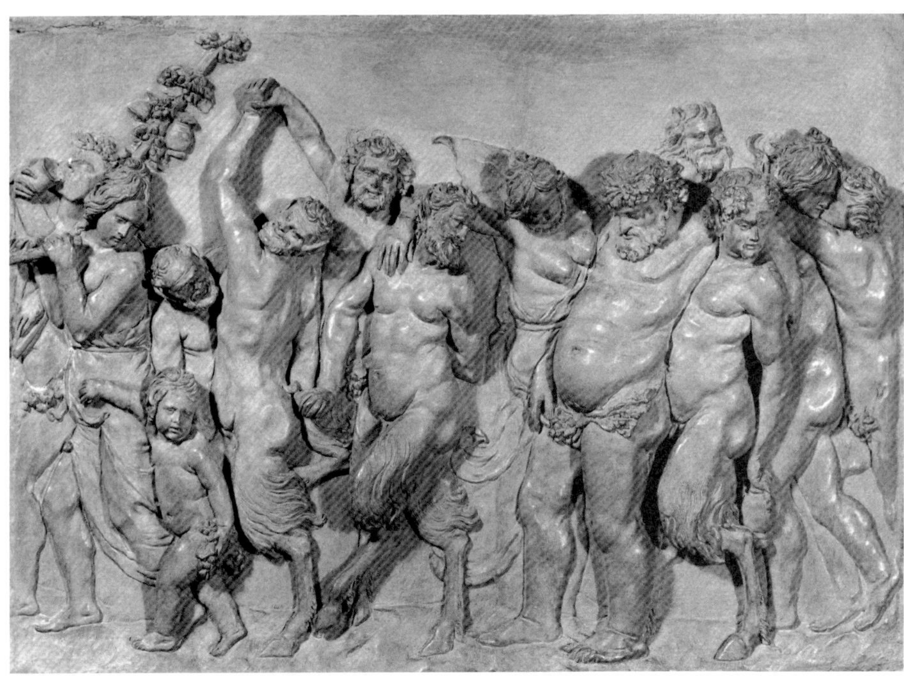

Fig. 62 *Silenus and his Followers*, follower of L. Faydherbe, 1640s, terracotta, 75 × 40 cm. Musées Royaux d'Art et d'Histoire, Brussels (V.1958)

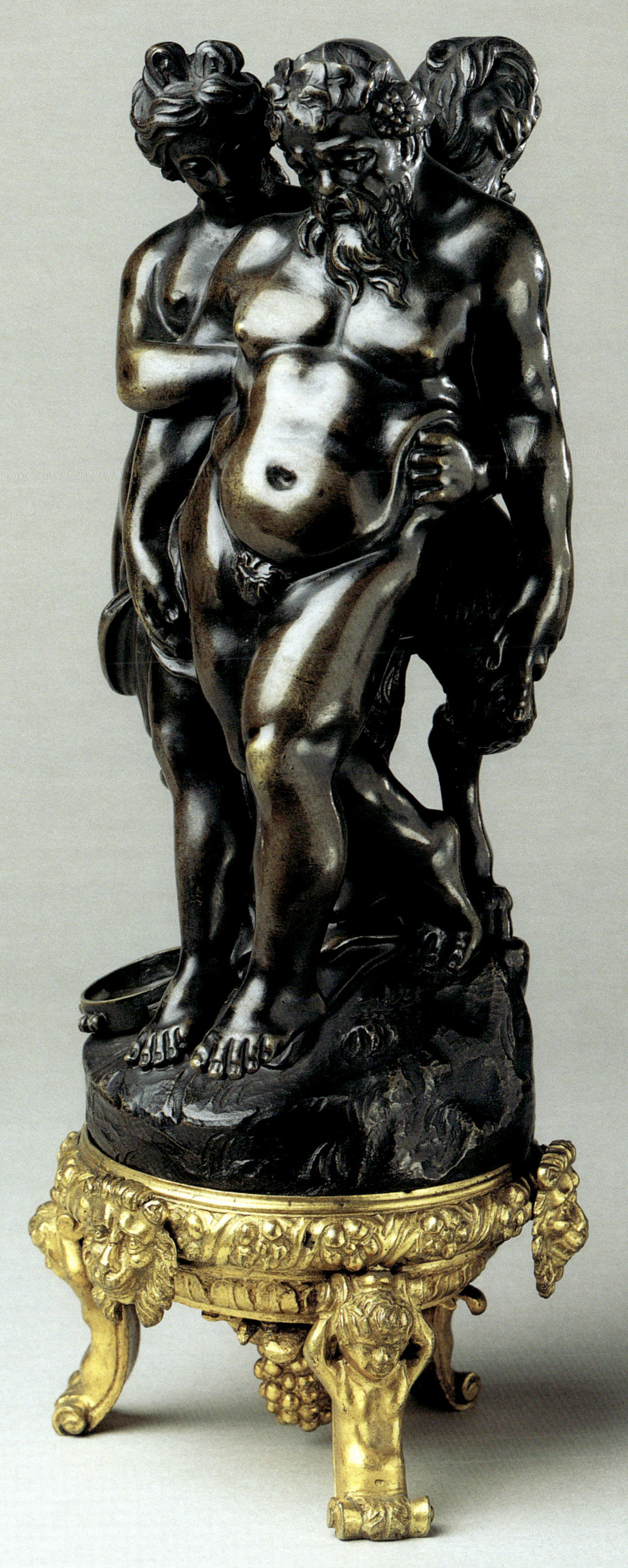

Mezzetino (Mezzetin)

MODEL & CAST:
French, perhaps *c.*1700–25

H.: 50.2 cm (20 in.)

Heavy lost-wax cast, possibly cast in a single pour. Dark-brown surface worn to orangey-chocolate brown natural patina.
On an integral square base.

The improvisational theatre of the *Commedia dell'arte*, which originated in renaissance Italy, proved immensely popular across northern Europe in the later 17th and early 18th centuries. This inspired the representation of the stock characters in a variety of media. The singing, guitar-strumming figure of this bronze wears the floppy beret and tight-fitting tunic and breeches typically worn by several of the *zanni* (comic servants), but is usually identified specifically as Mezzetino ('half-measure'), the rival of Harlequin.

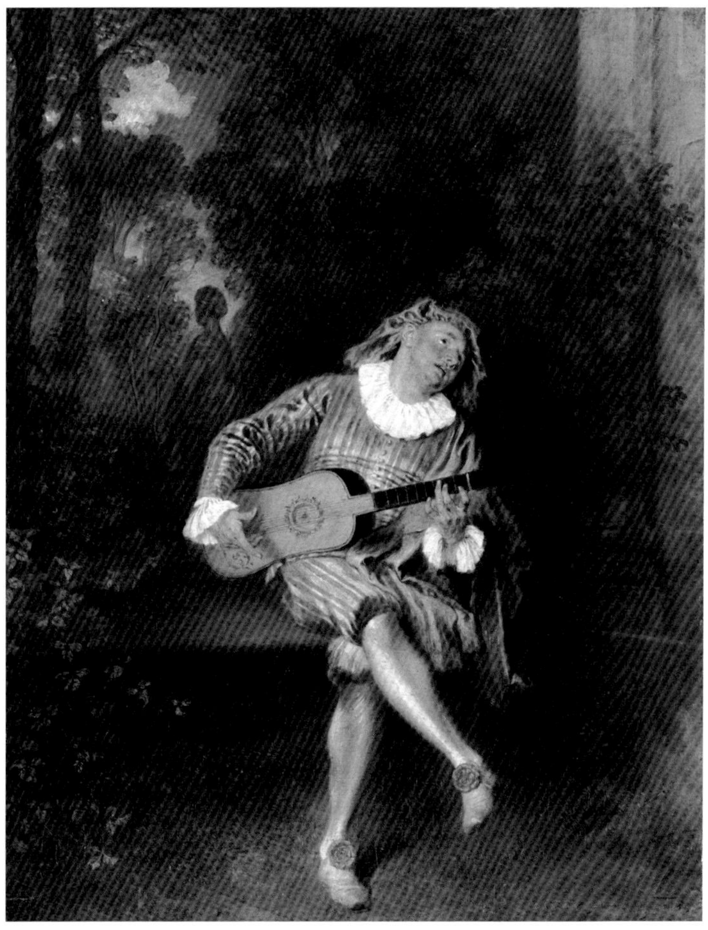

Fig. 63 *Mezzetino Playing the Guitar*, J.-A. Watteau, *c.*1717/19, oil on canvas, 55.2 × 43.2 cm. Metropolitan Museum of Art, New York, Munsey Fund, 1934 (34.138)

Mezzetino combined the roles of go-between and sentimental lover, often in the pursuit of unrequited love. Here he has an appropriately lovelorn attitude and heart-shaped pockets and patches. At his feet sits a monkey, symbolic of lust, who energetically blows into a sort of flute or oboe, mocking the aspirations of his human companion.

There are strong parallels between this bronze and the numerous *Commedia dell'arte* scenes by Jean-Antoine Watteau (1684–1721), in particular his celebrated *Mezzetino Playing the Guitar* (fig. 63). Monkeys also appear in Watteau's work and are in keeping with the prevailing French taste of the late Louis XIV period for such subjects (called *singeries*).

Bronze statuettes of *Commedia dell'arte* characters are surprisingly rare. Only one other cast of this model is known, although a variant exists, paired with the *commedia* figure of Columbine. A similar pair appeared in a succession of Paris sales in the 1780s, while a smaller figure of Mezzetino alone was sold in Paris in 1770. The posthumous inventory of Corneille Van Clève's property listed bronze figures of a Mezzetino and a Pierrot, and Jean Poultier (1653–1719) exhibited a 'Guitarist' at the 1704 Salon. Such evidence helps dispel arguments that this figure must be a revivalist piece of the early 19th century, and its method of facture seems consistent with early 18th century practice.

First documented in the collection of the 4th Marquess of Hertford, when lent to the 'Musée Rétrospectif' exhibition, Paris, 1865 ('*Scapin* [sic] *chante en s'accompagnant sur une guitare… Statuette dans le goût de Gillot. France (Commencement du XVIIIe siècle)*').

S234

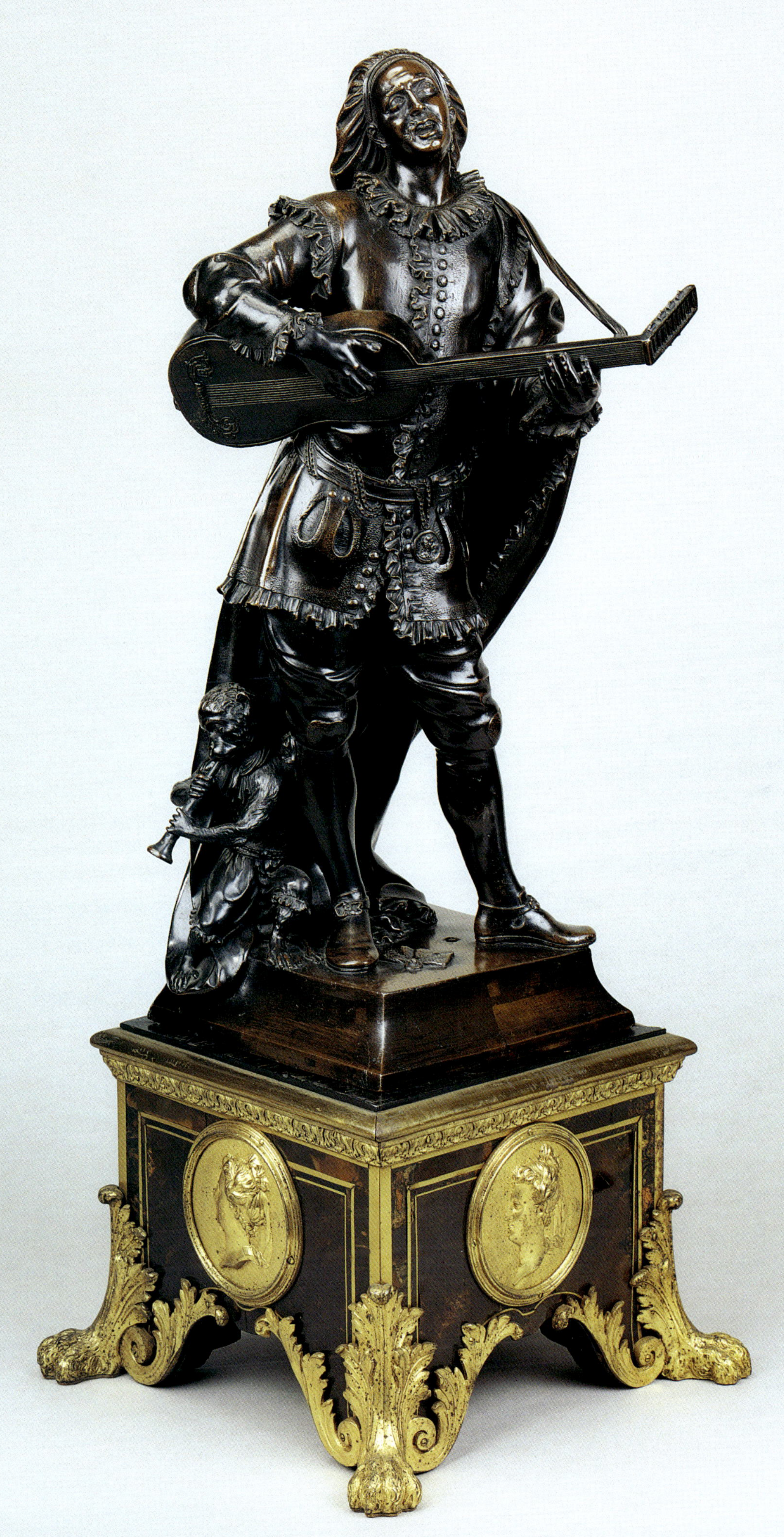

The Infant Bacchus and Cupid with his Bow

MODELS:
Attributed to François Duquesnoy (1594–1643), *c.*1620–40

CASTS:
French, probably early to mid-18th century

Bacchus
H. (excluding gilt base): 24.2 cm (9⅝ in.), L. (terrain base): 29.3 cm 11⅝ in.)

Cupid
H. (excluding gilt base): 24.7 cm (9¾ in.), L. (terrain base): 28.0 cm (11⅛ in.)

Lost-wax casts; cast in sleeve-joined sections. Smooth reddish-brown surfaces worn to a yellowish metal; blackish in recesses. Integral terrains.
On oval gilt-bronze bases in the neo-classical style. H.: 9.3 cm (3¾ in.).

As wine and love are happy companions in life, so too the decorative pairing of their infant gods in bronze. Bacchus is clearly identified by his attributes of vine-staff and upturned cup, Cupid by his familiar bow and arrows.

The compositions of both bronzes are closely comparable with statuettes of infants in the engravings of François Girardon's sculpture collection (*c.*1709) (e.g. fig. 64), where they are firmly stated to be by François Duquesnoy (see also p. 84). He was particularly celebrated for his statuettes of infants, to the extent that such figures were invariably attributed to him in 18th-century sale catalogues, although many probably originated with his contemporaries in Rome. But despite some similarities between the *Cupid* and Algardi's *Infant Hercules with a Snake* (c.1650), there seems no reason to modify the traditional attribution of both models for these bronzes to Duquesnoy.

That such *putti* were immensely popular in 18th-century France is demonstrated by their reproduction not only as bronzes, but also

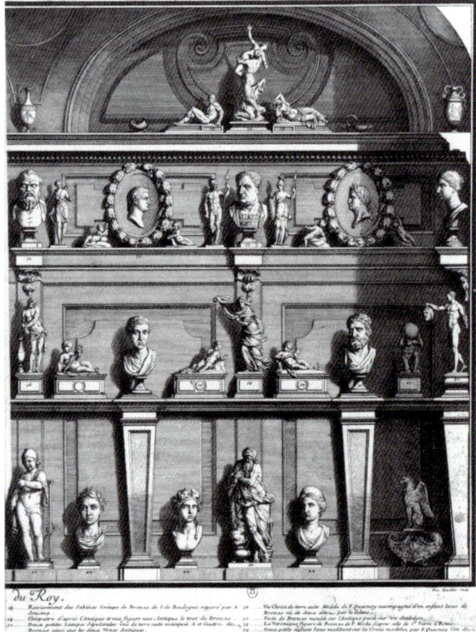

Fig. 64 *La Galerie de Girardon*, plate IV (detail), N. Chevallier after R. Charpentier (1680–1723), *c.*1709, engraving. Bibliothèque Nationale de France, Paris

as Sèvres biscuit porcelain figures and gilt-bronze clock mounts. A drawing by Claude Bertin (*fl.*1682–1705), *Sculpteur du Roi*, shows the essentials of the *Cupid* group, but it is so sketchy that it cannot be said with confidence whether it is a preparatory or record drawing. Bronzes of the *Cupid* model were certainly first cast before the late 1740s, since an example is documented that was stamped with the 'crowned-C' copper tax mark (see p. 74). These casts were probably made in France in the early to mid-18th century, although their neo-classical bases may imply a later date.

A pair of bronzes apparently of this subject was inventoried at Dorchester House after the death of the 3rd Marquess of Hertford in 1842 (and presumably acquired by him), and at Hertford House in 1870, after the death of the 4th Marquess. Unfortunately, in each case it is impossible to say whether the reference is to these bronzes or another, inferior pair, mounted on Louis XV style gilt-bronze bases (S200, S201). Sir Richard Wallace lent both pairs to the Bethnal Green Museum exhibition, 1872–5.

S199 (Bacchus)
S198 (Cupid)

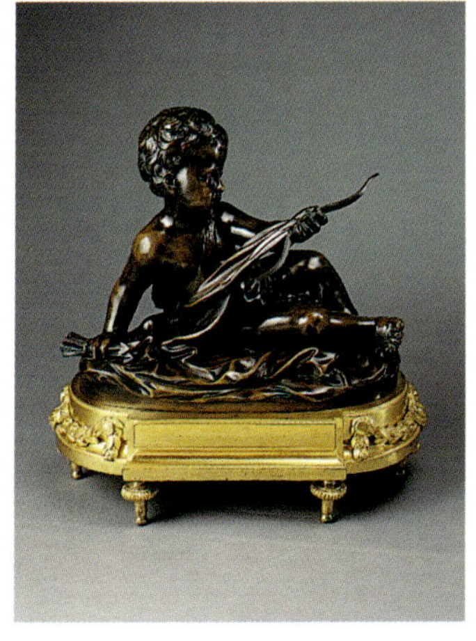

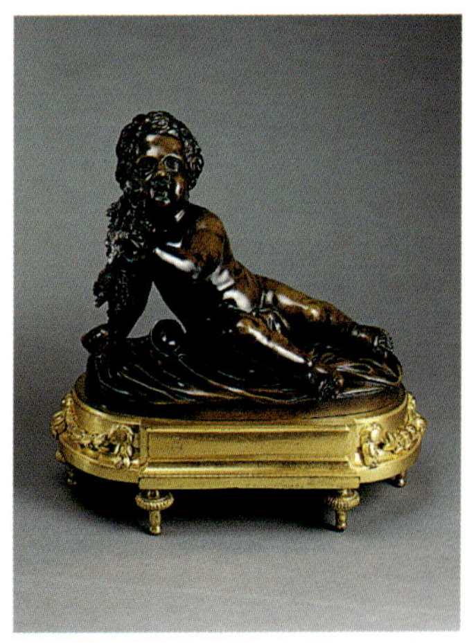

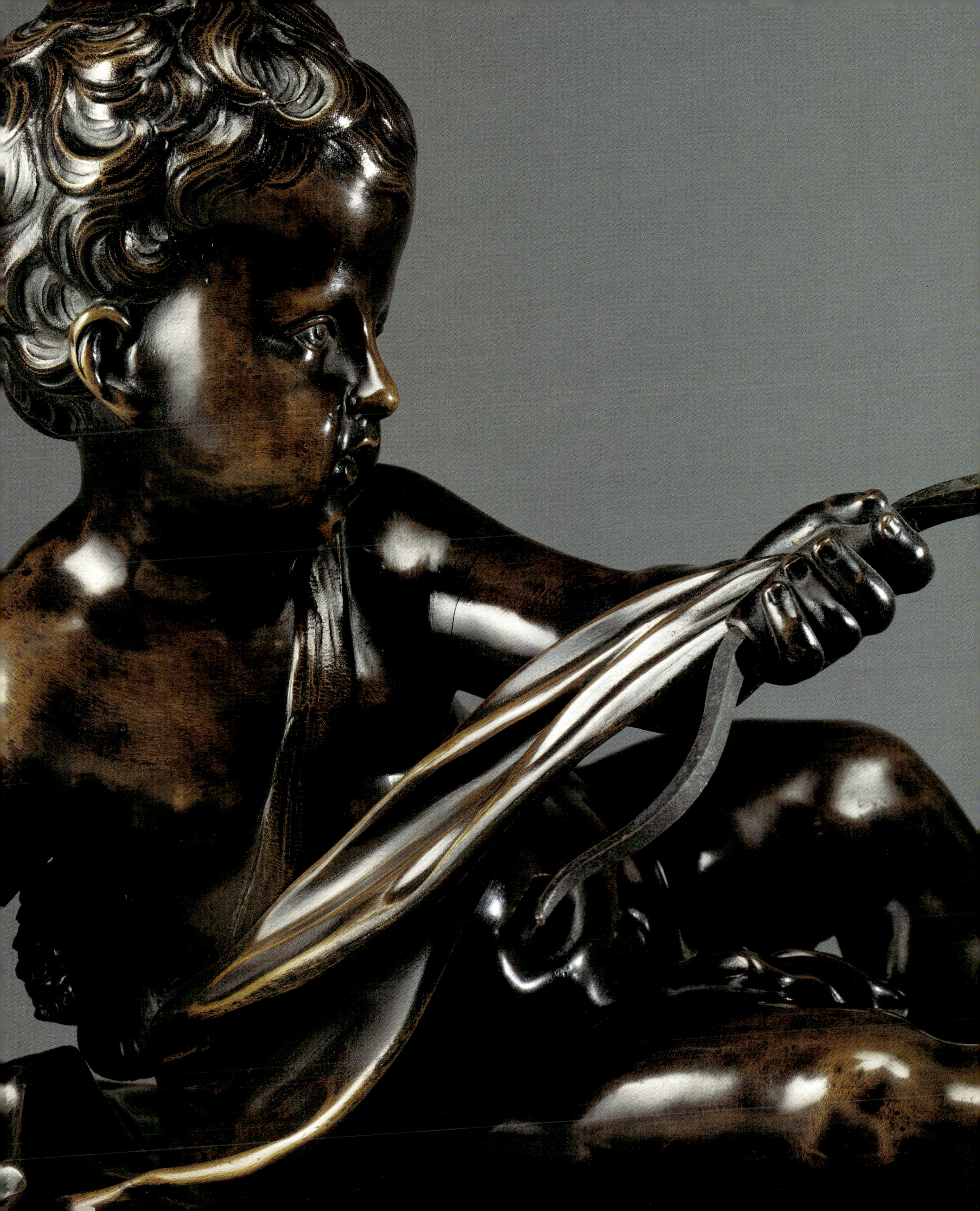

Infant Boys with Musical Instruments

MODELS:
Roman, mid-17th century

CASTS:
French, probably mid-18th century

Kneeling Boy Holding up a Shell
H. (excluding base): 26.4 cm (10⅜ in.)

Seated Boy Blowing a Double Conch Shell
H. (excluding base): 26.0 cm (10¼ in.)

Seated Boy Playing a Flute
H. (excluding base): 26.0 cm (10¼ in.)

Kneeling Boy Playing a Triangle
H. (excluding base): 28.0 cm (11⅛ in.)

Heavy, lost-wax casts; cast in sections joined in the metal. Reddish-brown patina, worn in parts to greyish-olive; brassy alloy beneath; blackish in recesses. Locks of hair and rockwork of integral terrains delicately punched in fine striations. Incised eyes. On rectangular gilt-bronze bases of spreading form, with a repeated acanthus-leaf motif. H.: 4.4 cm (1¾ in.).

While one hesitates to imagine the music this unorthodox quartet might produce, in their varied and lively postures these four infants make an agreeably harmonious ensemble. Nevertheless, it seems likely that they were not conceived together. Although such bronze *putti* were traditionally attributed to François Duquesnoy (see p. 82), they were certainly also modelled by several of his contemporaries who also worked in Rome. The *Boy Holding up a Shell* is the mirror-image of a terracotta *Hercules Strangling the Serpents* of *c.*1650 (Brussels) by his brother, Jérôme, *le jeune* (1602–1654). On the other hand, the *Boy Blowing a Double Conch Shell* is extremely close in form to a bronze *Putto on a Hippocamp*, generally accepted as cast from a model of *c.*1654 by Algardi (see pp. 34–7) (fig. 65). A close-variant cast of the conch-blower in the Louvre can be traced back to the

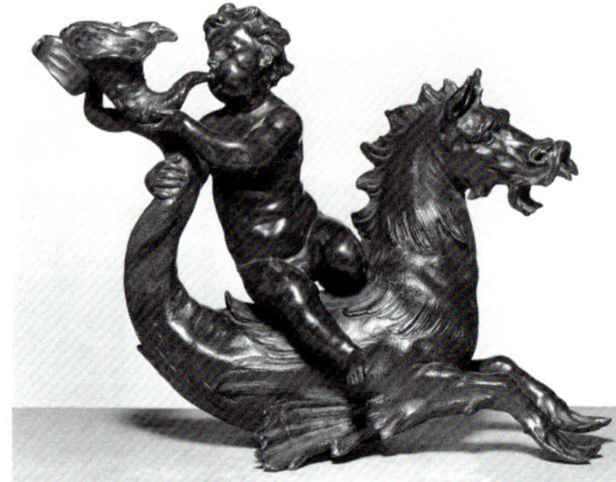

Fig. 65 *Putto on a Hippocamp*, after A. Algardi, *c.*1655, bronze, h.: 24.5 cm. The Walters Art Museum, Baltimore (54.942)

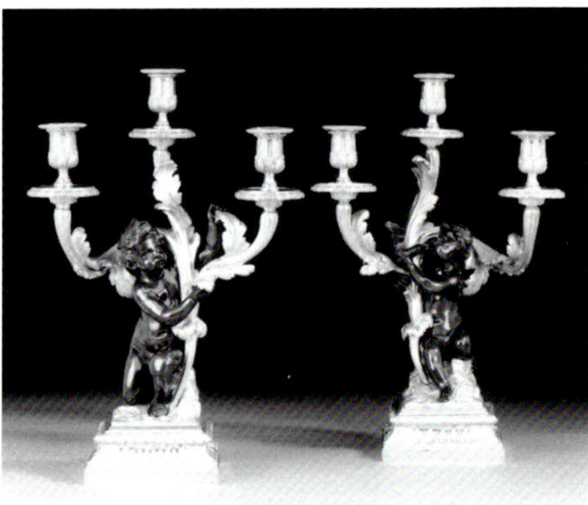

Fig. 66 Pair of Candelabra, French early 19th century, patinated and gilt bronze, h.: 47 cm. Sold Christie's, London, 13 December 2001 (434)

Randon de Boisset sale, Paris, 1777, when it was actually attributed to Algardi, whose *putti* have bodies that are distinctively lither and livelier than those by François Duquesnoy.

The Louvre bronze is thought to be a French cast, and clearly must date from the mid-18th century at the latest. A conch-blower was paired with an example of the flautist in the Jullienne sale, Paris, in 1767, and with a shell-holder in the Fortier sale, Paris, in 1770. All four models of the Wallace Collection bronzes were probably adapted (or conceived) in France in the mid-18th century for production as decorative pairings or quartets. The models were also much utilised as components of candelabra, with additional gilt-bronzes branches. Most of these candelabra in fact appear to be 19th century productions and many were supplied for the English market (fig. 66).

First recorded in the collection of the 4th Marquess of Hertford, by whom lent to the 'Musée Rétrospectif' exhibition, Paris, 1865.

S203 (Boy Holding up Shell)
S202 (Boy Blowing Double Conch Shell)
S204 (Boy Playing Flute)
S205 (Boy Playing Triangle)

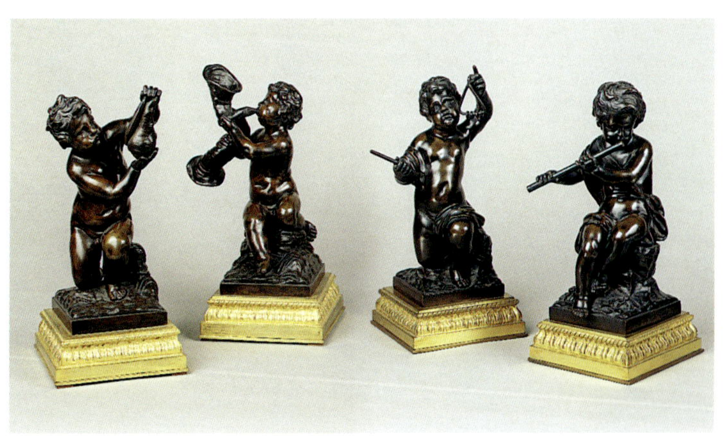

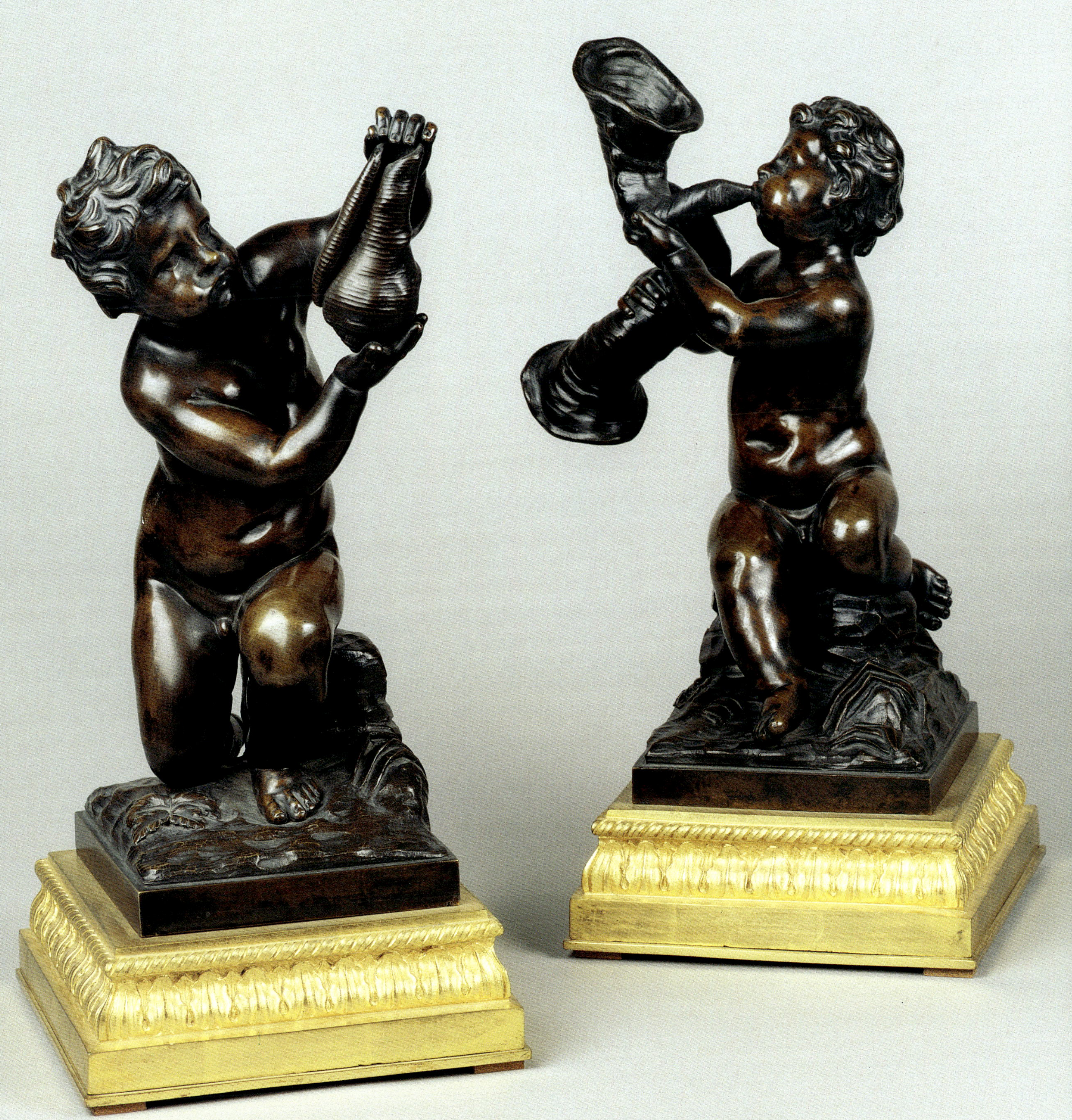

Cupid Vanquishing Pan ('Love Conquers All')

MODEL & CAST:
Jean-Jacques Caffiéri (1725–1792), 1777

signed & dated (inscribed, base, back): *I.I. Caffieri+/ invenit+ excudit 1777+*
inscribed (base, front): *OMNIA VINCIT AMOR./ l'Amour triomphe de tout.*

H.: 42.5 cm (16⅞ in.), Diam. (base): 21.5 cm (8½ in.)

Very thick, heavy, lost-wax cast, cast in two main parts: Pan and the terrain base; Cupid (except for lower right leg). Later blackish-brown surface coating now mottled on body of Cupid; original reddish-brown surface oxidised to mid-brown in worn areas.
Integral terrain and base. No socle.

'Omnia vincit Amor; Love conquers All. To convey this idea, the Artist has used the allegory of Pan, God of Shepherds. He was regarded by the ancients as the God of Nature, in accordance with … his name, which in Greek means All. His horns would indicate (they say) the rays of the Sun, and the horns of the Moon; his fiery face would designate the element of Fire; his stomach covered with stars [here absent], *would signify the Heavens, & his legs, covered with hair, the ground, the trees, the plants & the animals. He has Goat's feet, to suggest the solidity of the earth. Finally, the flute* [pan-pipes] *would represent the harmony of the Heavens, according to the opinion of several ancient Philosophers, & his hooked stick, the turning of the years.'*

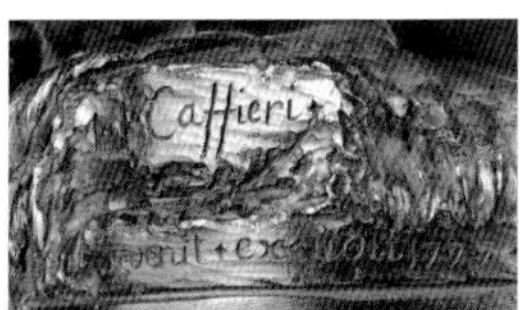

Fig. 67 *Cupid Vanquishing Pan*, detail of signature. Wallace Collection (S219)

Thus was the symbolism of Pan in this group explained in the Salon *livret* (catalogue) when Caffiéri exhibited a closely related terracotta version in 1771. The critics were unimpressed by the conceit, one even inviting his readers to 'laugh with me at the ineptitude of the conception of an allegory that is so mean, so cold, so fake'. Diderot was also critical of the obscurity of the sculptor's attempt to convey the 'motto', which can be read most simply as the triumph of spiritual over bestial love.

Diderot nevertheless conceded that 'the group is, like most of M. Caffiéry's works, modelled with fluency and intelligence'. The facture of the bronze version is particularly interesting since painstaking care has been exerted to salvage what was a defective and notably heavy cast. When considered together with the meticulous tooling of exterior details, especially the delicate punch-marking of the body hair, it is suggestive of an inexperienced founder but a prestigious commission. This is consistent with what we know of this remarkable bronze, which is fully signed by Caffiéri ('excudit' as well as 'invenit') (fig. 67), like its pendant, *Friendship Surprised by Love* (fig. 68). They were commissioned at the huge cost of 2000 *livres* each by the abbé Joseph-Marie Terray (1716–1778), who had been a powerful Finance Minister, and a lavish, if self-serving, patron of the arts between

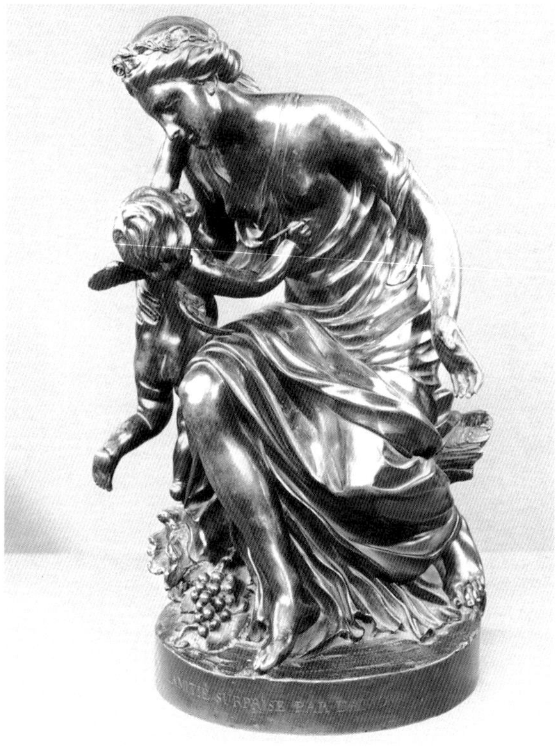

Fig. 68 *Friendship Surprised by Love*, J.-J. Caffiéri, 1777, bronze, h.: 42.5 cm. Toledo Museum of Art, Ohio (1971.160)

1773 (the year he also became *Directeur-Général des Bâtiments*, or 'Minister of Arts') and his death.

For Caffiéri, who usually worked in terracotta or marble, and most famously as a portraitist, the bronzes were somewhat exceptional commissions, even though he came from a celebrated family of metalworkers and so must have been familiar with casting processes. But the money and the *kudos* of working for Terray, one of the most powerful men in France, evidently were too significant to turn down.

Acquired by the 4th Marquess of Hertford at the Pembroke sale, London, 1851. The pendant bronze was also in this sale, but was not acquired by Lord Hertford.

S219

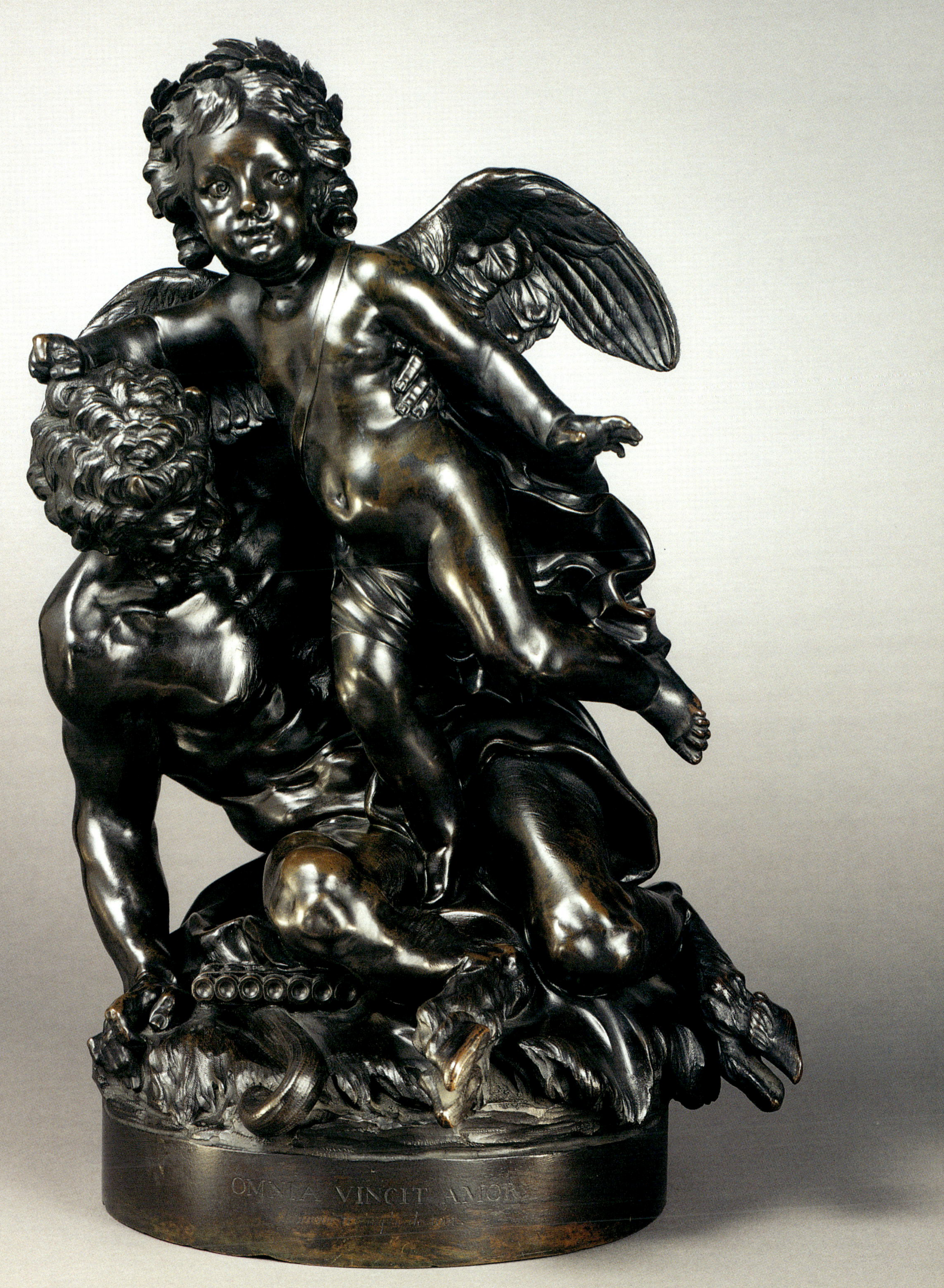
OMNIA VINCIT AMOR

Fidelity

MODEL & CAST:

Follower of Étienne-Maurice Falconet (1716–1791), c.1760–90

H. (excluding pedestal): 28.6 cm (11⅜ in.)

Fairly heavy, thick lost-wax cast; cast in sections, joined in the metal. Gilt-bronze (brassy-coloured metal within). Integral tight circular base.

On a stepped square-plan pedestal of Devonshire grey marble, with a bevelled cornice. H.: 15.3 cm (6 in.)

In this shimmering and graceful gilt-bronze statuette, Fidelity is represented as an idealised young female figure in classical dress holding a spaniel (symbolising Loyalty) in her left hand and a heart (for Truth) in her right. Beneath her left foot she tramples disdainfully the serpent of Deceit and the mask of Calumny.

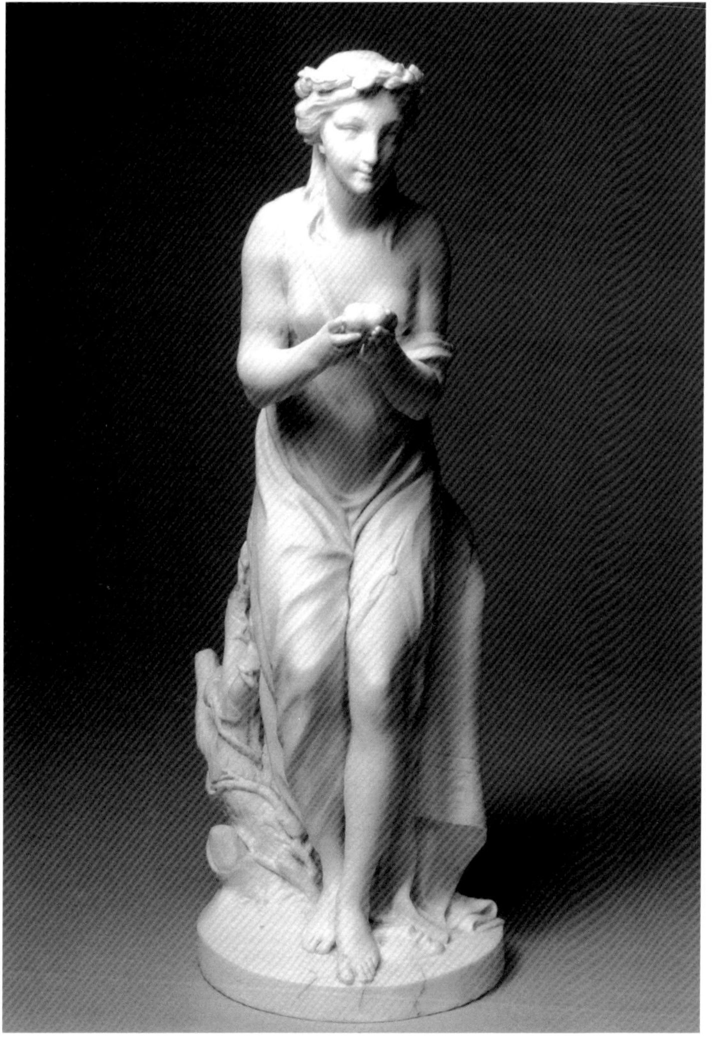

Fig. 69 *Friendship Holding Her Heart in Her Hands*, after E.-M. Falconet, 1765, Sèvres biscuit porcelain, h.: 35.5 cm. Musée National de Céramique, Sèvres (MNC 22433)

The statuette has been attributed to Houdon (see pp. 92–3) and, more plausibly, to Falconet. In style it relates to numerous other small-scale figures of slender young women – in marble, or in patinated or gilt-bronze – that traditionally have been attributed to him. Often found as clock mounts or incorporated into candelabra, they were produced in large quantities for the collectors' market in the late 18th century and beyond. They reflect the great influence of such successful marble sculptures as Falconet's *Sweet Melancholy* (Hermitage) and *Pygmalion and Galatea* (Louvre), both of 1763, and also of the many biscuit figures, including versions of the preceding, that he had modelled while Director of Sculpture at the Sèvres porcelain factory (1757–66). Among these were comparable figures of *Friendship with a Heart* (a portrait of Madame de Pompadour as 'Friendship') of 1755, and the yet closer *Friendship Holding Her Heart in Her Hands* of 1765, with its similarly-placed mask (fig. 69). But the facial features and exceptionally elongated body type (especially the long neck) of *Fidelity* are distinct from those favoured by Falconet who, furthermore, was in Russia between 1766 and 1778, and is not himself documented as having cast small bronzes, or supplied models for them. It was therefore perhaps a pupil or assistant at the Sèvres factory, or a younger follower working in his sweetened neo-classical style, who created this statuette.

Probably identical with a gilt-bronze statuette of this description in Richard Wallace's sale, Paris, 1857, where presumably bought by the 4th Marquess of Hertford. First certainly recorded at Hertford House in 1890.

S222

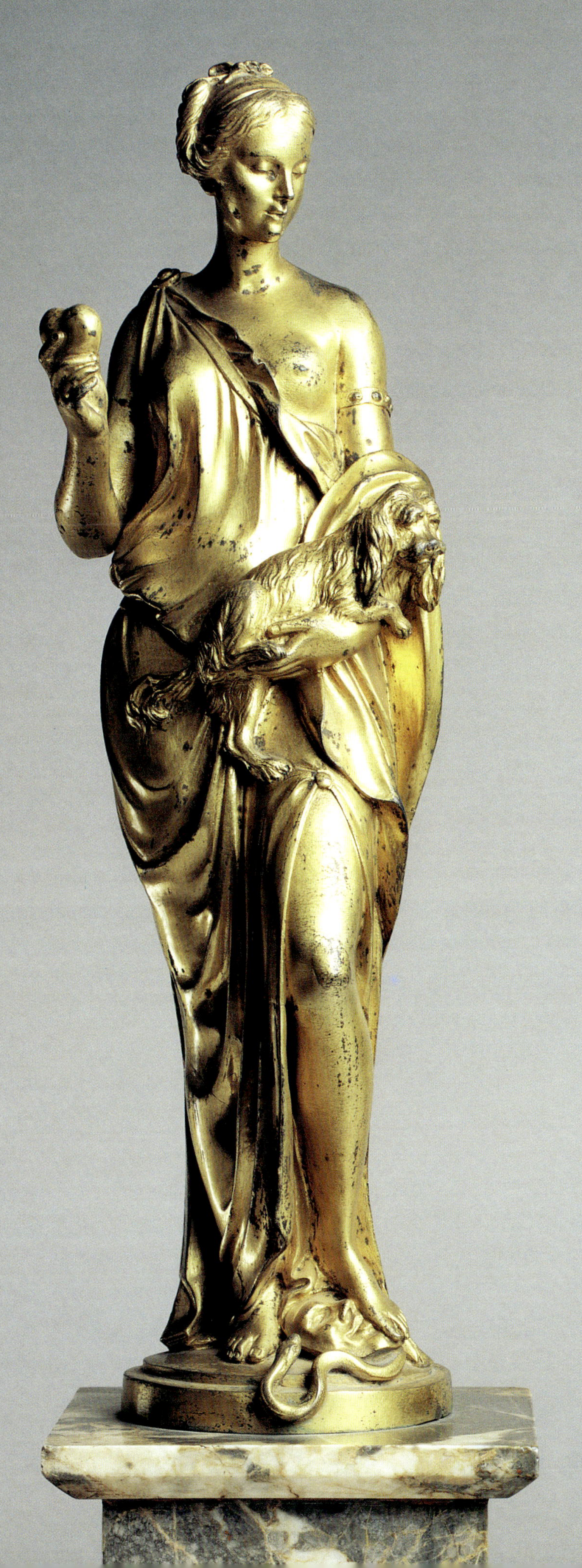

Bacchante with Pan-pipes and *Bacchante with Tambourine*

MODELS:
Attributed to Joseph-Charles Marin (1759–1834), *c*.1790

CASTS:
French, probably 1790s

Bacchante with Pan-pipes
H. (excluding pedestal): 46.0 cm (18⅛ in.)

Bacchante with Tambourine
H. (excluding pedestal): 43.8 cm (17⅜ in.)

Lost-wax casts; cast in sections, joined in the metal. Smooth deep dark-green patina with black streaks; brassy yellow high points. Bunches of grapes, wine-cups, pan-pipes and tambourine gilt. Integral terrains.
Cylindrical pedestals of green Genoa or verde antico marble, with gilt-bronze mounts in the neo-classical style. H.: 21.4 cm (8½ in.).

In classical mythology, bacchantes (Gk: *Maenads*, 'mad women') were the female devotees of Bacchus (Gk: *Dionysus*), god of wine, and, like their male equivalents, the satyrs, always followed him on his travels. They are characterised by their state of ecstatic abandon, induced by their vigorous participation in rituals that involved drinking, singing and dancing.

In basic posture one bronze is essentially a mirror image of the other, but each bacchante is individualised by different attributes and facial expressions. One is crowned with vine leaves, has a garment of drapery and animal skin, and carries a set of pan-pipes – an allusion to the satyr Pan, another associate of Bacchus. Her companion is crowned with ivy – also sacred to Bacchus – and wears an animal pelt, in reference to Bacchic ritual sacrifices. By the tree stump is her tambourine, which will be used to beat the rhythym of the ritual dances.

As is evident from their balanced pairing and elaborate pedestals, these bronzes are purely decorative in function, and were doubtless retailed to be placed on corner cupboards or chimneypieces. Indeed, the models are much more commonly found as elements of three- to six-light candelabra (fig. 70), indicative of the growing market for bronzes employed in this way, and reflecting the increasingly sophisticated reproduction techniques available at the end of the 18th century. The prominent *marchand-mercier* Dominique Daguerre (d.1796) may well have been involved in commissioning and retailing them since one pair of candelabra apparently utilising these models was in his London sale of 1791.

The models themselves traditionally have been attributed to Claude Michel, called Clodion (1738–1814). Although the success of Clodion's bacchantes undoubtedly inspired these models and the taste for such subjects as bronzes, their more insipid types and poses are actually closer to the terracotta figures and busts of his pupil, Joseph-Charles Marin. The svelte, running figures may also have been influenced by the terracotta (1778), marble (1780) or bronze (1782) versions of *Diana the Huntress* by Houdon (see fig. 13).

First recorded when lent by Sir Richard Wallace to the Bethnal Green Museum exhibition, 1872–5.

S215 (Bacchante with Pan-pipes)
S216 (Bacchante with Tambourine)

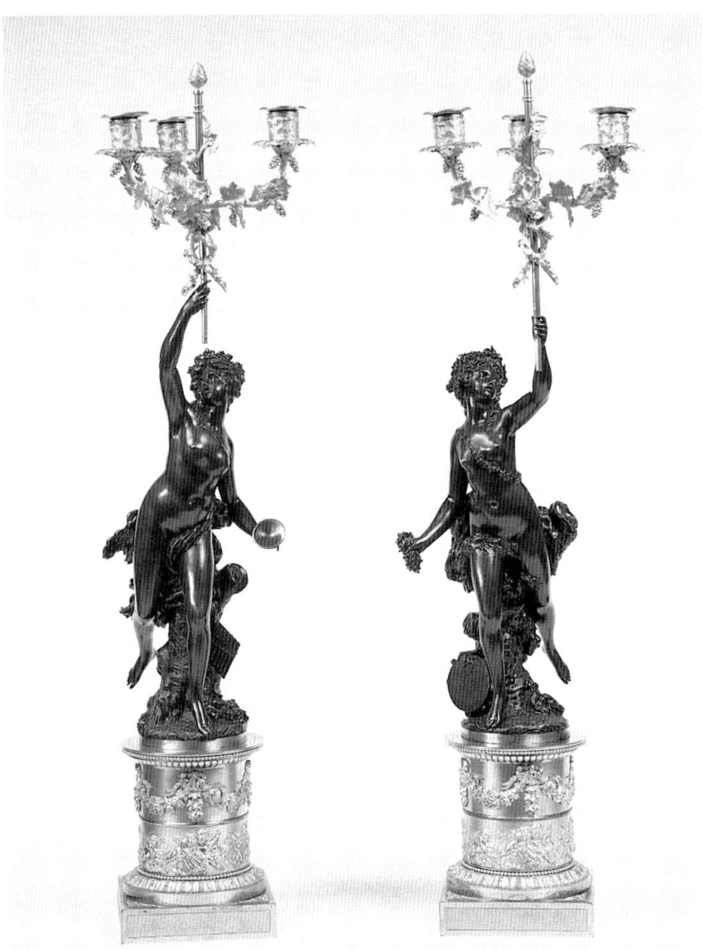

Fig. 70 Pair of Candelabra, French *c*.1790, patinated bronze and gilt-bronze, h.: 86.5 cm. Wallace Collection (F148, F149)

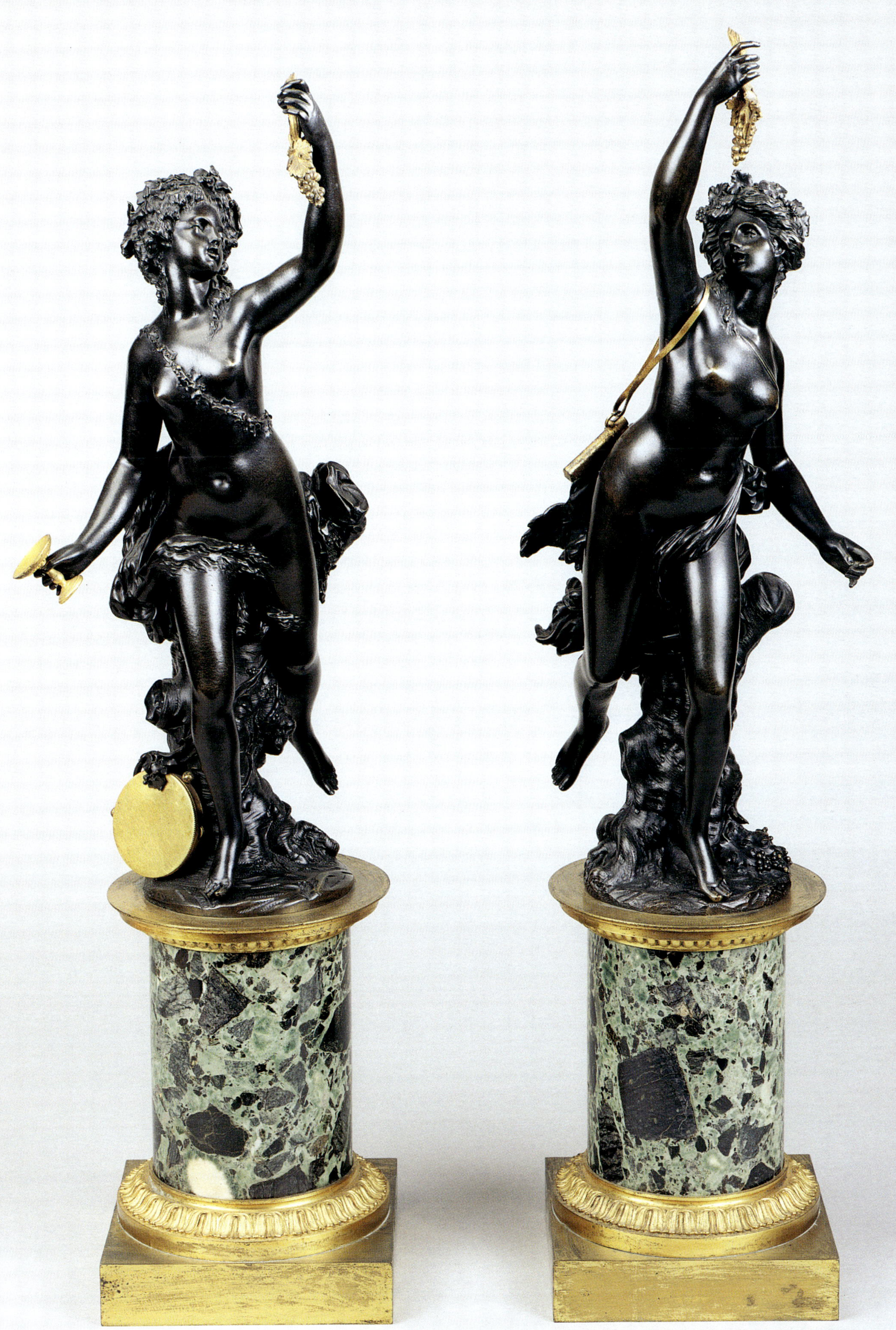

The Kiss Given ('Le Baiser Donné') and *The Kiss Received ('Le Baiser Rendu')*

MODELS:
Jean-Antoine Houdon (1741–1828), *c.*1774–80

CASTS:
Attributed to Pierre-Philippe Thomire (1751–1843), probably 1790s

The Kiss Given
H. (excluding pedestal): 10.9 cm (4⅜ in.)

The Kiss Received
H. (excluding pedestal): 10.8 cm (4¼ in)

Probably lost-wax casts, cast with open backs in two sections. Near-black patina, with natural copper-coloured oxidised-metal surface beneath; very brassy yellow in rubbed areas.
Cylindrical pedestal of striated grey marble, with gilt-bronze socle and mounts in the neo-classical style. H.: 15.8 cm (6¼ in.).

'Of an enervated stylistic period, rather lubricious and unworthy to figure in the Collections of the King [Louis-Philippe]', was the judgement made by Monsieur Dubois, Keeper of Antiquities, when the Louvre was offered a marble version of the *Kiss Given* in 1843. Although this severe view is unlikely to be shared by many today, the rococo sensibilities and swooning sensuality of these groups are undeniable – and irresistible. The lovers are represented as a bacchante and a satyr (the *Kiss Received*) and two rose-garlanded youths *à l'antique* (the *Kiss Given*). The subjects are drawn from the contemporary *Fables* of La Fontaine, specifically the story of the gardener Guillot, who ended up winning a kiss from his master's flirtatious wife, having earlier stolen one from her. It was a tale much reproduced by painters and sculptors of the period, and the numerous replicas of these groups in various media and contexts testify to their enduring market appeal.

In the inventory of his works that Houdon compiled *c.*1784, he listed for 1779 a group of 'a kiss of a bacchante [i.e. the *Kiss Received*]…model to be executed in marble', and under 1780, two groups representing the *Kiss Given* and the *Kiss Received* as 'executed several times in marble'. Since Dubois recorded that the version of the *Kiss Given* offered to him was dated 1774, it may be that it was conceived and made first, *c.*1774, and its 'pendant' created in 1779/80. Houdon appears usually to have subcontracted the casting of his smaller bronzes produced in multiple editions, such as this pair, to his former pupil, Thomire, a specialist *bronzier*. These bronzes are consistent with Thomire's work in their facture and finish, as are their neat pedestals, the style of which would indicate a date for these casts in the 1790s. A pair of bronze reductions of these subjects first appear in the Paris auction records at the Calonne sale of 1788.

First identifiable only in the 1890 inventory of Hertford House taken after the death of Sir Richard Wallace.

S217 (The Kiss Given)
S218 (The Kiss Received)

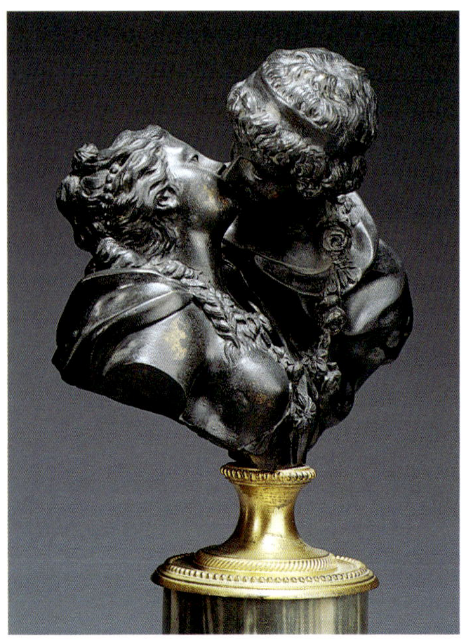
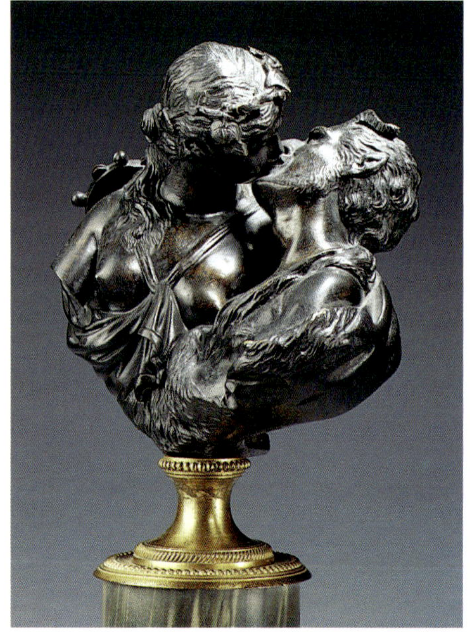

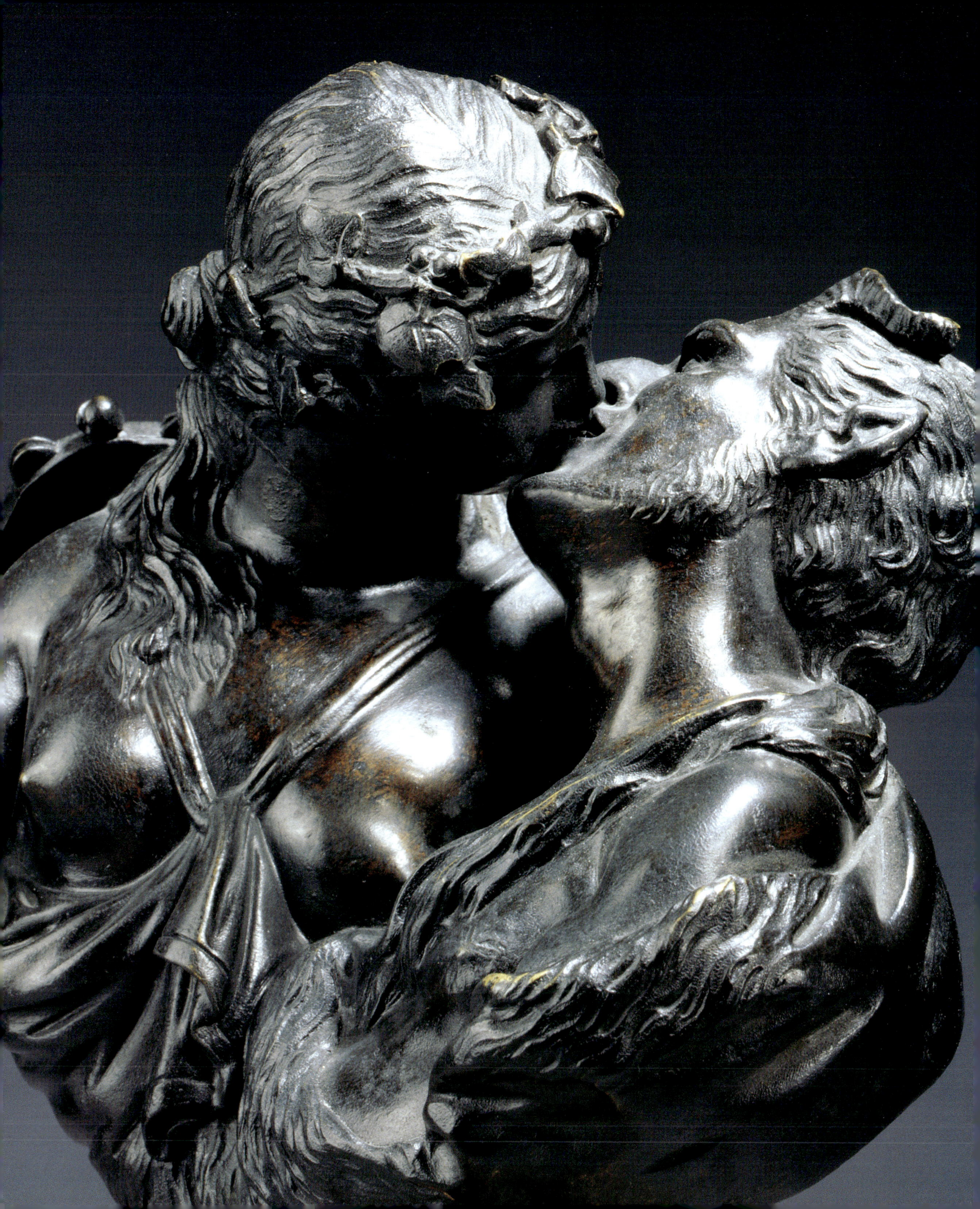

The Marly Horses ('Les Chevaux de Marly')

MODELS:
Guillaume I Coustou (1677–1746), 1740–5

CASTS:
Attributed to Pierre-François Feuchère (1737–1823), c.1800–15

(left-hand group)
H. (excluding plinth): 59.8 cm (23¾ in.), W. (terrain base): 47.9 cm (19 in.)

(right-hand group)
H. (excluding plinth): 58.4 cm (23⅛ in.), W. (terrain base): 46.0 cm (18¼ in.)

Lost-wax casts, cast in parts, sleeve-joined together. Gilt-bronze. Each hand of each figure is slotted, probably so as to grip reins, now lost. Each group bolted onto an integral terrain. Modern wooden plinths (not shown).

Instantly recognisable as one of the most famous symbols of France, the original 'Marly Horses' (Louvre) by Guillaume I Coustou (figs 71ab) became especially celebrated after their placement at the head of the Champs-Elysées in Paris in 1794 (from where they were removed 200 years later). In a period of heightened patriotism during the Napoleonic Wars, they came to be associated with '*la gloire de La France*', and thus to be seen as an allegory of France itself. Originally, when displayed on the terrace of the horse-pond (*abreuvoir*) in the Park at Marly, they were intended simply to represent the wild and free forces of nature. This was dramatically conveyed by the rocky ground, the staring eyes, jagged manes and rearing postures of the animals, and the muscular tensions exhibited in the bodies of the figures.

Patinated bronze reductions of the two groups were produced in the late 18th century, and as early as 1766 the collector Blondel de Gagny (1695–1776) owned a gilt pair mounted as firedogs, but the vast majority of casts were made after the Revolution. In an undated document, written before 1813, Feuchère wrote of them: 'these objects have never previously been made in gilt-bronze… I believe this would make the most magnificent and the richest effect, one opposite the other or on pedestals on the axes or angle of a *salon*…the price of one ungilt 1800fr. and gilt 3600, together 7200…'. One such pair was indeed supplied by Feuchère to the Würzburger Residenz in 1813, and further examples appeared in his workshop's sales of 1824 and 1829. The Wallace Collection groups are certainly 'rich' in 'effect', even if their gleaming surfaces do not entirely disguise the comparatively modest quality of their detailing, and it seems reasonable to attribute them to the Feuchère workshop.

The 3rd Marquess of Hertford bought a pair of *Marly Horses* at Christie's in 1814, but this was of patinated rather than gilt bronze, and evidently he gave it to his mother, after whose death in 1834 it passed out of the Collection. The present pair must also have been acquired by the 3rd Marquess, since after his own death in 1842 it was inventoried, under 'Ormolu Ornaments', at Dorchester House.

S191 (left-hand group)
S192 (right-hand group)

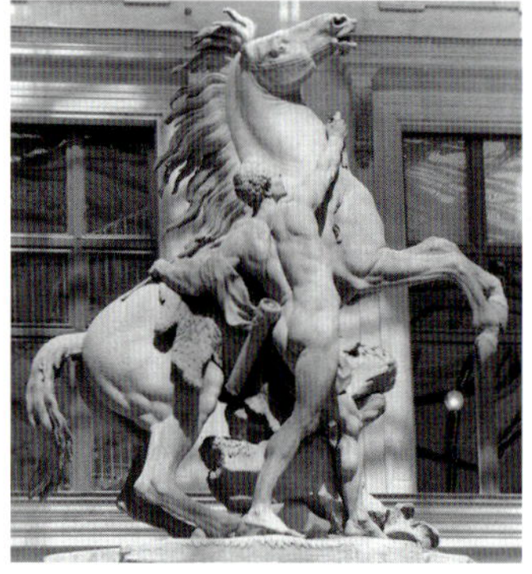 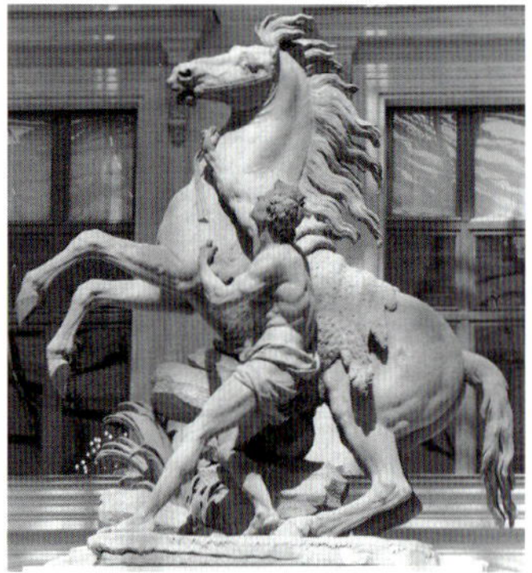

Figs 71ab *The Marly Horses*, G. I Coustou, 1740–5, marble, h.: 355 cm. Musée du Louvre, Paris (MR 1802, 1803)

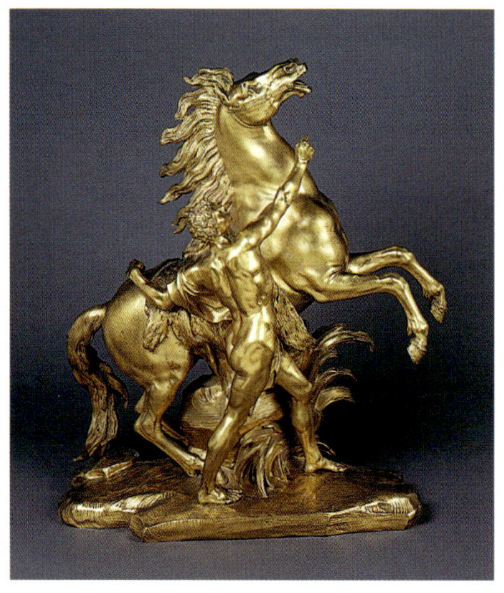 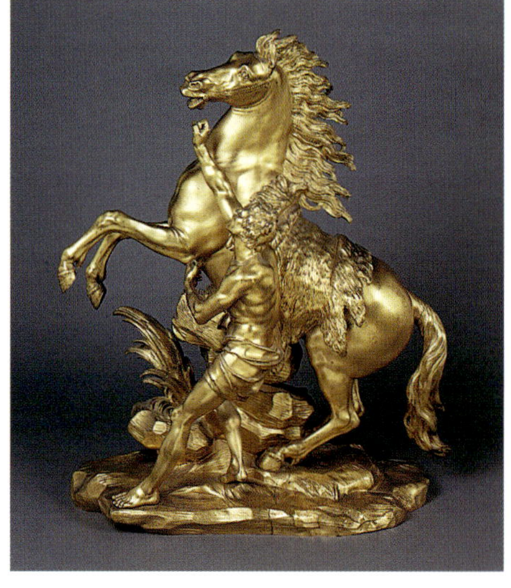

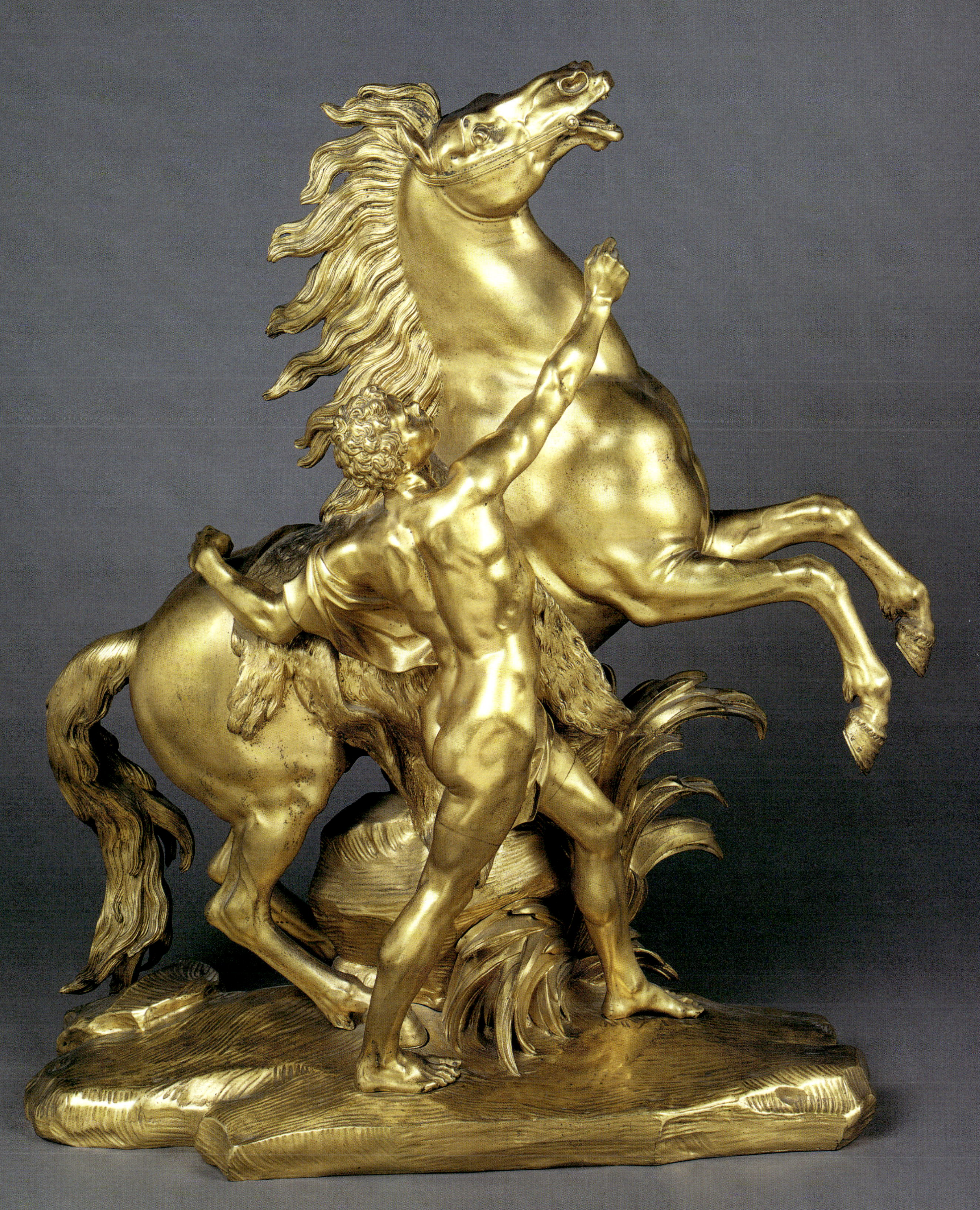

Sleeping Bacchante ('Bacchante endormie, sa tête posée sur son bras gauche')

MODEL:

Attributed to Joseph Broche (c.1740–after 1807), or Jean-Baptiste-Ignache Broche (1741–1794), c.1770

CAST:

French, perhaps c.1800–30

H.: 28.0 cm (11⅛ in.), L.: 32.8 cm (13 in.)

Sand-cast, the sections socketed and pinned together. Polished, dark-green patina. Integral terrain. No separate base.

Bacchantes, the passionate female followers of Bacchus, god of wine, were popular subjects for sculptors in late 18th century France (see pp. 90–1). Their classical origins provided the veneer of respectability beneath which the sculptor could represent the naked female form with varying degrees of eroticism. This bacchante, recognisable as such by her ivy-girt hair and lion skin, is represented sleeping off an excess of wine, an abandoned vessel by her side.

The general type and erotic pose of this bacchante derives from Falconet's work of the 1750s and '60s, in particular his many models for Sèvres biscuit figures (see fig. 69). Their success seems to have stimulated the demand among collectors for small marbles featuring naked females either singly or in groups representing Venus and Cupid. Many of these are now attributed to various of Falconet's followers, who were able to exploit his absence from France between 1766 and 1781. The model of the *Sleeping Bacchante* has recently been attributed to one of the Broche brothers, by comparison with a very similar marble figure of a *Seated Bacchante* signed 'Broche' (fig. 72). The model certainly dates back to at least 1774 since a close variant of comparable height in marble was sold in the du Barry sale that year, while a plaster version was depicted in two paintings by L.-L. Boilly (1761–1845), one of which is datable to 1785–8. The composition may derive from the work of François Boucher (1703–1770), from whose drawings and paintings Falconet and his followers drew inspiration for a number of their models. The facture of the Wallace Collection bronze, one of two examples known today, may indicate it was cast in the early 19th century. It has been given a lustrous dark-green surface colour, doubtless to suggest archaeological origins and antique associations.

First recorded in the Hertford House inventory of 1870 ('Second Room'), taken after the death of the 4th Marquess of Hertford, and probably acquired by him.

S214

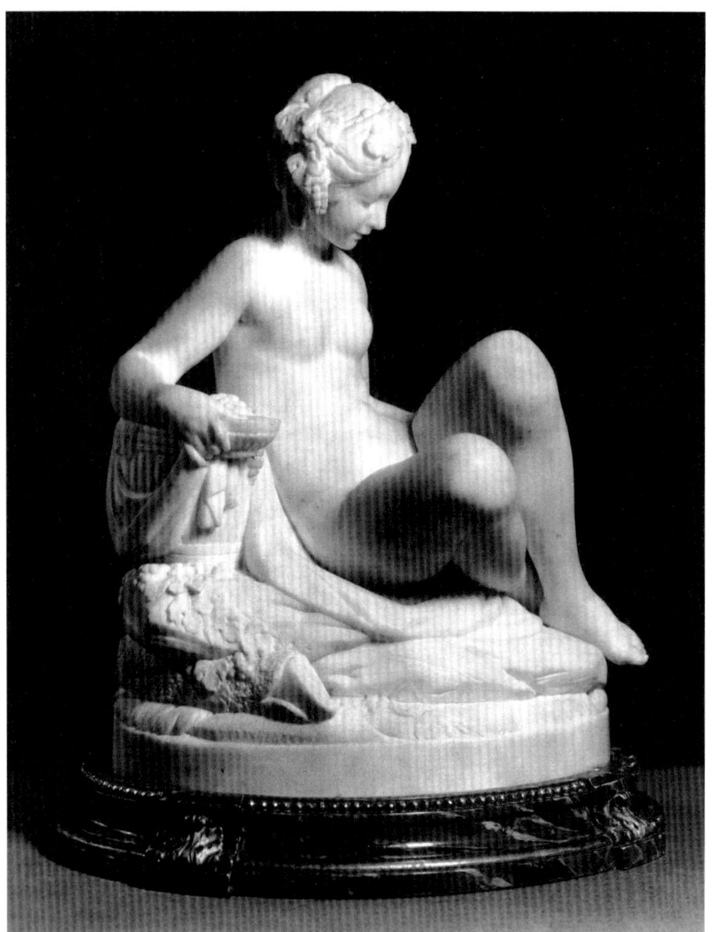

Fig. 72 *Seated Bacchante*, J. or J.-B.-I Broche, *c.*1770, marble, h.: *c.*30 cm. Location unknown

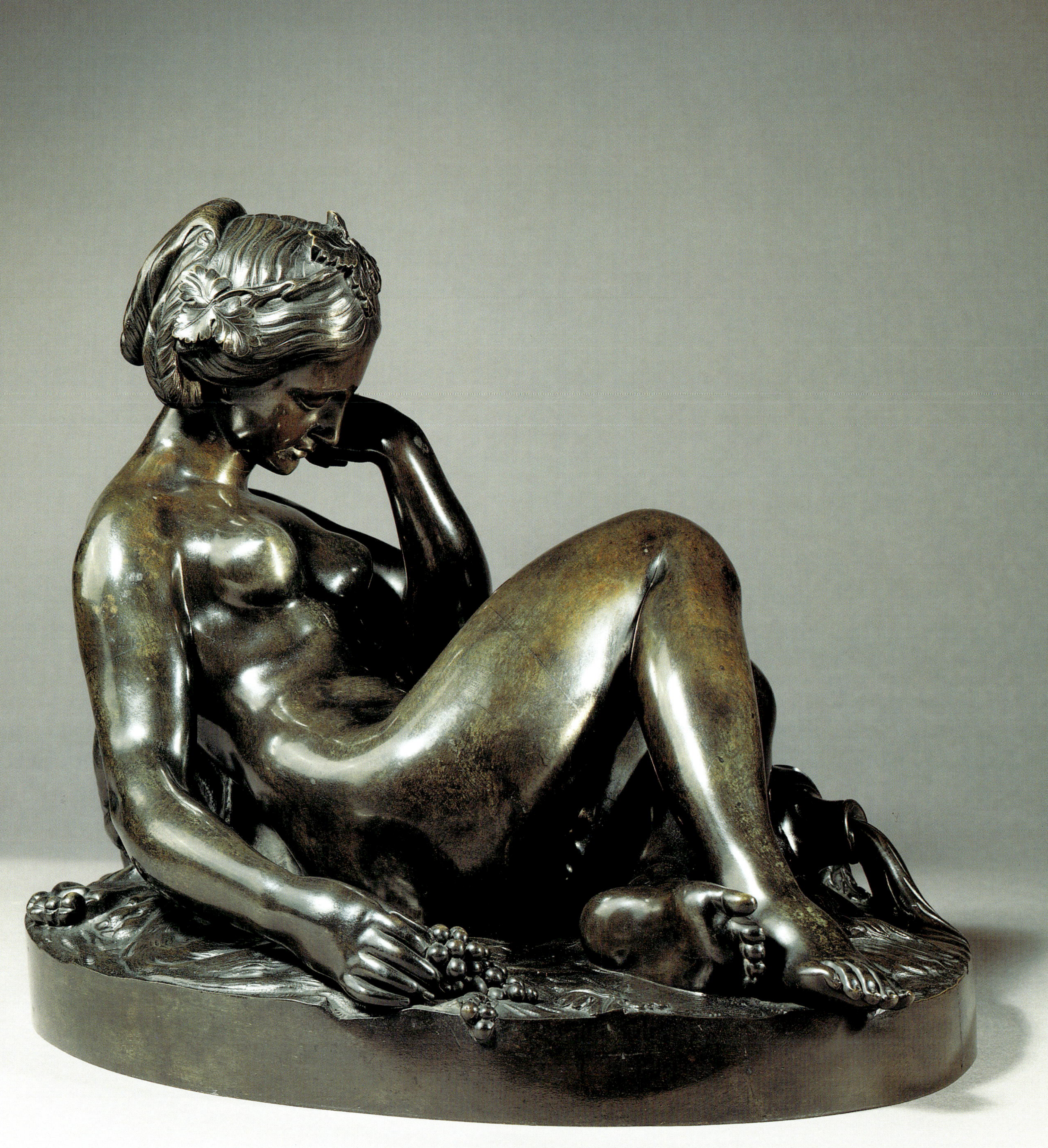

Pluto Abducting Proserpine and *Boreas Abducting Orithyia*

MODELS:
Louis-Simon Boizot (1743–1809), *c.*1786

CASTS:
French, *c.*1810–30

Pluto
H.: 49.2 cm (19½ in.), Diam.: 26.5 cm (10½ in.)

Boreas
H.: 57.2 cm (22⅝ in.), Diam.: 26.5 cm (10½ in.)

Sand casts; cast in sections and joined in the metal. The male figures are socketed into the terrain. Smooth, dark greenish patina; brassy yellow beneath. Circular integral terrains. No bases.

The subjects of these groups are exactly as for the pair of reductions after the marbles intended for the *Parterre d'Eau* at Versailles, by Girardon and Marsy and Flamen (see pp. 54–7), which were conceived about one hundred years earlier. Unlike the compact, independently-modelled compositions of those works, and in particular contrast to the helical arrangement of Girardon's figures, Boizot's essentially uniplanar groups are in each case open and carefully balanced, with the figures forming an X-shape pivoted on the vertical plane.

Between 1773 and 1800, Boizot was Director of Sculpture at the Sèvres porcelain factory, for which he made numerous models for biscuit groups (over 350 were designed during his directorship, but several were modelled by assistants). The models for this pair of bronzes, originally prepared for production as biscuit groups (now known only in plaster versions, see figs 73ab), were shown at the Salon in 1786, a mark of their significance to Boizot. However, he did not himself cast bronzes, and although he collaborated extensively with specialist *bronziers*, in almost all documented cases this was to supply models for the figural elements of clock cases and furnishing bronzes (see fig. 9). It therefore seems likely that these independent bronzes were produced after Boizot's death. Examples with circular bases, which imply a presentation in the round or at least atop circular pedestals, are perhaps earlier than those with square bases (often combined with evidently 19th-century Louis XV-style gilt-bronze mounts). Numerous examples of each type survive.

First identifiable only in the 1890 inventory of Hertford House taken after the death of Sir Richard Wallace.

S196 (Pluto)
S197 (Boreas)

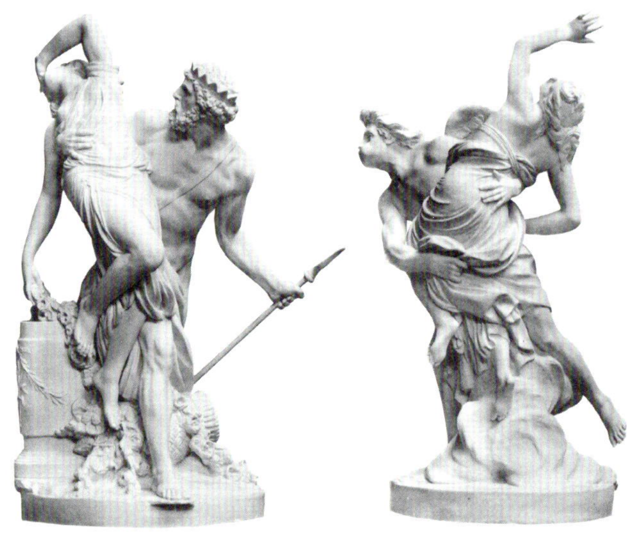

Figs 73ab (left) *Pluto Abducting Proserpine*, after L.-S. Boizot, plaster, h.: 44 cm. (right) *Boreas Abducting Orithyia*, after L.-S. Boizot, plaster, h.: 50 cm. From E. Bourgeois and G. Lechevallier-Chevignard, *Les Biscuits de Sèvres*, Paris, 1913, pl.32, nos 272, 271

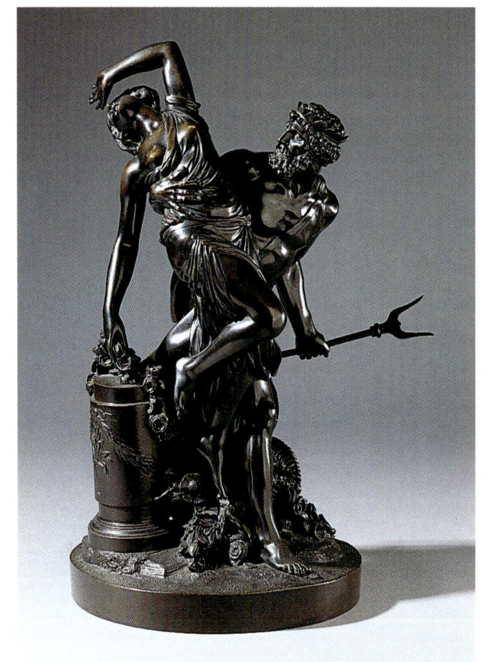

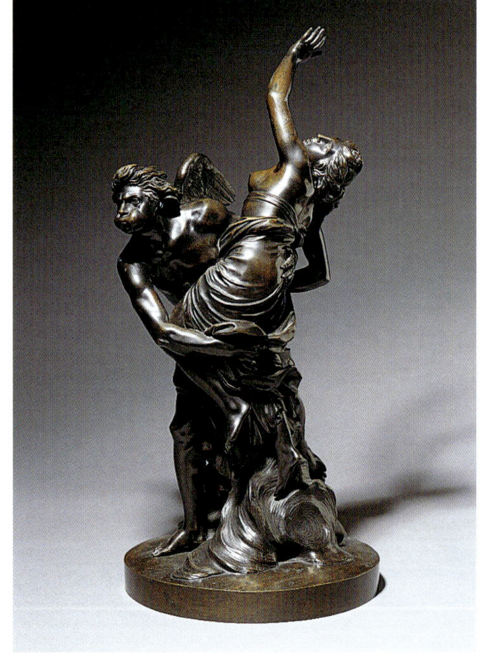

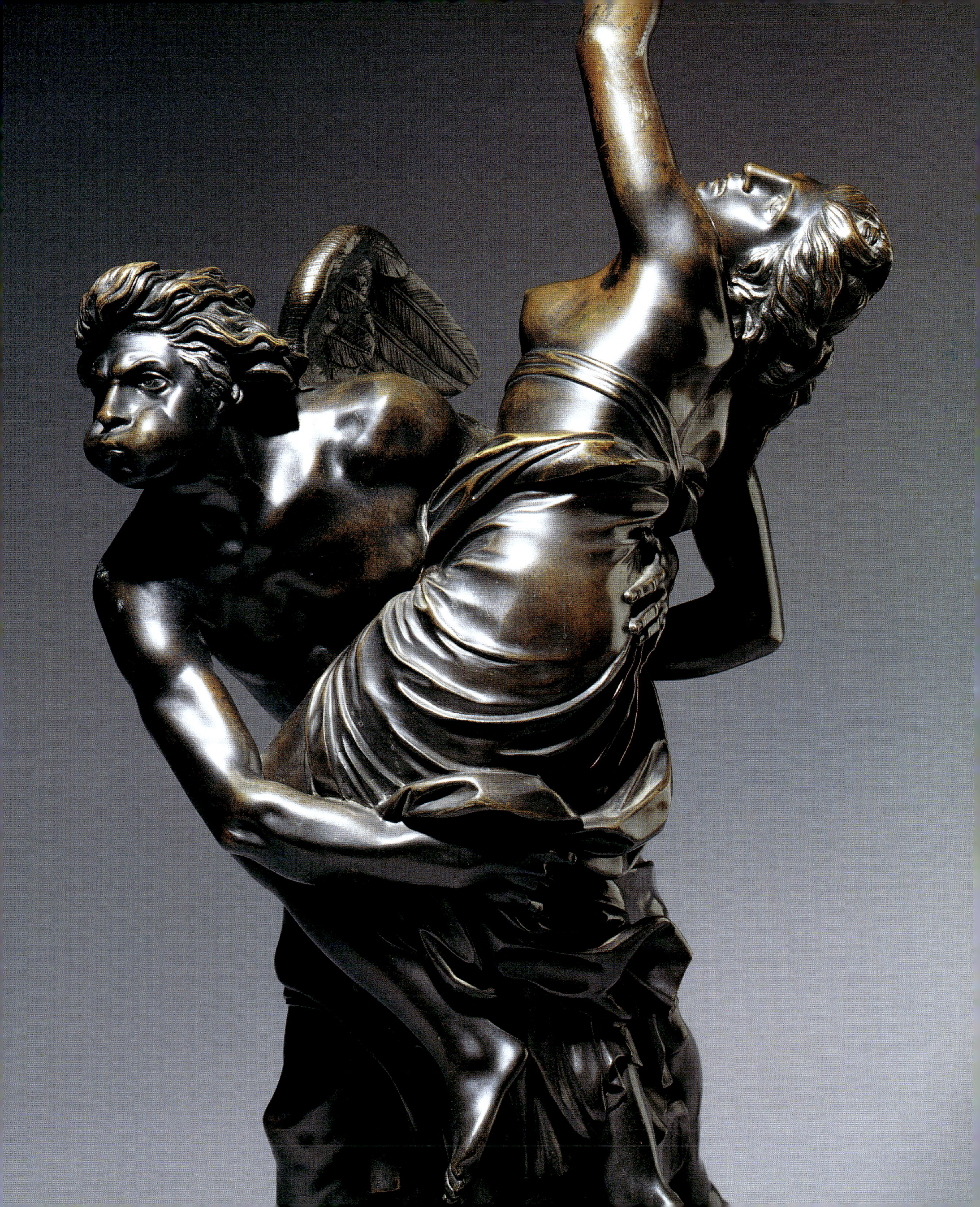

The Empress Marie-Louise (1791–1847)

MODEL:

(body) an antique bronze, 1st century AD

CAST:

Lacour, 1812; chased by François-Aimé Damerat (*fl*.1781–1819)

H.: 20.3 cm (8 in.), W. (base) 10.8 cm (4¼ in.), L. (base): 11.9 cm (4¾ in.)

The Emperor Napoleon I (1769–1821)

MODEL:

(body) an antique bronze, 1st/2nd century AD

CAST:

Lacour, 1812; chased by François-Aimé Damerat (*fl*.1781–1819)
signed (beneath): *Damerat-Cœlavit*

H.: 22.9 cm (9⅛ in.), W. (base) 11.9 cm (4¾ in.), L. (base): 15.2 cm (6 in.)

Lost-wax casts; cast in sections and joined in the metal. Smooth dark greenish-brown patina; coppery-brown metal within. Original plain, straight-sided rectangular bases.

These exquisite statuettes represent Napoleon and his second empress with the attributes of the Sciences and Arts, and of the Art of Painting, respectively. As such they presumably allude to the Emperor's pacific role as Protector of the Sciences and Arts and to Marie-Louise's interest in painting, in which she was tutored by Prud'hon and Isabey. The bronzes are one of five such pairs cast in 1812 and intended for the imperial palaces. They appear to have been made on the initiative of baron Dominique-Vivant Denon (1747–1825), Napoleon's Minister of Fine Arts. He was also an important if eclectic collector and, while the portrait heads were probably derived from contemporary official busts, the figures were copied directly from antique Roman bronze statuettes in his collection: a naked, seated *Mercury* for Napoleon (fig. 75), and a seated *Young Woman* for his empress (fig. 74).

Each of the five pairs, of which one was of silver and the other four of bronze, was cast by an obscure goldsmith named Lacour. The chasing of the bronze versions was shared between two specialists, L.-F. Jeannest (1781–1856), who executed two pairs, including versions now in the Louvre, and Damerat (fig. 76), who

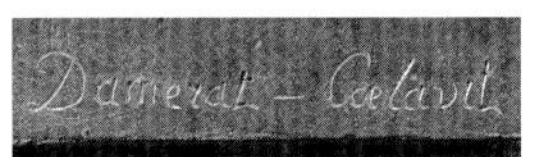

Fig. 76 *The Emperor Napoleon I,* detail of signature. Wallace Collection (S228)

also chased the silver pair (Fontainebleau). Damerat's finishing of the Wallace Collection pair is particularly meticulous and refined.

Ironically, Denon's attempt at flattery backfired. Napoleon objected to the nudity of his portrayal as being 'too indecent', declaring that to be shown in anything other than the dress of his own day was 'ridiculous and bizarre', and ordered the statuettes to be melted down. Marie-Louise was evidently more appreciative: two pairs were delivered to her at the château de Saint-Cloud in 1813. Denon kept one pair for himself which appeared in both his own posthumous sale in 1826, and (presumably having been bought in) that of his nephew and heir, baron Brunet-Denon, in 1846. This was possibly the pair now in the Wallace Collection, and could even have been acquired at the latter sale by the 4th Marquess of Hertford, although the bronzes are first definitely recorded in the Collection when lent to the Bethnal Green Museum exhibition, 1872–5.

S229 (Marie-Louise)
S228 (Napoleon I)

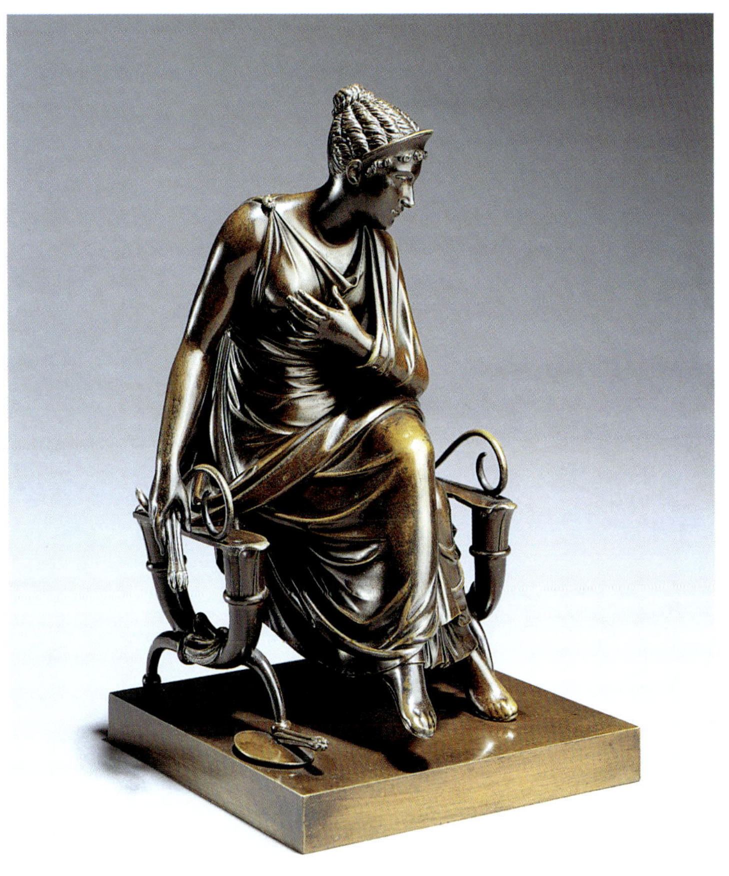

S229

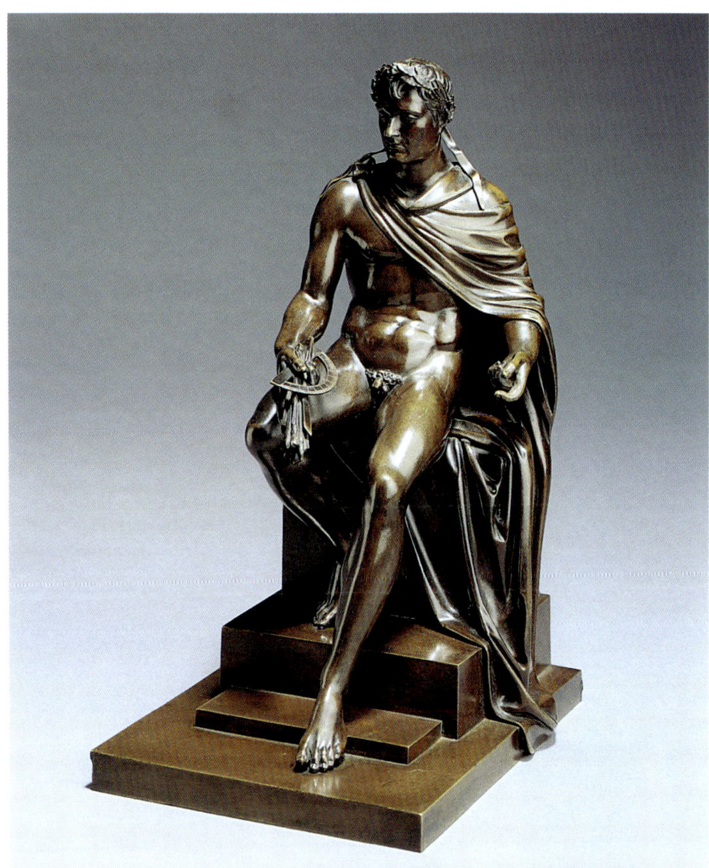

S228

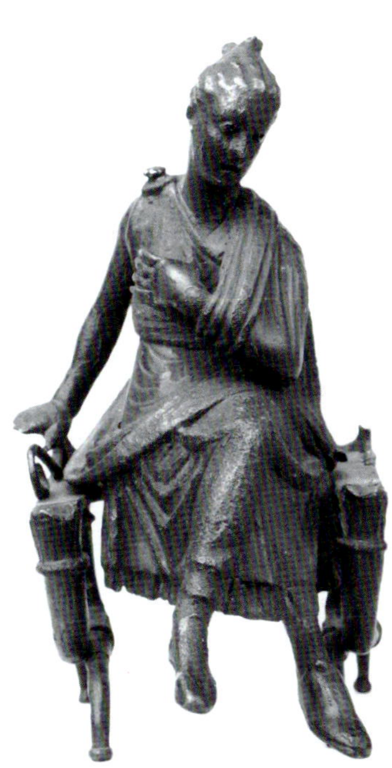

Fig. 74 *Young Woman*, Roman 1st century AD, bronze, h.: 17 cm.
Musée du Louvre, Paris (Br 1081)

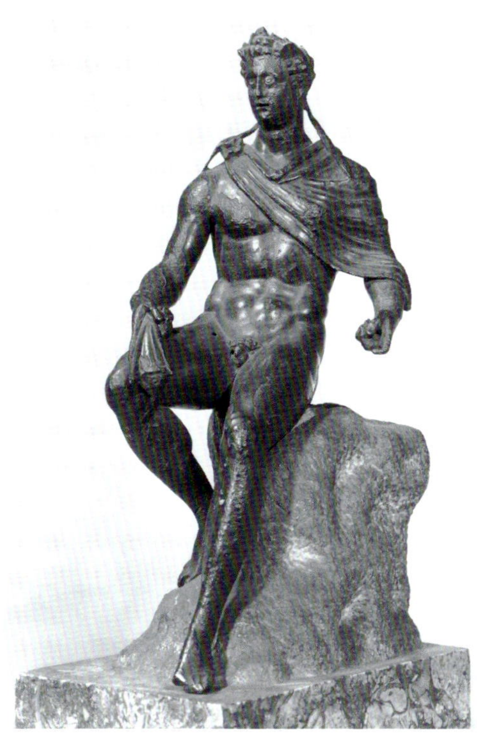

Fig. 75 *Mercury*, Roman 1st–2nd century AD, bronze, h.: 24 cm.
Bibliothèque Nationale de France, Paris (Bronze 837)

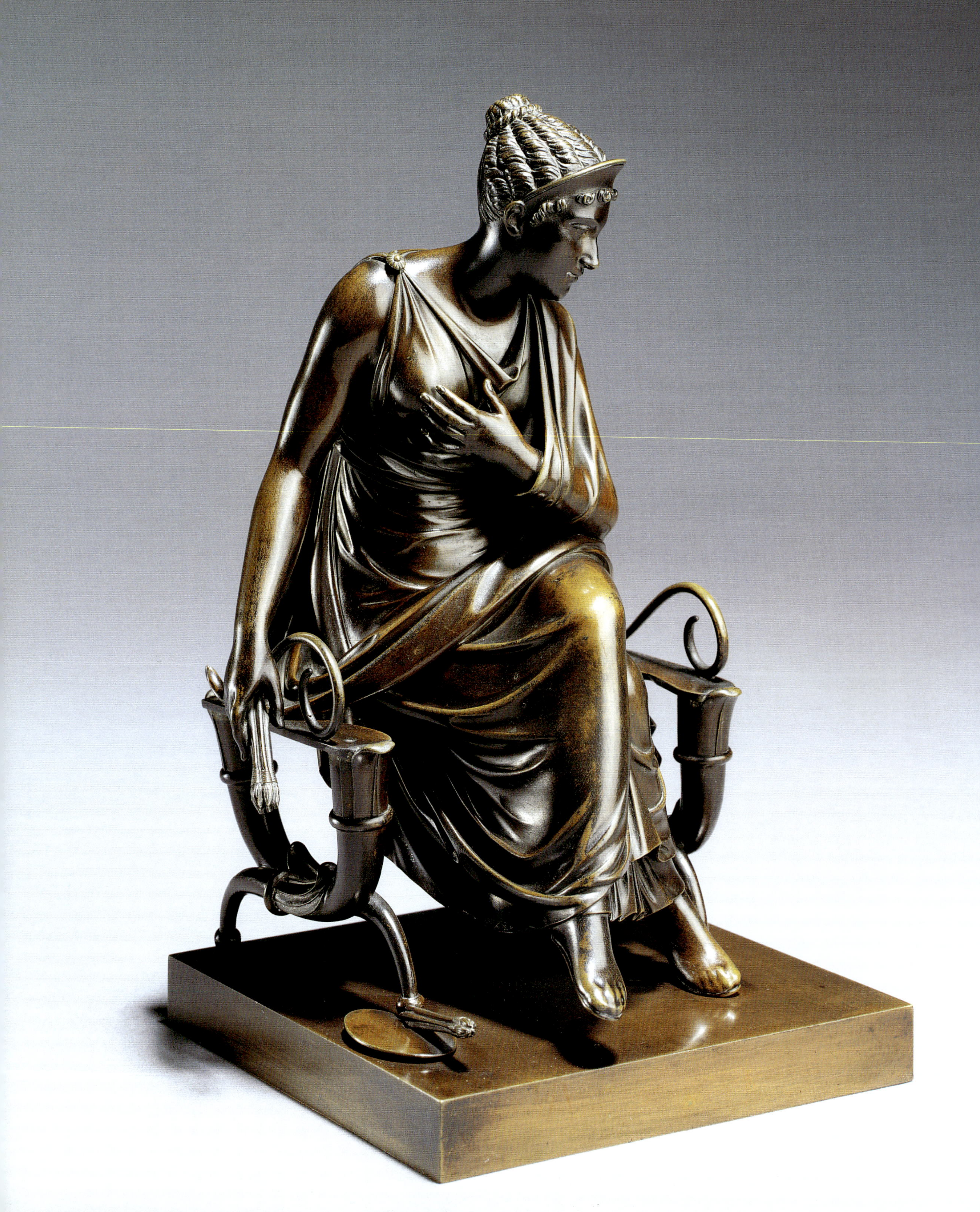

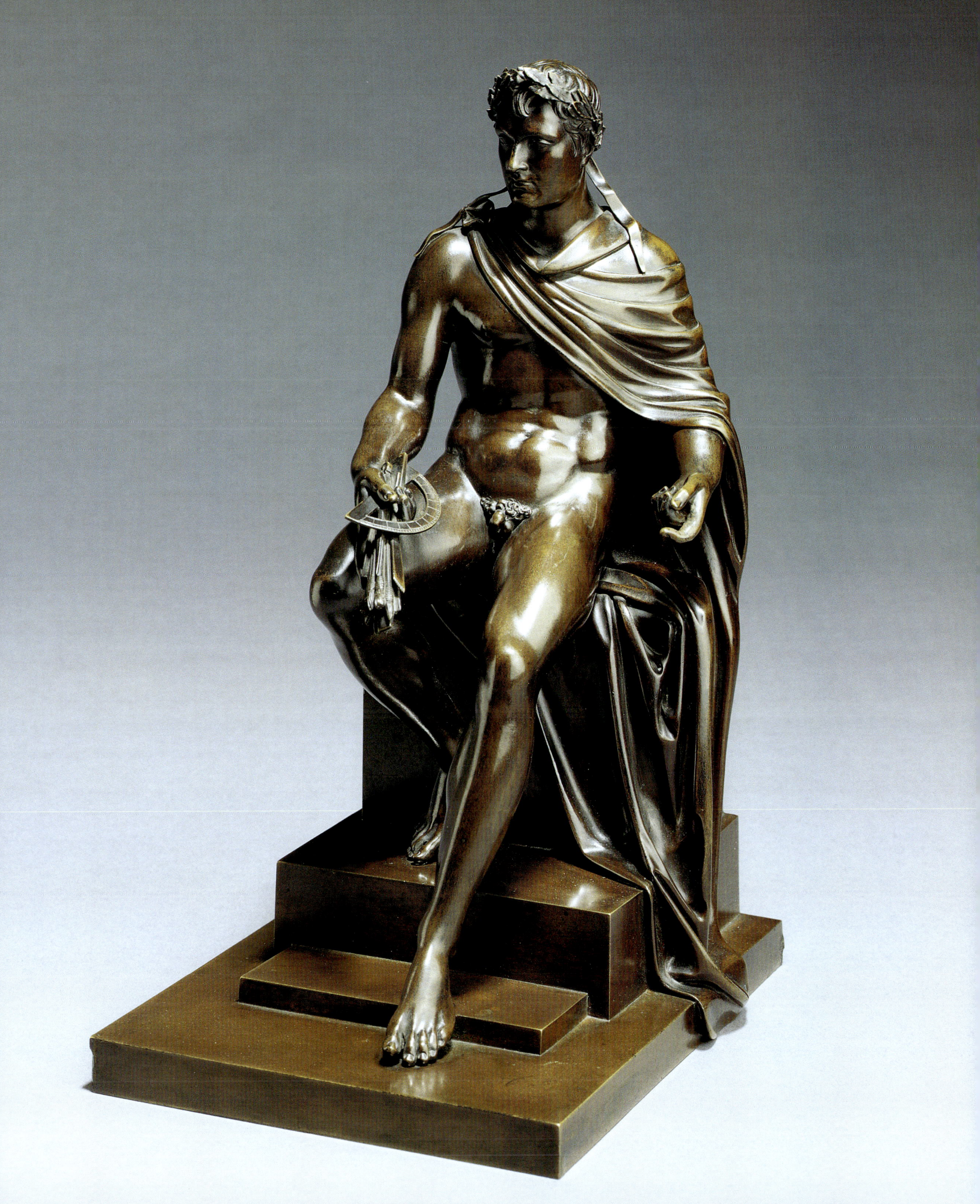

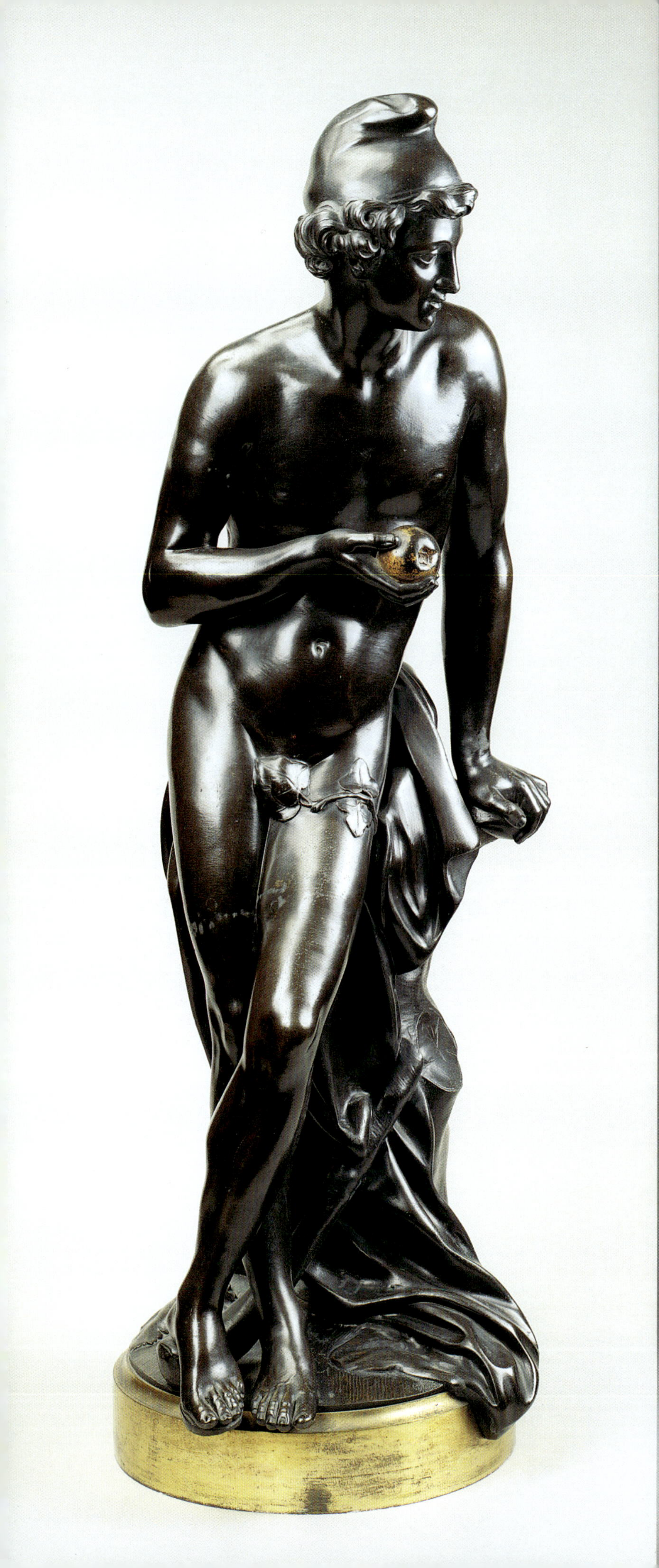

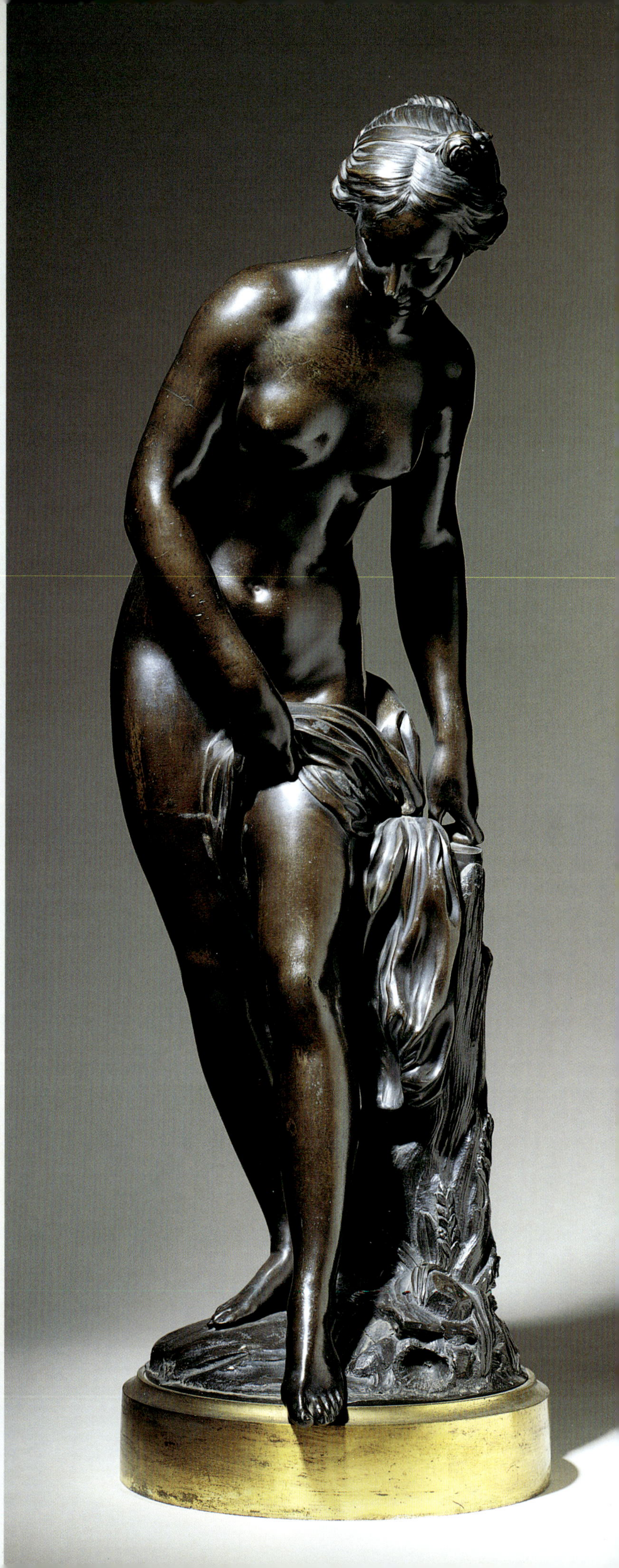

The Shepherd, Paris ('Le Berger Pâris, prêt à donner la pomme qui doit être le prix de la beauté')

MODEL:
Nicolas-François Gillet (1709–1791), 1757

CAST:
French, c.1840–60

H. (excluding base): 79.3 cm (31½ in.)

The Bather ('La Baigneuse', or 'La Nymphe qui descend au bain')

MODEL:
Étienne-Maurice Falconet (1716–1791), 1757

CAST:
French, c.1840–60

H. (excluding base): 78.1 cm (31 in.)

Light sand-casts, each limb socketed into the torso and secured by rivets. Polished dark brown patina. The apple held in Paris's right hand is gilt.
Integral patinated circular terrains, mounted on plain, straight-sided cylindrical gilt-bronze bases. H.: 6.3 cm (2½ in.), Diam.: 27.1 cm (10¾ in.)

Both bronzes are same-scale copies of compositions that were first exhibited as marble sculptures in 1757 – by sculptors who co-incidentally both spent a significant part of their careers in Russia. Gillet's *Paris* (Louvre) (fig. 77) was his reception piece submitted to the French Academy; the relaxed pose is essentially that of a classical marble of *Ganymede* in the Museo Pio-Clementino, Rome. The original marble of Falconet's *Bather*, like his celebrated *Cupid*, was also exhibited at the 1757 Salon. Both his works were triumphant critical and popular successes and were thereafter much replicated. 'Everyone wanted to enjoy this appealing object, and one saw it multiplied by casts in all the apartments of Paris', a contemporary wrote of the *Bather*, which was reproduced in both marble and Sèvres biscuit porcelain in the 18th century. The Wallace Collection bronze reproduces the variant with a rose in the figure's hair of which the original may be the version in London (fig. 78).

These casts probably were produced in one of the several Paris foundries active in the mid-19th century that were able to supply the growing market for reproductions of popular classical, 'old master' and contemporary bronzes. The pairing of two elegant and well-balanced, but thematically unrelated figures was clearly made for purely decorative purposes. It seems first to have been made with smaller, marble versions in the collection of the baron de Besenval (1721–1791), in whose posthumous sale they appeared in 1795 (untraced).

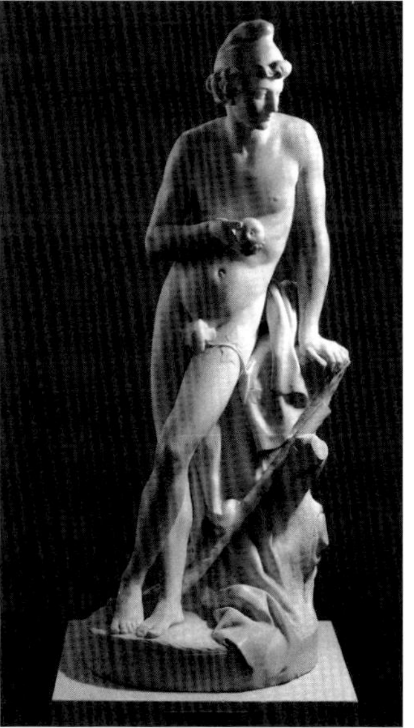

Fig. 77 *The Shepherd Paris*, N.-F. Gillet, 1757, marble, h.: 84 cm. Musée du Louvre, Paris (MR 1863)

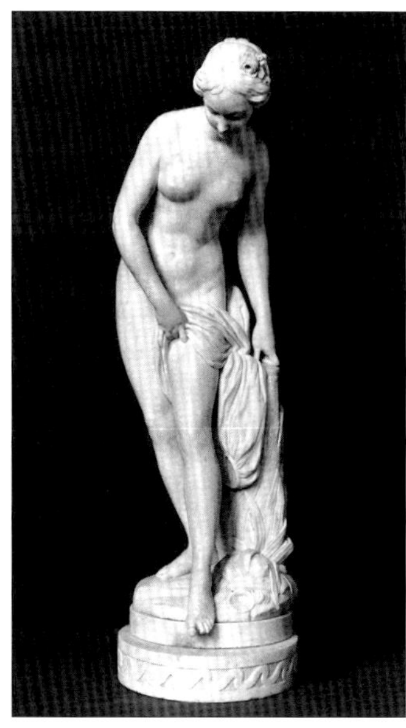

Fig. 78 *The Bather*, attributed to E.-M. Falconet, c.1757, marble, h.: 89.5 cm. Victoria and Albert Museum, London (1131–1882)

Not certainly documented until loaned by Sir Richard Wallace to the Bethnal Green Museum exhibition, 1872–5 (both as by Falconet, French 18th century).

S220 (Paris) S221 (Bather)

Alessandro Algardi (1602–1654)
Born in Bologna, then moved to Mantua and finally settled in Rome, where he became the greatest sculptor of the mid-17th century in the city, after Bernini. Working in a less flamboyant style than Bernini, he was able to express his talents in a great variety of commissions ranging from small-scale designs for metalwork to huge statues and reliefs for St Peter's, Rome.

François Anguier (1604–1669)
Brother of the sculptor Michel Anguier (see p. 12), with whom he studied under **Algardi** in Rome. He produced many funerary monuments, and is best known for the mausoleum of Henri II, duc de Montmorency (Moulins).

Philippe Bertrand (1663–1724)
His work for the *Bâtiments du Roi* (chapel, Versailles; Nôtre-Dame, Paris, etc) is now less appreciated than the elegant small-scale bronzes and terracottas he made for collectors. These include versions of an *Abduction of Helen* group that was his reception piece for the Académie Royale (1701), and four groups of the *Seasons* (Royal Collection, Windsor Castle).

Louis-Simon Boizot (1743–1809)
Exhibited regularly at the Salon, 1773–1806. Director of Sculpture at the Sèvres porcelain manufactory, 1773–1800, for which he designed numerous models for biscuit figures and groups. He also designed clock cases and furnishing bronzes, was a skilled portraitist and executed several large-scale official commissions.

Jean-Jacques Caffiéri (1725–1792)
From a celebrated family of skilled bronze-casters and chasers. He was a ceaseless petitioner for official commissions, which included marble figures of *Corneille* (1779) and *Molière* (1787) (both Louvre). Executed several marbles and small bronzes for private clients, including Mme du Barry and the abbé Terray. He is most celebrated for his lively and naturalistic portrait busts.

Guillaume I Coustou (1677–1746)
Like both his famous uncle, Antoine **Coysevox**, and his brother, Nicolas, he worked mainly and extensively for the Crown (chapel, Versailles; Nôtre-Dame, Paris). Within the Académie Royale rose to become Rector, 1733. The *Marly Horses* (1740–5) (Louvre) are his most famous works.

Antoine Coysevox (1640–1720)
Sculpteur du Roi, 1666. Highly successful career as the leading sculptor under Louis XIV, for whom executed numerous commissions in the great châteaux and gardens. A remarkable and sensitive portrait sculptor, the finest of the reign. In 1702 elected Director of the Académie Royale, the highest possible office for a sculptor.

François-Aimé Damerat (*fl*.1781–1819)
One of three brothers who were all specialist metal-chasers. He supplied furniture mounts under Louis XVI, and assisted the leading *bronzier* François Rémond (1747–1812) on various projects during the Empire period.

Martin Desjardins (1637–1694)
Born in Breda, trained in Antwerp. Various official commissions for public buildings in Paris, and at Versailles. Rector of the Académie Royale, 1686. Acclaimed for his monuments to Louis XIV in Paris (Place des Victoires, 1682–5) and Lyons (1688–91). Died a very rich man, and in recognition of his work, his descendants were ennobled by Louis XIV (1704).

François Duquesnoy (1597–1643)
Born in Brussels, the son and brother of sculptors, but settled in Rome in 1618. He became one of the outstanding sculptors of that city, working in style influenced by, but more restrained than that of Bernini. He was particularly renowned for his many small sculptures of *putti*.

Étienne-Maurice Falconet (1716–1791)
Successful early career making small and large-scale marbles for private and public commissions. Director of Sculpture at the Sèvres porcelain manufactory, 1757–66, for which he designed many models for biscuit groups. He worked for Catherine II in Russia, 1766–78, for whom he made his masterpiece, the *Equestrian Statue of Peter the Great* in St Petersburg (unveiled 1782). Falconet was also an impassioned writer on sculpture.

Pierre-François Feuchère (1737–1823)
Learnt his skills as a gilder and chaser from his goldsmith father-in-law. Made furnishing bronzes from the 1770s, assisted in the family workshop by his brother and son.

Anselme Flamen (1647–1717)
Pupil of Gaspard **Marsy**, 1669. Studied in Rome, 1675–9. Worked on royal commissions at Versailles, Marly and elsewhere, from 1679. Professor at the Académie Royale, 1701.

Giovanni Battista Foggini (1652–1725)
Florentine sculptor, who studied in Rome,
1673–6. Appointed First Sculptor to the
Florentine Court, 1687. He thereby took over the
foundry set up by **Giambologna**, the centre of
bronze production in the city, and made many
bronze groups. As First Architect (from 1694/5),
he also controlled the court hardstone workshops.

Giambologna (Jean Boulogne; 1529–1608)
Born and trained in Flanders, he became court
sculptor to the Medici dukes of Florence, and
the dominant sculptor of his day. From the
1560s, he sculpted several powerful marble
groups and bronze statues, and his style was
spread across Europe by the numerous small
bronze statuettes that he and his pupils and
followers produced.

Nicolas-François Gillet (1712–1791)
Studied in Rome, 1746–52. In 1757 he was
accepted into the Académie Royale with his
marble of *Paris*, but that year was invited to
Russia, where he established the new Academy
of Fine Arts in St Petersburg. He is considered
the father of the Russian neo-classical school of
sculpture, and executed many mythological
groups and historical portraits.

François Girardon (1628–1715)
Son of a metal-founder, trained under the
Anguiers, and worked closely with his friend
Charles Le Brun (*Premier Peintre du Roi*). From the
1660s, he supervised much of the sculptural
work commissioned under Louis XIV,
especially at Versailles, Marly and The Invalides,
Paris. Made a *chevalier*, 1690; Chancellor of the
Académie Royale, 1695. Died a very rich man,
with an important collection of works of art.

Jean-Antoine Houdon (1741–1828)
Although he executed a number of fine marble
and bronze statues in his early career, official
commissions were lacking, and it is as the
greatest portrait sculptor of the age that he is
famous. From the early 1770s, he produced a
remarkable series of busts of his leading
contemporaries, not just from France, but also
from America and at the German and Russian
courts. His fortunes wavered after the French
Revolution, but he continued to sculpt superb

busts, exhibiting at the Salon for the last time
in 1814.

Robert Le Lorrain (1666–1743)
Grandson of a goldsmith; trained under
Girardon. Although he worked at Versailles
(chapel), much of his ouput was directed at
private clients, for whom he created several fine
bronze statuettes. His best-known work is
probably the superb stone *Horses of the Sun* relief
for the *hôtel* de Rohan, Paris (1735–7). Rector of
the Académie Royale, 1737.

Joseph-Charles Marin (1759–1834)
A close follower of Clodion (1738–1814), to
whom his terracotta statuettes have often been
attributed. They similarly feature figures of
bacchantes, vestals and other youthful female
subjects. In the 1800s he studied and worked in
his Rome, where he adopted a more austere,
neo-classical style. He continued to exhibit at
the Salon into the 1830s.

Gaspard Marsy (1624–1681)
Son and brother of sculptors; trained under,
among others, **François Anguier**. Executed
several major tomb monuments, but worked
mainly for Louis XIV, especially at Versailles,
where he was one of the leading sculptors.
Briefly Rector of the Académie Royale (1678).

Henri Perlan (1597–1656)
From a family of goldsmiths. Worked for Marie
de Médici at the hôtel du Luxembourg, and
under Nicolas Poussin at the Louvre (1641–2).
Appointed *Sculpteur du Roi*, *c*.1647. A specialist
bronze-caster, his surviving works are
technically superb.

Germain Pilon (*c*.1525–1590)
Trained under his sculptor father, and
influenced by the first School of Fontainebleau
(see p. 11). Executed the Monument to the *Heart
of Henri II* (1561–5) and the Mausoleuum of *Henri
II and Catherine de Médici* (completed 1570; St-
Denis Abbey), both after Primaticcio's designs.
Appointed *Contrôleur Général des Effigies* at the
Royal Mint, 1573. Also many commissions for
churches and private individuals. The
predominant French sculptor from the mid-
1560s until his death.

Barthélemy Prieur (*c*.1536–1611)
The most prolific French manufacturer of
bronze statuettes in the decades around 1600.
Appointed *Sculpteur du Roi*, 1591. The
posthumous inventory of his property lists
about one hundred small figures of 'men or
women' at various stages in the casting process,
which can be associated with an extensive
surviving œuvre of small genre bronzes.

Roger Scabol (*fl*.1680s–1713)
Born in Brussels, worked in Paris from the mid-
1680s; *Sculpteur et fondeur du Roi*, by 1692.
Assisted with the casting of several important
monuments, including those to Louis XIV by
Desjardins for the Place des Victoires, Paris
(1682–5) and for Lyons (1688–91), and by
Girardon for the Place Louis-le-Grand, Paris
(cast 1692).

Antonio Susini (*fl*.1580–1624)
Specialist Florentine caster-chaser, who worked
for **Giambologna**, *c*.1580–1600. He then set up
his own workshop, using several of
Giambologna's models for small bronze
statuettes and groups. His bronzes are notable
for their superb technical quality and finish.

Pierre-Philippe Thomire (1751–1843)
Trained under **Houdon** and Pajou, but followed
his father in becoming a specialist bronze-
worker. Supplied numerous mounts for Sèvres
porcelain vases during the 1780s. His business,
which now also made furniture, grew rapidly
and prospered under Napoleon I. His later years
were less successful.

Corneille Van Clève (1646–1732)
From of a family of goldsmiths of Flemish
origin. His many royal commissions included
work at Versailles (1680s, 1700s), The Invalides,
Paris (1700s) and Nôtre-Dame, Paris (1710s). His
smaller-scale work included several fine
bronzes for collectors and designs for
candlesticks.

Bibliography

D. Alcouffe, *Un Temps d'Exubérance: Les Arts Décoratifs sous Louis XIII et Anne d'Autriche*, exh. cat., Paris, 2002

H.H. Arnason, *The Sculptures of Houdon*, London, 1975

C.B. Bailey, 'The abbé Terray: an enlightened patron of modern sculpture', *Burlington Magazine*, CXXXV, 1993, pp. 121–32

S. Baratte, *et al.*, *Les Bronzes de la Couronne*, exh. cat., Paris, 1999

M. Beaulieu, *Musée du Louvre: Description raisonée des sculptures, II: Renaissance française*, Paris, 1978

M. Beaulieu, *Robert Le Lorrain (1666–1743)*, Paris, 1982

A. Blunt (revised R. Beresford), *Art and Architecture in France 1500 to 1700*, New Haven & London, 1999

G. Bresc-Bautier, *et al.*, *Masterpieces from the Louvre*, exh. cat., Brisbane, 1988

G. Bresc-Bautier, *Germain Pilon et les sculpteurs français de la Renaissance* (colloquium papers, musée du Louvre, 1990), Paris, 1993

D. Diderot & J. d'Alembert, *Encyclopédie*, 35 vols, Paris, 1751–80, *s.v. Bronze, Fonte, Sculpture*, etc

[Düsseldorf] *Europäiche Barockplastik am Niederrhein: Grupello und seine zeit*, exh. cat., Düsseldorf, 1971

A. Félibien, *Principes de l'architecture, de la sculpture…*, Paris, 1676 [etc]

J. Fischer, *The French Bronze 1500–1800*, exh. cat., Knoedler's, New York, 1968

J.-R. Gaborit, *Musée du Louvre: Sculpture Française, II: Renaissance et Temps Modernes*, 2 vols, Paris, 1998

F. Haskell & N. Penny, *Taste and the Antique*, New Haven & London, 1981

V. Krahn, *'Von allen seiten schön': Bronzen der Renaissance/Barock*, exh. cat., Berlin, 1995

A. Lefébure, 'Louis-François Jeannest, Napoléon Ier et Marie-Louise', *Musée du Louvre: Nouvelles acquisitions du département des Objets d'art 1990–1994*, Paris, 1995, pp. 234–7

M. Levey, *Painting and Sculpture in France 1700–1789*, 2nd ed., New Haven & London, 1993

J.G. Mann, *The Wallace Collection: Catalogue of Sculpture*, 2nd ed. (with Supplement by J.A.S. Ingamells), London, 1981

M. Martin, *Les Monuments équestres de Louis XIV*, Paris, 1986

Ministère de la Culture, *La Sculpture: Méthode et Vocabulaire*, Paris, 1978

H. Ottomeyer & P. Pröschel, *Vergoldete Bronzen die Bronzearbeiten der Spätbarok und Klassizismus*, 2 vols, Munich, 1986

[Paris] *L'école de Fontainebleau*, exh. cat., Paris, 1972

A. Schnapper, *Curieux du grand siècle, Collections et collectionneurs dans la France du XVIIe siècle*, Paris, 1994

L. Seelig, 'L'Inventaire après décès de Martin van den Bogaert dit Desjardins', *Bulletin de la Société de l'Histoire de l'Art Français*, 1972, pp. 161–82

L. Seelig, 'Studien zu Martin van den Bogaert gen. Desjardins', thesis, Munich, 1973 [publ. Hamburg, 1980]

[Sèvres] *Falconet à Sèvres 1757–1766 ou l'art de plaire*, exh. cat., Musée national de Céramique, Sèvres, 2001

F. Souchal, 'La collection du sculpteur Girardon d'après son inventaire après décès', *Gazette des Beaux-Arts*, juillet–août 1973, pp. 1–98

F. Souchal, *French Sculptors…: The Age of Louis XIV*, 3 vols, London, 1977–87, and Supplement, London, 1993

[Versailles] *Louis-Simon Boizot (1743–1809)*, exh. cat., Musée Lambinet, Versailles, 2001

D. Walker, 'The early career of François Girardon, 1628–1686…', thesis, New York Univ., 1982

Index of Names and Places

NOTE

Names from titles of works of art and of mythological figures have been excluded. Names in bold have biographical entries on pp. 106–7.

Académie Royale, *see* Paris
Algardi, Alessandro, 12, 18, 34, 35, 56, 82, 84, 106
Ammannati, Bartolommeo, 35
Anguier, François, 32, 106, 107
Anguier, Michel, 12, 106
Antwerp, 106
Apuleius, Lucius, 74
Aranjuez (near Madrid), Gardens, 35
Arcambal (Arcambale), marquis d', (sale, Paris, 1776), 70
Augustus 'the Strong', Frederick-Augustus I, Elector of Saxony and Augustus II, King of Poland, 13, 40, 44, 48, 56, 62, 74

Baltimore, Walters Art Museum, 84
Bargello, *see* Florence
Beauvau, François-Victurnien-Charles Just, prince de Craon and prince de, (sale, Paris, 1865), 48
Beckford, William, (sale, London, 1823), 64
Beringhen, Henri-Camille, marquis de, (sale, Paris, 1770), 78
Bernini, Gianlorenzo, 12, 56, 64, 106
Berry, Charles-Ferdinand de Bourbon, duc de, 24
Bernard, Thomas, 70
Bertin, Claude, 82
Bertrand, Philippe, 13, 66, 68, 70, 106
Besenval, Pierre-Joseph-Victor, baron de, (sale, Paris, 1795), 105
Bethnal Green Museum, *see* London
Bibliothèque National de France, *see* Paris

Blondel de Gagny, Augustin, 14, 94
Boilly, Louis-Léopold, 96
Boizot, Louis-Simon, 14, 98, 106
Bologna, 106
Bologna, Giovanni, *see* Giambologna
Bonaparte, Napolcon, *see* Napoleon I
Bone, Henry, 17
Borghese, Cardinal Scipio, 32
Botticelli, Sandro, 66
Boucher, François, 96
Boulle, André-Charles, 14
Boulogne, Jean, *see* Giambologna
Braunschweig, Herzog Anton-Ulrich Museum, 78
Breda, 106
Broche, Joseph, 96
Broche, Jean-Baptiste-Ignache, 96
Brunet-Denon, baron, (sale, Paris, 1846), 100
Brussels, 106, 107
Brussels,
    Musées Royaux d'Art et d'Histoire, 78
    Musées Royaux des Beaux-Arts de Belgique, 84

Caffiéri, Jean-Jacques, 18, 21, 22, 86, 106
Calonne, Charles-Alexandre de, (sale, Paris, 1788), 92
Carlier, Martin, 38, 40
Carjat, Étienne, 17
Catherine 'the Great', Catherine II, Empress of Russia, 106
Catherine de'Medici, *see* Medici
Cellini, Benvenuto, 11
Chambellan, Jean-Claude, *see* Duplessis
Chantilly, musée Condé, 68
Chapeaurouge, Jacques de, 35
Charlemagne, King of the Franks and Emperor, 11
Charles I, King of England, 12

Charles IX, King of France, 24
Clodion, Claude Michel, *called*, 90, 107
Colbert, Jean-Baptiste, 54
Copenhagen, Statens Museum for Kunst, 52
Cosimo I de' Medici, *see* Medici
Coustou, Guillaume I, 4, 94, 106
Coustou, Nicolas, 106
Coypel, Charles-Antoine, 58
Coysevox, Antoine, 42, 44, 64, 106

Daguerre, Dominique, 14, 90
Damerat, François-Aimé, 100, 106
Delaroche (dealer), 52
Denon, baron Dominique-Vivant, (sale, Paris, 1826), 100
Desjardins, Jacques, 52
Desjardins, Martin, 50, 52, 64, 106, 107
Detroit, Institute of Arts, 74
Diderot, Denis, 86
Dijon, musée des Beaux-Arts, 64
Dorchester House, *see* London
Dresden,
    Grünes Gewölbe, 21, 48, 62
    Skulpturensammlung, 40, 44, 74
Du Barry, comte, (sale, Paris, 1774), 96
Dubois, Jean-Joseph, 92
Duplessis, Jean-Claude, *père*, 56
Dupré, Guillaume, 12
Duquesnoy, François, 12, 60, 82, 84, 106
Duquesnoy, Jérôme, *le jeune*, 84

Ephesus, Temple of Artemis, 28

Falconet, Étienne-Maurice, 14, 88, 96, 105, 106
Faydherbe, Lucas, 78
Félibien, André, 22
Feuchère, Pierre-François, 14, 94, 106
Flamen, Anselme, 54, 56, 98, 106

Florence,
    Gallerie degli Uffizi, 42, 44, 66
    Museo Nazionale del Bargello, 34
Foggini, Giovanni Battista, 13, 42, 74, 107
Fontainebleau, château de, 11, 12, 38
Fortier, Alexandre, (sale, Paris, 1770), 84
Fould, Louis, (sale, Paris, 1860), 18, 58, 78
François Ier, King of France, 11, 26, 38
Frederick-Augustus I, *see* Augustus 'the Strong'
Frémin, René, 68, 76

Gaignat, Louis-Jean, (sale, Paris, 1768/9), 48
George IV, King of Great Britain and Ireland, 17, 18
Gersaint, Edme, 14
Giambologna, 12, 14, 17, 46, 56, 62, 107
Gillet, Nicolas-François, 105, 107
Girardon, François, 12, 18, 38, 40, 46, 48, 52, 54, 56, 58, 82, 98, 107
Grand Dauphin, *see* Louis
Grünes Gewölbe, *see* Dresden
Guise, Henri I, duc de, 24

Hals, Frans, 18
Hardouin-Mansart, Jules, 50
Henri II, King of France, 24
Henri III, King of France, 24
Henri IV, King of France, 11
Hermitage, *see* St Petersburg
Hertford,
    3rd Marquess of, 17, 18, 32, 44, 56, 64, 82, 94
    4th Marquess of, 18, 22, 24, 30, 35, 40, 48, 52, 56, 58, 60, 62, 64, 66, 68, 70, 72, 76, 78, 80, 82, 84, 86, 88, 96, 100
    House, *see* London
Hesiod (Hesiodus), 66
Houdon, Jean-Antoine, 14, 18, 35, 88, 90, 92, 107
Huntington Library and Art Gallery, *see* San Marino

Isabey, Louis-Eugène-Gabriel, 100

Jacquiot (Jacqueau), Ponce, 11, 30
Jarry, abbé Juilhard du, 70
Jeannest, Louis-François, 100
Jullienne, Jean de, (sale, Paris, 1767), 84
Julius II, Pope, 26

Koucheleff, Countess Katherine, 56

Lacour, 100

Laffitte, No.2 rue, *see* Paris
La Fontaine, Jean de 74, 92
La Granja Palace (near Segovia), Gardens, 76
La Live de Jully, Ange-Laurent, 58
Le Brun, Charles, 54, 107
Le Lorrain, Robert, 4, 13, 66, 68, 72, 107
Le Marié, (sale, Paris, 1776), 56
Le Nôtre, André, 11, 12, 62
Lespingola, 13, 76
Le Sueur, Hubert, 12
Lewis, L. and R.J., 12
London,
    Bethnal Green Museum (exhibition, 1872–5), 56, 66, 74, 82, 90, 100, 105
    Christie's (sale, 13 December 2001), 84
    Dorchester House, 18, 44, 82, 94
    Hertford House, 32, 35, 40, 60, 62, 66, 72, 82, 88, 92, 96, 98
    Pantechnicon, 56
    Victoria and Albert Museum, 12, 30, 105
Louis, Grand Dauphin, 12, 35
Louis XII, King of France, 11
Louis XIII, King of France, 12, 32, 70
Louis XIV, King of France, 12, 38, 42, 46, 50, 52, 106, 107
Louis XV, King of France, 14, 35
Louis XVI, King of France, 35, 106
Louis-Philippe, King of the French, 92
Louvre, *see* Paris
Lyons, place Bellecour, 50, 106, 107

Mantua, 106
Marcus Aurelius, 50
Marie-Antoinette, Queen of France, 35
Marie-Louise, Empress of the French, 18, 100
Marin, Joseph-Charles, 90, 107
Marly, château and parc de, 12, 38, 44, 106, 107
Marsy, Gaspard, 54, 56, 98, 107
Mauger, Jean, 70
Max Emanuel, Elector of Bavaria, 50, 52
Mazarin, Cardinal Jules (Giulio Mazarini), 35
Medici (Médici),
    Catherine de', 24
    Cosimo I de', 35
    Marie de, 107
Metropolitan Museum of Art, *see* New York
Meudon, château de, 35
Michel, Claude, *see* Clodion
Michelangelo (Buonarroti), 24, 44
Moinville, baron Boissel de, (sale, Paris, 1861), 30
Montmorency, Anne de, 26, 30

Montmorency, Henri II de, 106
Moulins, Lycée Banville (formerly Couvent de la Visitation), 106
Musée Rétrospectif, *see* Paris

Napoleon I (Napoleon Bonaparte), Emperor of the French, 18, 100, 107
New York, Metropolitan Museum of Art, 18
Nieuwerkerke, Alfred-Émilien, comte de, 26
Nôtre-Dame Cathedral, *see* Paris

Ovid (Publius Ovidius Naso), 13, 34, 46, 54, 72

Pajou, Augustin, 107
Paris,
    Académie Royale (French Academy), 13, 70, 105, 106, 107
    Bibliothèque Nationale de France, 7, 40, 48, 82, 101
    Champs-Elysées, 94
    Elysée Palace, 72
    Invalides, The, 107
    Louis-le-Grand, place, 107
    Louvre, musée du, 11, 13, 24, 26, 28, 30, 32, 42, 46, 56, 58, 68, 84, 88, 94, 101, 105, 106, 107
    Musée Rétrospectif (exhibition, 1865), 26, 64, 80, 84
    Nôtre-Dame, Cathedral, 70, 106, 107
    Palais de Trianon (exhibition, 1867), 68, 70
    Rohan, *hôtel* de, 107
    Rue Laffitte, No. 2, 76
    Saint-André-des-Arcs, 28
    Tuileries, Gardens, 38, 56
    Victories, place des, 106, 107
Pembroke, Robert Henry Herbert, 12th Earl of (sale, London, 1851), 18, 86
Perlan, Henri, 12, 21, 32, 107
Petel, Georg, 78
Philip (Felipe) IV, King of Spain, 34
Pilon, Germain, 11, 18, 21, 24, 107
Pliny the Elder (Gaius Plinius Secundus), 38
Poultier, Jean, 80
Pourtalès-Gorgier, James-Alexandre, comte de (sale, Paris, 1865), 18, 24
Poussin, Nicolas, 107
Primaticcio, 11, 28, 107
Prieur, Barthélemy, 4, 11, 12, 18, 21, 26, 28, 30, 107
Prince Regent, *see* George IV
Prud'hon, Pierre-Paul, 100
Puget, Pierre, 68

Randon de Boisset, Pierre-Louis-Paul, (sale, Paris, 1777), 84
Regnaudin, Thomas, 54
Rémond, François, 106
Richelieu, Armand-Jean du Plessis de, Cardinal, 46
Rome,
    French Academy, 40
    St Peter's, 106
    Vatican Museums, 38, 42, 105
    Villa Medici, 42
Rouen, Cathedral, 11
Roussel, Jérôme, 70
Rubens, Peter Paul, 78

Saint-Auban, Gabriel de, 46
Saint-Cloud, château de, 100
Saint-Denis, Abbey, 107
St Petersburg,
    Academy of Fine Arts, 107
    State Hermitage Museum, 72, 88
San Marino (California), Huntington Library and Art Gallery, 18
Scabol (Schabol), Roger, 50, 52
Selle, Marcellin-François-Zacherie de, (sale, Paris, 1761), 72
Sèvres,
    musée national de Céramique, 88
    porcelain manufactory, 98, 106, 107
Seymour-Conway, Francis, *see* Hertford, 3rd Marquess of
Seymour-Conway, Richard, *see* Hertford, 4th Marquess of
Soldani-Benzi, Massimiliano, 13, 68
Soret, René, (sale, Paris, 1863), 68
Spingola, François, *see* Lespingola
Stockholm, Nationalmuseum, 62, 78
Stoskopff, Sébastien, 11
Susini, Antonio, 46, 107

Tacca, Ferdinando, 13, 60
Terray, abbé Joseph-Marie, 18, 86
Tessin, Count Carl Gustav, 62
Thomire, Pierre-Philippe, 14, 90, 107
Thomson, John, 18
Toledo (Ohio), Museum of Art, 86
Tuby, Jean-Baptiste, 54
Tuileries, *see* Paris

Uffizi, *see* Florence

Van Clève, Corneille, 13, 66, 68, 80, 107
Vatican Museums, *see* Rome
Versailles, château and parc de, 12, 14, 18, 32, 35, 42, 54, 56, 58, 98, 106, 107
Victoria and Albert Museum, *see* London
Vinache, Joseph, *père*, 44
Voltaire, François-Marie Arouet de, 18, 70

Wallace
    Sir Richard, 18, 26, 28, 32, 56, 66, 74, 82, 88, 90, 92, 98
    Amélie-Julie-Charlotte, Lady, 18
Washington, National Gallery of Art, 52
Watteau, Jean-Antoine, 68, 80
Werff, Adriaen van der, 14
Winckelmann, Johann Joachim, 32
Windsor Castle, The Royal Collection, 66, 106
Würzburg, Residenz, 94

Photographic Acknowledgements

NOTE

All colour photographs of Wallace Collection objects are by Richard Valencia, except the detail on p.53 (Alastair Johnson), and where otherwise credited.

Baltimore, The Walters Art Museum: fig. 65

Brussels, Musées Royaux d'Art et d'Histoire: ©IRPA-KIK, Brussels: fig. 62

Copenhagen, Statens Museum for Kunst: Photo: SMK: fig. 41

Detroit, Detroit Institute of Arts: Photo © 1990 The Detroit Institute of Art: fig. 58

Dijon, Musée des Beaux-Arts: fig. 49

Dresden, Staatliche Kunstsammlungen, Grünes Gewölbe: figs 47–8

Dresden, Staatliche Kunstsammlungen, Skulpturensammlung: figs 35, 57, 61

Florence, Museo Nazionale del Bargello: su concessione del Ministero dei Beni e le Attività Culturali: fig. 28

London, Christie's Images: fig. 66

London, The Royal Collection: © 2002, Her Majesty Queen Elizabeth II: fig. 50

London, Victoria and Albert Museum: V&A Picture Library: figs 4, 24, 78

New York, Metropolitan Museum of Art: All rights reserved: fig. 63

Nuremberg, Germanische Nationalmuseum: fig. 39

Paris, Bibliothèque Nationale de France: figs 32, 36, 38, 64, 75

Paris, Musée du Louvre, Documentation du Département des Sculptures: figs 33, 72

Paris, Musées de la Ville de Paris (Petit Palais): © PMVP / Ladet: fig. 37

Réunion des Musées Nationaux:

Paris, Musée du Louvre: Photo RMN: figs 3, 5, 6, 20–1, 22 (Photo: Michèle Bellot), 23ab, 25–7, 31, 33–4, 42, 44–5, 52, 71ab, 74, 77

Sèvres, Musée National de Céramique: Photo RMN (M. Beck-Coppola): fig. 69

Versailles, Châteaux de Versailles et de Trianon: Photo RMN (Arnaudet/ Lewanowski): fig. 43

Toledo (Ohio), Toledo Museum of Art: fig. 68

St Petersburg, State Hermitage Museum: fig. 56

San Marino (California), Huntington Library and Art Gallery: Photo courtesy of the Huntington Library, Art Collections, and Botanical Gardens, San Marino, California: fig. 13

Vatican City, Monumenti Musei e Gallerie Pontificie: fig. 30

Washington (D.C.), National Gallery of Art: Photograph © Board of Trustees: Fig. 40

Author's Acknowledgements

My greatest debts are to John Lewis, for his enthusiastic support of this book from its inception, and to Richard Valencia (photography) and Tim Harvey (design) whose outstanding skills have considerably enhanced the visual appeal of this book. I am very grateful to Francesca Bewer for providing an excellent technical diagram and advice. I would also like to extend my sincere thanks for their valuable and varied assistance to Sergei Androssov, Emmanuelle Delapierre, Jean-René Gaborit, Mark Gunning, Richard Harris, Hayden Hopkins, Andrew Hunter, Alastair Johnson, Donald Johnston, Jonathan Marsden, Jennifer Montagu, Rosalind Savill, Guilhem Scherf, Dirk Syndram, Jeremy Warren and to fellow members of the French Bronze Study Group, from whose Argus-like eyes and solomonic wisdom I have hugely benefited. My final debt of gratitude is to my partner, and former colleague, Jo Charlton, for her constant encouragement, advice, support and love.